LÉON WALRAS
1834-1910

Advanced Textbooks in Economics

Series Editors: C.J. Bliss *and* M.D. Intriligator

Currently Available:

Volume 2 : *Lectures on Microeconomic Theory* (Second Revised Edition)
E. MALINVAUD

Volume 5 : *Applied Consumption Analysis* (Second Revised Edition)
L. PHLIPS

Volume 11 : *Collective Choice and Social Welfare*
A.K. SEN

Volume 12 : *General Competitive Analysis*
K.J. ARROW and F.H. HAHN

Volume 14 : *Distributed Lags* (Second Revised Edition)
P.J. DHRYMES

Volume 15 : *Notes and Problems in Microeconomic Theory*
P.B. DIXON, S. BOWLES, D. KENDRICK, L. TAYLOR and M. ROBERTS

Volume 17 : *Stochastic Methods in Economics and Finance*
A.G. MALLIARIS and W.A. BROCK

Volume 19 : *International Trade and Resource Alloccation* (Second Revised Edition)
A.D. WOODLAND

Volume 20 : *Introduction to the Use of General Equilibrium Analysis*
R.R. CORNWALL

Volume 22 : *Lectures in Econometrics*
L.R. KLEIN and W. WELFE

Volume 23 : *Public Enterprise Economics* (Second Revised Edition)
D. BÖS

Volume 24 : *Optimal Control Theory with Economic Applications*
A. SEIERSTAD and K. SYDSÆTER

Volume 25 : *Capital Markets and Prices: Valuing Uncertain Income Streams*
C.G. KROUSE

Volume 26 : *History of Economic Theory*
T. NEGISHI

Volume 27 : *Differential Equations, Stability and Chaos in Dynamic Economics*
W.A. BROCK and A.G. MALLIARIS

Volume 28 : *Equilibrium Analysis*
W. HILDENBRAND and A.P. KIRMAN

Volume 29 : *Economics of Insurance*
K.H. BORCH

EQUILIBRIUM ANALYSIS
Variations on themes by Edgeworth and Walras

ADVANCED TEXTBOOKS IN ECONOMICS

VOLUME 28

NORTH-HOLLAND
AMSTERDAM · NEW YORK · OXFORD · TOKYO

EQUILIBRIUM ANALYSIS

Variations on themes by Edgeworth and Walras

W. HILDENBRAND

University of Bonn

A. P. KIRMAN

European University Institute, Florence

NORTH-HOLLAND
AMSTERDAM · NEW YORK · OXFORD · TOKYO

ELSEVIER SCIENCE PUBLISHERS B.V.
Sara Burgerhartstraat 25
P.O. Box 211, 1000 AE Amsterdam, The Netherlands

Distributors for the United States and Canada:
ELSEVIER SCIENCE PUBLISHING COMPANY, INC.
655 Avenue of the Americas
New York, N.Y. 10010, U.S.A.

First edition 1988
Second impression 1991

ISBN: 0 444 70511 2

PRINTED IN THE NETHERLANDS

INTRODUCTION TO THE SERIES

The aim of the series is to cover topics in economics, mathematical economics and econometrics, at a level suitable for graduate students or final year undergraduates specializing in economics. There is at any time much material that has become well established in journal papers and discussion series which still awaits a clear, self-contained treatment that can easily be mastered by students without considerable preparation or extra reading. Leading specialists will be invited to contribute volumes to fill such gaps. Primary emphasis will be placed on clarity, comprehensive coverage of sensibly defined areas, and insight into fundamentals, but original ideas will not be excluded. Certain volumes will therefore add to existing knowledge, while others will serve as a means of communicating both known and new ideas in a way that will inspire and attract students not already familiar with the subject matter concerned.

The Editors

Preface

This book had its origins in our "Introduction to Equilibrium Analysis". In that book we stated our aim as being to give "a simple but formal account of work done to date in that part of economics which we have chosen to call equilibrium analysis". Three things have changed since that time. Firstly the "work done to date" has considerably expanded and we have naturally had to take account of this. Secondly, our view of the relative importance of some of the results presented in that book has changed and indeed some no longer figure in this book. Thirdly, our view of the general topic has necessarily changed. Although we still believe that the exchange economy is the best means to present equilibrium analysis, its limitations and indeed the limitations of the whole "individualistic" approach which underlies equilibrium analysis have become more apparent. This should be evident to the reader when he tackles our chapter on structure, uniqueness and stability, topics which did not figure at all in our earlier book.

The structure of this book is then as follows. Within the context of the exchange economy we develop two solutions or themes due to Walras and Edgeworth. The first consists of finding those allocations obtained through the decentralization of the choices of individuals by prices. The second of allocations which are not objected to coalitions by individuals. We use essentially the same mathematical tools as before although the differentiable approach has now appeared in our last chapter. Thus if we had to give a description of this book we might call it "Variations on themes by Walras and Edgeworth scored for modern instruments, convex sets, fixed points, with further variations on Walras' theme for earlier instruments".

Our book is still limited to what we consider to be at the heart of modern economic theory, it does not contain a description of all those developments in economics which are founded on equilibrium analysis. Nevertheless a thorough understanding of the material treated here will be invaluable to the reader in appreciating the economic literature. In particular, he will learn to treat with caution many of the assertions found in that literature.

The book should be suitable for final year undergraduate courses or for graduate students. Our previous book has been used widely and in particular in Berkeley, Bonn, Brussels, Marseille, Paris and Warwick. The comments, corrections and criticisms of students and colleagues there and at other universities have been of great value in preparing this book.

We have kept our earlier aim in mind, that the book should be readable by anyone who has a logical mind and who is reasonably persistent. Again, often at the cost of generality, we have kept the mathematical treatment as simple as possible.

As a guide for preparing a course we give an outline of the contents. Chapter 1 contains a simple geometric presentation in a very special case of most of the results in the book. Parts of this chapter may be redundant for those well trained in microeconomics. However, it should give most readers an intuitive feel for the problems treated in the book. Indeed the mathematician may well, after reading this chapter, feel that this will suffice to understand the problems involved and that their formalisation is relatively simple. In Chapter 2 we develop the formal basis of our model. In Chapter 3 we prove the existence of competitive equilibrium that is of Walras' theme. In Chapter 4 we present Edgeworth's theme, the core, and in Chapter 5 we explain the relationship between the two.

Chapter 6 is concerned with the structure, uniqueness and stability of equilibrium. This should not be thought of as a mere encore for it plays a crucial role in the programme. In fact it is only after hearing this work that the reader will begin to appreciate the limitations of the earlier pieces. There are appendices to chapters in which somewhat more technical material is presented, and mathematical appendices which are useful not only for reading this book but for much of the literature in theoretical economics.

Our fundamental debt intellectually is still obviously to Edgeworth and Walras. The names of certain recent mathematical economists still occur and recur, in particular those of Aumann, Debreu, Scarf and Shapley.

Finally we should thank those institutions who supported our work: The Deutsche Forschungsgemeinschaft, Sonderforschungsbereich 303, the European University Institute, Florence, La Fondation les Treilles, and our collaborators. We cannot list the names of all those who have read various sections and offered comments but we would like, in particular, to thank the following: Christiane Beyer, Felicitas Bayer, Christoph Balk and Jessica Spataro for the careful typesetting in TEX, Dario Paternoster for the preparation of the figures in the first chapter, Valerie Hildenbrand for the meticulous drawing of all the figures, and Heike Schmidt for overseeing and organizing the preparation of the various versions of the manuscript. We are particularly indebted to Kurt Hildenbrand for his skill in organizing the structure and lay–out of the book and for solving the many problems that arose in producing the camera–ready manuscript.

Contents

Preface v

Chapter 1. Introduction 1

1. Introduction 1
2. A Simple Example 2
3. First Theme: Decentralization by Prices (Walras) 7
4. Second Theme: Improving by Cooperation (Edgeworth) . . . 13
5. The Relation between the Two Themes 18
6. A Conjuring Trick 29
7. Limit Economies and the Importance of Being Insignificant . . 32
8. Back to Walras 34
9. Less Well Behaved Individuals 38
10. What Other Features Does Walras' Theme Have? 42
11. What Hope for Uniqueness? 46
12. Stability 48
13. To What Avail? 49

Chapter 2. Exchange Economies 51

1. Introduction 51
2. The Commodity Space 53
3. Agents' Characteristics 54
4. An Exchange Economy and its Core 70
5. Prices and Demand: The Competitive Model 76
6. Walras Equilibrium 82
7. Appendix to Chapter 2 85

Chapter 3. Existence of Competitive Equilibrium 89

1. Introduction 89
2. Individual Demand 91
3. Total Demand 96
4. Existence of Equilibria: Strongly Convex Preferences 98
5. Economies without Convex Preferences 115
6. Conclusion 122

Chapter 4. The Core of a Game 123

1. Introduction 123
2. Balancedness 128
3. Some Non–classical Exchange Economies 139
4. Appendix to Chapter 4 152

Chapter 5. Core and Competitive Equilibria 163

1. Introduction 163
2. Replica Economies 165
3. Economies with a Continuum of Agents 178
4. Finite Economies 185
5. More General Limit Theorems 190

Chapter 6. Structure, Uniqueness and Stability 199

1. Introduction 199
2. Structure: Properties of Excess Demand 202
3. Income Distribution and Properties of Excess Demand . . . 212
4. Uniqueness 222
5. Stability 232
6. Tâtonnement in Continuous Time 236
7. Conclusions 239

Mathematical Appendix I. Topological Concepts in $\mathbb{R}^\ell$. 241

1. Convergence in $\mathbb{R}^\ell$ 242
2. Closed and Open Sets 243

Mathematical Appendix II. Separation of Convex Sets . 251

Mathematical Appendix III. Continuous Correspondences 257

1. Introduction 257
2. Upper Hemi–Continuous Correspondences 259
3. Lower Hemi–Continuous Correspondences 269
4. Continuous Correspondences 273

Mathematical Appendix IV. Fixed Point Theorems . . . 277

List of Mathematical Symbols 285

References 289

Author Index 293

Subject Index 295

Chapter 1

Introduction

1. Introduction

In this chapter we will follow the practice of our earlier book and present the topics that we treat in a simple geometric framework. We shall make extensive use of a device created by the composer of our second theme Edgeworth. The arguments used are sometimes specific to the geometric case we consider but, in any event, they should give an insight into the nature of the problems involved. The economist who wishes simply to have a general idea of the topics presented in the book or the mathematician who feels that the formalisation and generalisation of these arguments should not be difficult, may wish to stop after this chapter. We have written the rest of the book in the belief, and the hope, that there are other readers. The economist with a sound training in micro-economics may prefer to start from the outset with Chapter 2.

As we have already said, we shall confine ourselves to the analysis of one economic activity – the exchange of goods. Although there may be many who object to this restriction, as the theory currently stands it enables us to do justice to most of the essential content of equilibrium analysis. Throughout the book we shall consider a situation in which a group of individuals, each of whom possesses quantities of various goods, meets and exchanges these goods with a view to their consumption. Each individual has preferences as to the various bundles of goods he might obtain. We shall analyse the possible outcomes of the exchange of goods and shall evaluate these allocations in terms of criteria which are related to individual preferences. To give a little life to these ideas let us look at the following simple example.

2. A Simple Example

Consider two individuals, Ada and Bill, whom we shall sometimes refer to, somewhat impersonally, as a and b, each of whom possesses quantities of two goods, bread and wine. Between them they have 25 loaves of bread and 19 bottles of wine. Now suppose that we wish to represent this situation geometrically. Look at Figure 1.1 where we have drawn a box.[1] The vertical axis represents quantities of wine and the horizontal one, quantities of bread. Now, if we measure quantities for Ada from the origin, then any point in the box tells us not only the quantities that Ada receives but also those that go to Bill. This is obvious since we know the total of both goods in the economy. Hence, Bill simply gets those amounts not included in Ada's bundle. In other words we can consider the quantities received by Bill as measured from the "origin" represented by (25,19) as represented in Figure 1.1. No point outside the box would represent a feasible distribution since it would represent a negative allocation of some good to one of the agents.

---

[1] The box device is often said to be a development by Bowley of an idea of Edgeworth and is sometimes referred to as an Edgeworth Bowley box. However, a careful reading of Edgeworth shows that he fully developed the idea and it should therefore properly be called an Edgeworth box.

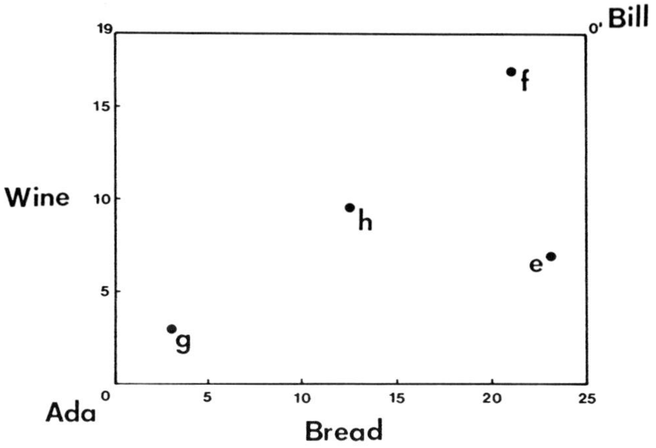

Figure 1.1

To say that every point in the box represents a possible distribution of the goods implies that we are assuming that the goods may be divided up as finely as we wish, that is, they are not only available in "units". The size of the box again is given by the total quantities of the two goods that Ada and Bill possess. In our case we have 25 units of bread and 19 units of wine, but the box may, of course, be any size. Indeed, if there were only one good it would be a line segment!

We have not yet specified how the goods are originally divided between the two individuals. Suppose, however, that Ada starts with 23 loaves and 7 bottles whilst Bill's initial endowments are 2 loaves and 12 bottles. This is the position indicated by e in Figure 1.1. We could write this a little more formally as

$$e(a) = (23, 7), \qquad e(b) = (2, 12) .$$

As yet we have said nothing about the outcome of the exchange and if, for example, Ada is very aggressive or Bill is very generous the result could be point f, in which she gets almost everything. This allocation f we would describe by

$$f(a) = (21, 17), \qquad f(b) = (4, 2) .$$

Alternatively, Bill might be very persuasive and the final position might be $g(a) = (3, 3)$ for example in which almost all the goods go to him. There is, of course, always the possibility that neither would dominate to this extent and the result could, for example, be an equal division of the goods as at point h. If we are to make any progress towards analyzing the outcome of the exchange we must know more about the desires of the two individuals. Our first assumption is that they are able to make choices between any of the various bundles of goods that they might obtain in the exchange. In other words, consider any two combinations of goods, for example one loaf and two bottles of wine (bundle x) and two loaves and one bottle of wine (bundle y). Ada and Bill can each make one of the following statements: "I prefer x to y", "I prefer y to x", or "I am indifferent between x and y". These statements may be written symbolically as $x \succ y$, $y \succ x$ and $x \sim y$. In general, we will work with the basic comparison between bundles "preferred or indifferent to" written as $\succsim$. We will index this by a or b to indicate the individual in question, e.g., $x \succsim_a y$, x is preferred or indifferent to y for Ada.

Now take any bundle for Ada, i.e., some point x in our box as in Figure 1.2 and consider all the other bundles which for her are equivalent to x, that is all the bundles y such that $y \sim_a x$ for Ada. Link all these bundles together and with all the assumptions we will make they will form a line which is the familiar indifference curve of economics textbooks. Now we shall assume throughout that Ada and Bill prefer more goods to less, and this assumption of greed or more technically "monotonicity" will play an important role in what follows. Given this, then the set of bundles preferred by a to x lies above the curve, to the north–east and those inferior, from her point of view, below and to the south–west. The opposite would be true if we looked at one of Bill's indifference curves. Note that both Ada and Bill are perfectly capable of com-

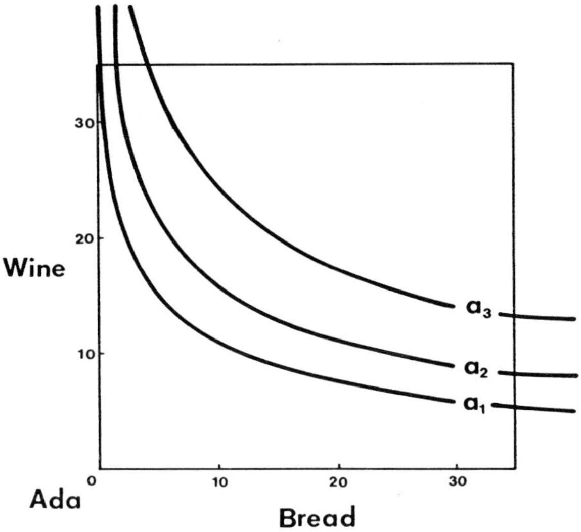

Figure 1.2

paring bundles outside the box, even though these are not available to them. Thus, in Figure 1.2, Ada's indifference curves extend beyond the box. In fact, throughout the book we will assume that individuals can compare any two bundles with positive or zero amounts of all goods.

However, in this chapter we will not bother to extend the curves outside the limits of the box since those bundles are not actually available to our agents. The fact that we can draw nice continuous curves to represent Ada's and Bill's preferences follows, as we have said, from the assumptions that we shall make about preferences and we will discuss this in some detail in Chapter 2. We can now fill the whole box with Ada's indifference curves since every bundle must lie on one of these curves. Bill is equally comprehensive in his ability to choose and his preferences may be similarly represented, observing that the allocation in the north–east corner of the box will be least preferred and the most preferred allocations lie to the south–west from his point of view as shown in Figure 1.3.

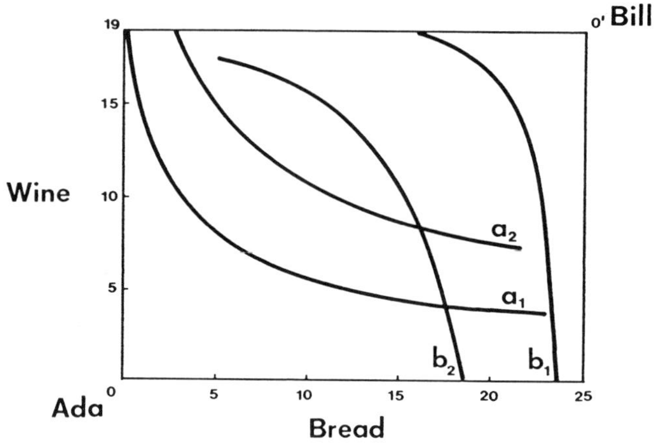

Figure 1.3

Now observe that although we have assumed that goods are desirable, that is that bundles containing more of the goods are preferable to those containing less, we have attributed no further particular shape to the indifference curves or surfaces in the general case. We will in much of the book add an assumption in this direction. We will assume that these curves are strongly convex. In other words, they have the shape shown in Figures 1.2 and 1.3 for Ada. The basic idea involved in this assumption is that people prefer mixtures to extreme bundles. Thus, if an individual is indifferent between two bundles, he would strictly prefer the average of these two bundles to either of them. The reader will have no difficulty in finding cases where this assumption does not make sense, but we will show that it is not essential to many basic results. Nevertheless, it simplifies our analysis greatly and we are certainly not breaking with any traditions in making it. Returning then to our example and to the special preferences that we have now assumed for Bill and Ada let us first look at the results of trading.

3. First Theme: Decentralization by Prices (Walras)

Our first theme, due to Walras, is the decentralization by prices of the exchange problem. The idea, which will be familiar to the reader, is that the individuals in the economy take prices as given. They evaluate their endowments at those prices and this determines their income. They then choose the best bundle available which costs no more than their income. Thus, an individual need only know the going prices and need not consider the other individuals in making his choices. We make the point at the outset that this price–taking behaviour only makes sense when individuals view themselves as an insignificant part of a large market. Thus, our first theme is like Wagner – it can only be played with any success by large orchestras.

Our aim is to find prices which give rise to a "competitive equilibrium". What does this mean? Now, going back to our simple example, assume that in some mysterious way Ada and Bill know at what prices wine and bread may be exchanged. They both accept the prices as given and only contemplate trades at these prices. Recall our warning that this sort of behaviour cannot make real sense in a two–man world. Indeed, we will show later why this is true. We are doing what is often done in texts, interpreting a theme in an inappropriate context, to simplify the explanation. Throughout this discussion, the reader should bear in mind that we are trying here to explain the nature of a competitive equilibrium, and he should set aside, without forgetting, the problem of inappropriateness.

In the simple two–commodity world of our example we need only one price. We need simply to know the rate at which bread exchanges for wine. Taking the basic price unit in terms of bottles of wine then obviously the price of a bottle of wine is one. In other words, we are setting the price of our second good, wine, as one, written $p_2 = 1$. Our interest will be focused on the price of bread, i.e., p_1. Now let us see how Ada and Bill behave when faced with different prices. Consider the case when $p_1 = \frac{1}{2}$, that is the price of a loaf of bread is half a bottle of wine.

Ada, as the owner of 23 loaves of bread and 7 bottles of wine, can at this price trade all her wine for bread and finish in total with 37 loaves of bread, if this were available, or she could sell all her bread and finish with $18\frac{1}{2}$ bottles of wine or she could make some intermediate trade. Thus since she may, if she chooses, throw things away, she can consume any bundle in the dotted area of Figure 1.4. This we can call Ada's budget set. Bill, on the other hand, could trade off all his wine and wind up with 26 loaves of bread if this were available. His trading possibilities are given by the dotted area in Figure 1.5.

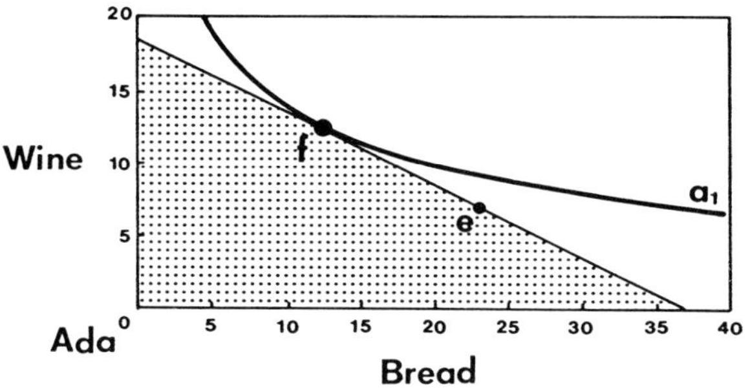

Figure 1.4

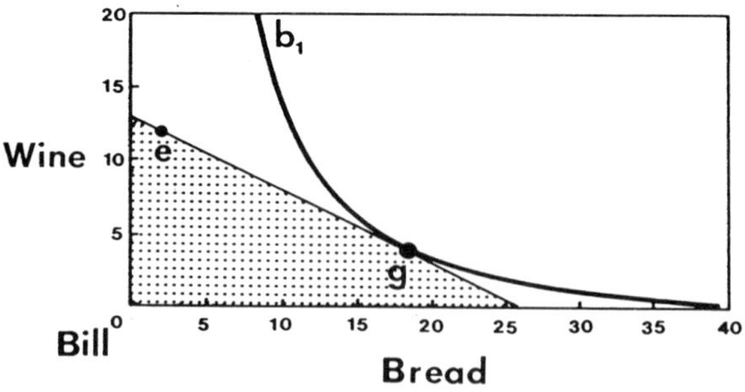

Figure 1.5

However, since only 25 loaves exist in our economy, Ada can never attain any more than this, she could at most trade off one of her bottles for all of Bill's bread. No equilibrium could involve a bigger trade.

Now, given the possible trades, which will Ada and Bill choose? The answer is, obviously, that which they each find most desirable. In Figure 1.4 we observe that the bundle $f = (\frac{37}{3}, \frac{37}{3})$ is the best available for Ada. It is the bundle in her budget set which is on her highest "indifference curve". Thus, when the price of bread is $\frac{1}{2}$ she would choose the bundle f which is the best that she can afford.

Note that,

$$p \cdot f = p_1 f_1 + p_2 f_2 = p_1 e_1 + p_2 e_2 = p \cdot e(a)$$

with our values, $(\frac{1}{2}, 1) \cdot (\frac{37}{3}, \frac{37}{3}) = (\frac{1}{2}, 1) \cdot (23, 7) = \frac{37}{2}$. Bear in mind the obvious consequences of our remarks that anything better than what she chose at these prices must cost more. The bundle that Ada did choose we refer to as her *demand* at prices p, written $\varphi(a, p)$ and the difference $z(a, p) = \varphi(a, p) - e(a)$, her "*excess demand*". The excess demand is, of course, the trade which she wishes to make at the given prices. Thus, in our example when $p_1 = \frac{1}{2}$ Ada wishes to trade in $10\frac{2}{3}$ of her loaves of bread for $5\frac{1}{3}$ bottles of wine, i.e., $z(a, p) = (-\frac{32}{3}, \frac{16}{3})$. Bill, on the other hand, faced with the low price of bread, wants to trade to g his demand in Figure 1.5. He wants to consume $\frac{23}{6}$ bottles of wine and $\frac{55}{3}$ loaves of bread. Thus,

$$\varphi(b, p) = (\frac{55}{3}, \frac{23}{6})$$

and

$$z(b, p) = \varphi(b, p) - e(b) = (\frac{55}{3}, \frac{23}{6}) - (2, 12) = (\frac{49}{3}, -\frac{49}{6}) .$$

Now it is clear that these two trades are incompatible. If we add the trades we see that

$$z(a, p) + z(b, p) = (-\frac{32}{3}, \frac{16}{3}) + (\frac{49}{3}, -\frac{49}{6}) = (\frac{17}{3}, -\frac{17}{6}) .$$

Thus, there is an excess supply of $\frac{17}{6}$ bottles of wine and an excess demand of $\frac{17}{3}$ loaves of bread. If we want the trades to balance, i.e., the markets to clear, we must change the prices. Intuitively, it is apparent that the problem is caused by the bread being relatively too cheap. Now suppose that we can find prices which generate a zero excess demand for both commodities. Now we have constructed Ada's and Bill's preferences such that when $p_1 = \frac{2}{3}$ their demands are as follows

$$\varphi(a,p) = (11,15)$$
$$\varphi(b,p) = (14,4) .$$

Then

$$z(a,p) = (-12,8) \text{ and } z(b,p) = (12,-8)$$

and we have

$$z(a,p) + z(b,p) = (0,0) .$$

What precisely does an equilibrium allocation look like in terms of our Edgeworth box? Drawing Ada's and Bill's preferences and budget constraints in the box we have the situation shown in Figure 1.6.

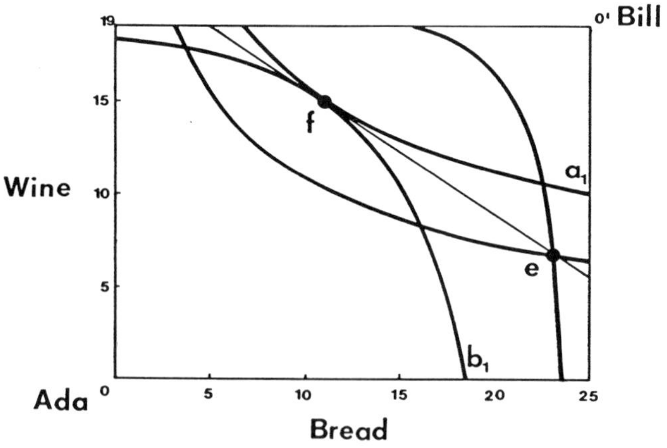

Figure 1.6

The indifference curves of the two individuals are tangent at the point f which measured from each origin is the best point in the respective individual's budget set. Recall that Bill's budget set is the area to the north–east of the diagonal price line. The fact that these two points coincide means that the two agents demand between them exactly the total quantity of goods available. In other words, there is zero total excess demand. Note that the price line through the initial endowment point separates the set of allocations which Ada prefers to f and the set which Bill prefers to f. We will come back to the significance of this later.

Now, at the risk of belabouring the point, recall that, when explaining the competitive equilibrium, we asserted that Ada and Bill behaved as if prices were given to them, and they simply had to accept them. Now, as we have said, this obviously makes no sense for two people since each of them knows that he or she can affect the outcome of the trade and hence can affect the terms on which goods are exchanged.

Example 1.1. This example shows how an individual can influence the competitive outcome in a small economy. In this case suppose that Ada starts with four loaves of bread and Bill with three bottles of wine. The competitive equilibrium is shown in Figure 1.7 as f where Ada receives

$$f(a) = (1\frac{1}{2}, 1\frac{1}{4}) \text{ and } p_1 = \frac{1}{2} \, .$$

Now suppose that Ada throws away a loaf of bread. The new situation is shown in Figure 1.8. Now the competitive equilibrium is at g where Ada receives

$$g(a) = (1\frac{1}{2}, 1\frac{1}{2}) \text{ and } p_1 = 1 \, .$$

Clearly, Ada by her apparently bizarre course of action, has influenced the situation in her favour. The reader will recall examples of such behaviour. Coffee was burnt as fuel in trains in Brazil to keep up its price, farmers throw away tons of produce to do the same. But the real point is that in small economies the individual's behaviour does affect the outcome. In fact the reader will easily be able to construct an example in which Ada gives a loaf of bread to Bill and the competitive outcome is better for her! The only situation where accepting prices as beyond one's influence seems reasonable is in a large market. If there are many participants it becomes less plausible that one individual can have a significant impact on the market price of a commodity.

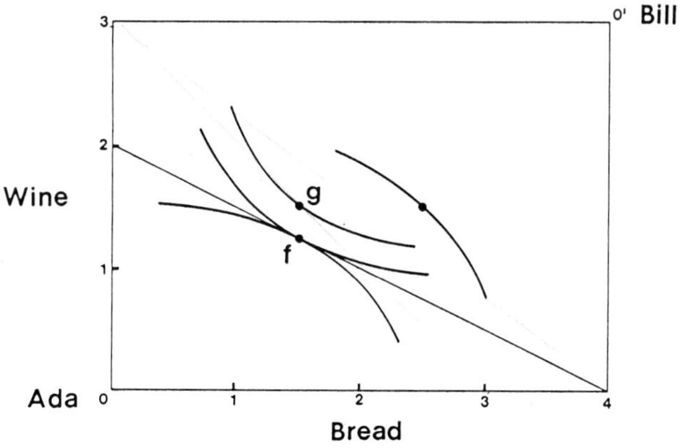

Figure 1.7

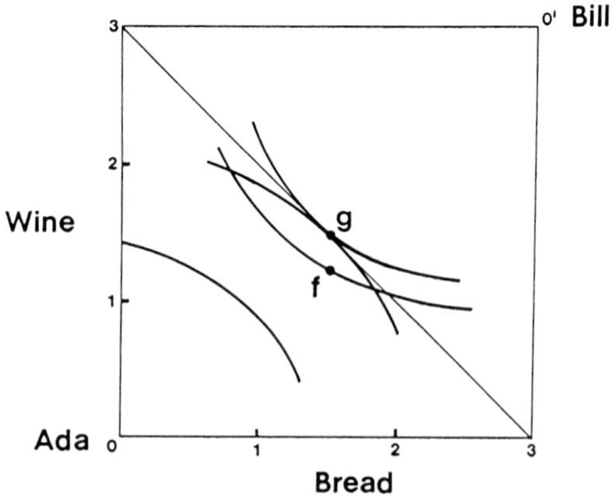

Figure 1.8

4. Second Theme: Improving by Cooperation (Edgeworth)

Our second theme, due to Edgeworth, involves the idea that individuals independently or cooperatively may be able to improve upon redistributions of goods. This simple idea leads to certain redistributions being acceptable as solutions to the exchange problems. Look at our example (Section 2) to see how this works.

Let us start again with Ada and Bill having initial bundles given by $e(a) = (23, 7)$, $e(b) = (2, 12)$. Observe first that it is safe to assume that neither will trade if they would finish up with a worse bundle from their own point of view than their initial endowments. Now, looking at Figure 1.9 we see that this must mean that the individuals trade into the lens–shaped area in the centre of the box.

This area, of course, is the intersection of the set of bundles preferred by Ada to her initial endowments and the analogous set for Bill. As long as this intersection is not empty both Ada and Bill can profit from trade. Suppose that they trade from their initial endowments to a position g in their preferred set as in Figure 1.9. From g they may again be able to

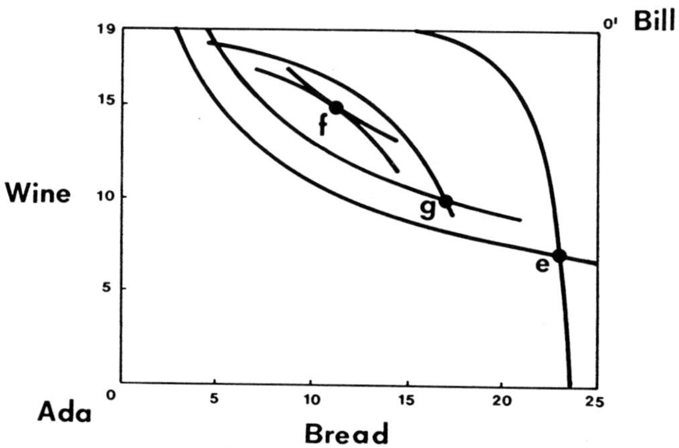

Figure 1.9

make mutually profitable trades. However, if they arrive at f no further trading would be possible without either Ada or Bill being worse off. There are many such positions and the set of all such allocations is known as the set of Pareto optima, which is shown by the line 0,0' in Figure 1.10.

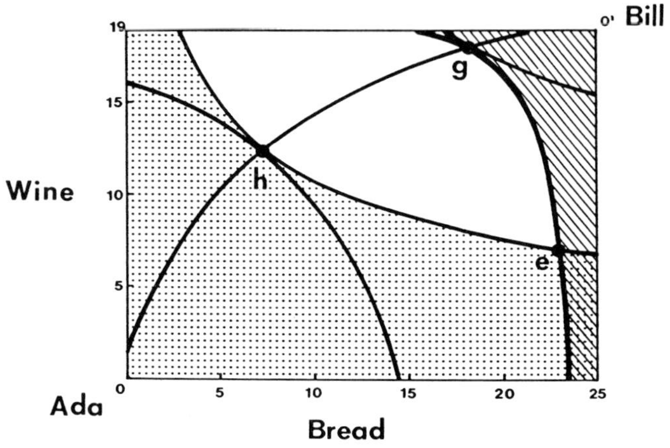

Allocations which can be improved upon by Ada

Allocations which can be improved upon by Bill

Allocations which can be improved upon by Ada and Bill acting together (not those on the line hg)

Figure 1.10

Note that some of these allocations will not be countenanced by Ada and Bill since they place these individuals in a worse position than they were with their initial endowments. Nevertheless, if any of these positions were to occur, the two agents together could not move profitably to any other position.

We have then two types of allocations to which there are objections. Firstly, there are those which can be improved upon by both individuals acting together and secondly, those which Ada or Bill would refuse since they could improve their lot by simply keeping their initial bundle. The first set of allocations are those off the line 0,0' in Figure 1.10. The second are those outside the lens in the same figure. The remaining unobjectionable allocations consist of the line *hg*, that is the Pareto optima which cannot be objected to by either Ada or Bill. Notice that the set of Pareto optima or "contract curve", as it is often called, is independent of how the goods are distributed initially. However, the power of Ada or Bill to object is based entirely on what they can manage by themselves. Hence, the lens–shaped area depends on the initial endowments, i.e., the initial distribution of "income" or resources. To see this more clearly, suppose that the initial position had been *h* as in Figure 1.11.

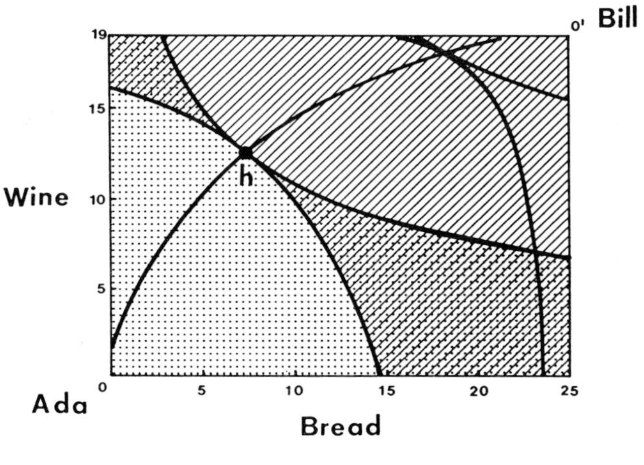

Allocations which can be improved upon by Ada

Allocations which can be improved upon by Bill

Figure 1.11

Then Ada would have objected to any allocation in the dotted area to the south–west of h, but Bill would have objected to anything in the diagonally shaded area to the north-east of h in Figure 1.11. Clearly, h is the only allocation which could not be improved upon. Thus, to repeat, the allocations to which the community as a whole, for the moment Ada and Bill, cannot object, are unaffected by the initial distribution of resources between them. However, the allocations upon which the individuals can improve and hence to which they would raise objcctions depend essentially upon their initial holdings.

Now with only two individuals in the economy the situation is very simple. There are only two basic sources of objection to proposed allocations: either one of the two individuals or the two acting together. Suppose, however, that there were more people in the economy. How then can we define those allocations which are unexceptionable? The natural extension to our previous discussion is to say that any coalition of individuals can object to a suggested allocation if that coalition could redistribute its initial resources among its members so as to improve the lot of each of its members. In other words, the coalition *could improve upon* the suggested allocation. Now if we eliminate all allocations which could be improved upon in this way we are left with a set of allocations which provide a solution to the problem of exchange. We can summarize this in the following which is our first theme, that attributed to Edgeworth. Its title and the nationality of its author suggest that it would be best played on the *cor anglais*.

Definition 1.1. The core of an exchange economy is that set of allocations which can be improved upon by no coalition of individuals.

The core is then a "solution" to the problem in the sense that it consists of a set of allocations which meet a criterion for acceptability. Whether this criterion is the appropriate one is for the reader to decide.

In fact we devote a chapter of the book to showing that, with the sort of assumptions we have already made, there are always allocations in the core. The value of a solution concept is reduced if we cannot specify assumptions under which there are allocations providing such a solution. Once we have specified such assumptions we have to move on to discuss whether they are reasonable and this will occupy our attention later in the book. An assumption which is crucial to the demonstration of the existence of core allocations is that of the convexity of preferences. The reader, as we have already said, will be able to think of examples where mixtures of bundles, between which he is indifferent, are indeed worse than those bundles in his eyes, thus contradicting the assumption of convexity. We will discuss this again at length, but for the moment let us simply note the basic role that convexity plays. We will also discuss in Chapter 4 what happens to the idea of the core when other difficulties present themselves. If goods are only available in discrete quantities and cannot be arbitrarily finely divided, for example, then our example looks very different. Suppose that wine can be traded only in units of one bottle and bread in units of one loaf. The possible allocations then look, in our example, as in Figure 1.12. When such indivisibilities are present the core may not exist (and we will give an example in Chapter 4). We will, however, also discuss an example where there are core allocations which do have properties of special interest.

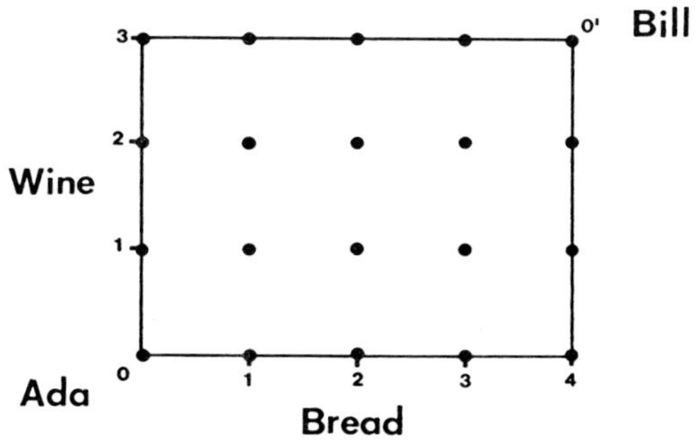

Figure 1.12

5. The Relation between the Two Themes

Now, having examined our two themes, competition and cooperation, let us have a look at the relation between the two.

The first observation is that the competitive allocation is in the core. To see this in our example note that when we found the competitive allocation f in the Edgeworth box the price line separated the allocations preferred by Ada to f from those preferred by Bill. Thus the competitive allocation is a Pareto optimum. The coalition of all agents, in our case Ada and Bill, cannot improve upon it together. Furthermore, the two remaining coalitions in our example, Ada and Bill each on their own, will never at any price choose something worse than their initial bundle. Therefore the bundle that they demand at the competitive equilibrium is at least as good as their initial endowments. Thus neither of them can improve upon it and the allocation f must be in the core.

Can we say more? Recall that we argued that the competitive theme made more sense in large economies, Wagner should not be performed by small ensembles.

Suppose, for the moment, that we look at an exchange market with many traders none of whom is exceptionally well endowed. This is a situation in which competitive behaviour, i.e., the acceptance of prices as given, makes sense, but what we would like to know is whether the character of our other solution concept, the core, is changed. In fact, what we will show is that, in a certain sense, the core "shrinks" as an economy becomes large, and in particular those allocations which are not competitive disappear from the core. The astute reader will be very suspicious of this claim as he will want to know whether the statement "the core shrinks" has any meaning. At first sight, it would seem to make little sense. What after all is an allocation? In a two–person economy it is a list of the quantities of each commodity assigned to each of the two traders. In our two–commodity example an allocation is the two pairs of quantities assigned to Ada and Bill. If we add another agent we need to expand our list and an allocation will now consist of three pairs of numbers. How can we decide whether a set of allocations for the two–man economy is bigger or smaller than a set for the three–man economy?

We will now take a very special sort of large economy and show that the statement that "the core shrinks" is, in fact, meaningful. In Chapter 5, however, we will prove results for rather more general economies. It will become clear that these results correspond to the idea of the core reducing to the set of competitive equilibria.

Let us return to our example and increase the number of participants. We will choose a very special way of doing this which will enable us to make statements about the core in large economies. Suppose that, instead of Ada and Bill being alone in our economy, Ada has a twin sister and Bill has a twin brother. These twins not only have identical preferences to those of their counterparts but have identical endowments of goods. Thus, we now have a four–person economy but we only have two *types* of individuals. An economist looking at these people would only be able to say "that woman is an Ada" or "that man is a Bill". He would not be able to distinguish between the two women, for example. Remember that the economist is only concerned with two aspects of people, their preferences and their endowments. Ada's sister may well be considerably more attractive than Ada, but if the two women have the same tastes and resources they will be classified, for we "dismal scientists", as identical.

Remember, before we consider the problem of this new four–person economy, that a competitive equilibrium is in the core. The argument is slightly different from the one employed above and carries over to more general economies. The first thing to observe is that if any bundle $g(a)$ is preferred by an individual a to $f(a)$, his competitive allocation, then at the competitive prices this bundle $g(a)$ must cost more than his initial resources. This is obvious since otherwise he would have chosen $g(a)$ at the competitive prices and $f(a)$ would not have been the best available. Now, if some coalition S can improve upon the competitive allocation, they must be able to redistribute their initial resources amongst themselves to find for each individual something, say g, preferred to f. But if g is preferred to f by all the individuals in S, then g must cost more for each of them than their initial bundles. Hence, in total, S by redistributing its resources amongst itself achieves something higher in value than those resources – an obvious nonsense! Thus a competitive allocation must be in the core.

Furthermore, note that the competitive allocation must assign identical bundles to the two Adas. Obviously neither can get something better than the other since they both choose from the same budget set and have the same preferences. Neither can they get bundles which are different but lying on the same indifference curve, for with the strongly convex preferences we have assumed the average of the two bundles would be strictly better than their choice and still affordable. Hence, they could not have chosen the best bundle in the first place. The same obviously applies to the two Bills. This takes us on to an important point. If we are interested in competitive allocations in our four–man economy we need look only at the allocation of one of the Adas and that of one of the Bills. In other words, the competitive allocation for this economy can still be described in our familiar Edgeworth box.

The question now arises, is this true for core allocations as well? In other words, if a core allocation gives identical bundles to people of the same type then we just choose one of each type, in our case one Ada and one Bill, and by looking at their allocations we know all there is to be known about the allocation for the whole economy. If this is the case in our four-person economy we can still concentrate our attention on the Edgeworth box and need only consider allocations in that framework. This gives a certain sense to the idea of looking at the behaviour of the core as the number of participants if an economy grows.

The argument that the core does have this *equal treatment* property is most easily given in the context of our example and extends directly to the more general situation discussed in later chapters.

Suppose that there is an allocation f which does not assign identical bundles to identical individuals, can it be in the core? There are two possible ways in which this unequal treatment could arise. Suppose that Ada $(a,1)$ and her sister $(a,2)$ receive bundles which are different but which they rank equally. In other words,

$$f(a,1) \neq f(a,2) \text{ but } f(a,1) \sim_a f(a,2) \,.$$

Clearly, with strongly convex preferences the average of these two bundles would be strictly preferred by both Ada and her sister, and the allocation g which gives this to the two females and the previous f to the two Bills would represent an improvement, is obviously feasible, and therefore provides the basis for an objection to f by the whole group. Hence, f is not in the core.

The second possibility is that there is unequal treatment in a stronger sense. Thus, for example, if Ada 1 were to receive something worse than Ada 2, could the allocation f be in the core? Now if we look at the two Bills, since they have the same preferences we can compare their at-

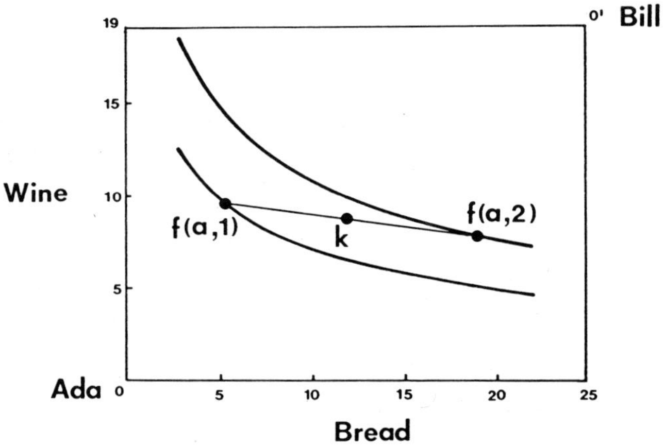

Figure 1.13

titudes to what they receive in f. In particular one of the two Bills must be no better off than the other: suppose that this is Bill 1. They may well be equally treated in this allocation of course. Bill 1 and Ada 1 can surely achieve for themselves the average Bill and Ada allocation respectively. But this must be strictly better for Ada 1 and can be no worse for Bill 1. Therefore, these two can improve upon f and f cannot be in the core.

The fact that the average k of the two Adas' bundles will be strictly preferred to the worst of these bundles is, indeed, a consequence of the strong convexity of preferences and is illustrated in Figure 1.13. We may summarize this argument as follows:

$$\sum_{i=1}^{2} f(a,i) + \sum_{i=1}^{2} f(b,i) = 2e(a) + 2e(b)$$

$$f(a,2) \succ_a f(a,1) \quad \text{and} \quad f(b,2) \succsim_b f(b,1) \; .$$

Hence $$\frac{1}{2}\sum_{i=1}^{2} f(a,i) \succ_a f(a,1) \quad \text{and} \quad \frac{1}{2}\sum_{i=1}^{2} f(b,i) \succsim_b f(b,1) \; ,$$

but $$\frac{1}{2}\sum_{i=1}^{2} f(a,i) + \frac{1}{2}\sum_{i=1}^{2} f(b,i) = e(a) + e(b) \; .$$

Therefore, $(a,1)$ and $(b,1)$ can improve upon f. The fact that we only have two Adas and two Bills is obviously immaterial. If we had some arbitrary number n of both we could still use this argument. Just order the people of each type in terms of the satisfaction derived from their bundles and a coalition made up of the worst off of each type will be able to improve upon any allocation with unequal treatment.

All this shows that if we have equal numbers in each type then it is enough, when considering core allocations, to look at the allocation to one representative of each type. Thus, no matter how many identical replicas of Bill and Ada we have, we may continue to represent core allocations in our original Edgeworth box.

Observation. To return to our original analogy, what we have said is that if we have a certain number of instruments in the orchestra then for our purposes it is enough to look at the score for one of each instrument. It does not matter how many first violins there are since they are all playing the same thing. Our statement is in fact more restrictive than this in that we are really saying it does not matter if we replicate the orchestra, but it does matter if we increase some instruments and not others.

In our example, had Ada had a sister and Bill no brother then there might well be core allocations which did not treat Ada 1 and Ada 2 equally. We will show an example of this in the text. However, for the moment we shall focus on replications of our Bill–Ada economy.

In our four–man economy let us try to see which are the core allocations. We may, for the reasons just given, look at the Edgeworth box (Figure 1.14). Now it is clear that the allocations in the core must be "contained in" the old core of the two–person economy. Otherwise, whoever objected in the two-person situation would object in the four–

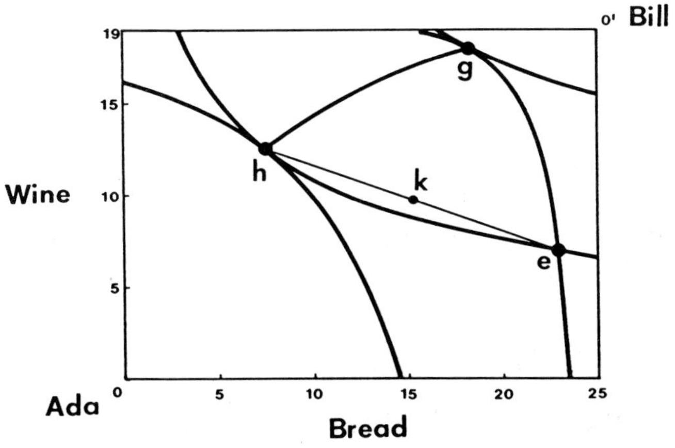

Figure 1.14

person framework. The question is, are there allocations which were in the core originally but now, with the introduction of two new players, disappear?

Look at the allocation h which in the original economy was the worst in the core for Ada. It was that which was on the same indifference curve as her initial resources. Could this allocation, now to two Adas and to two Bills, be in the core? The answer is no, and the reasoning is simple. Think of the coalitions that could form in the two–person economy. They were Bill or Ada alone or the two of them together. Now, however, we have a new possibility. The coalition of two Adas and one Bill will ensure that the old endpoint of the core is now removed. It will make sure that any allocation in the core gives something better to each Ada than her initial resources. Brotherhood or sisterhood is not to be despised!

How does this coalition improve upon the allocation in question? Note first that any point on the line between the initial Ada resources and the point h would be strictly preferred by Ada to her initial bundle. In particular, this is true of the halfway point k in Figure 1.14. Thus,

$$(1) \qquad k(a,1) = k(a,2) = \frac{1}{2}e(a) + \frac{1}{2}h(a,1) \succ_a h(a,1) = h(a,2) \ .$$

But consider the allocation for the three–man coalition (the two Adas with, say, Bill 1 which gives k to the Adas and h to Bill 1. This is feasible since

$$k(a,1) + k(a,2) + h(b,1) = e(a) + h(a,1) + h(b,1)$$

and h was an allocation for the two–person economy, i.e.,

$$h(a,1) + h(b,1) = e(a) + e(b) \ .$$

Therefore,

$$k(a,1) + k(a,2) + h(b,1) = 2e(a) + e(b) \ .$$

Then the fact that Bill 1 still receives $h(b,1)$, together with equation (1), means that this coalition, two Adas and a Bill, can improve upon h and that allocation is not in the core of the four–person economy.

In fact, as is clear from Figure 1.15, every allocation f as in Figure 1.15 is not in the core of the four–person economy. The argument is the same as the one we gave for the allocation h.

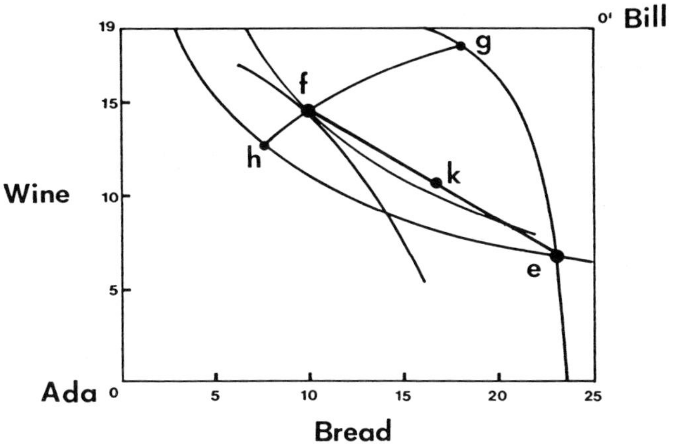

Figure 1.15

Now we make the argument to show that all allocations in the core except the competitive equilibria are removed if we replicate our economy still further. Thus, if we add more Adas and more Bills all non-competitive allocations disappear from the core. Concentrating our attention on those allocations below, i.e., to the south–west of the competitive allocation, we notice the following crucial fact. The line through e to any non–competitive Pareto optimal allocation f must cut the Ada indifference curve passing through f and must be above that curve near f. Thus, there must be a point close to f on that line which is preferred to f by Ada. In other words, for any f if we look at a bundle

$$k(a) = \frac{1}{n}e(a) + \frac{n-1}{n}f(a)$$

this would, if n were very large, have the property that

$$k(a) \succ_a f(a) .$$

We drop the index i since all people of the same type are equally treated in f. The above idea is illustrated in Figure 1.16.

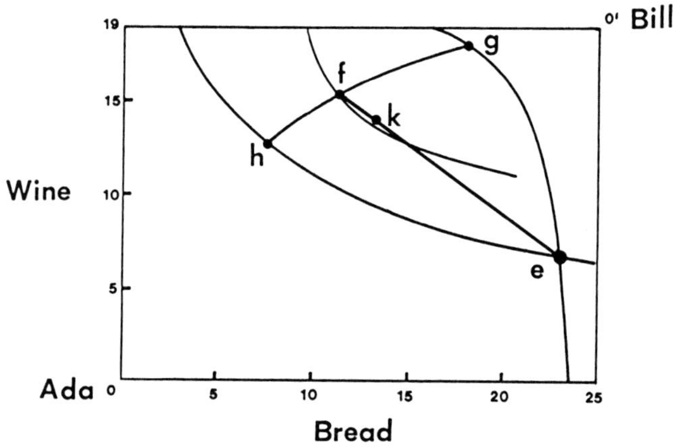

Figure 1.16

But the coalition consisting of n Adas and $n-1$ Bills can improve upon f by giving g to the Adas and f to the Bills. We have only to show that this is feasible for such a coalition. We know that

$$\begin{aligned} nk(a) + (n-1)f(b) &= n(\frac{1}{n}e(a) + \frac{n-1}{n}f(a)) + (n-1)f(b) \\ &= e(a) + (n-1)(f(a) + f(b)) \\ &= e(a) + (n-1)(e(a) + e(b)) \\ &= ne(a) + (n-1)e(b) . \end{aligned}$$

Hence, f is not in the core. Similarly, on the other side of the competitive allocation the coalition of $n-1$ Adas and n Bills will improve upon any allocation that is not competitive. The competitive allocation is just that Pareto optimum where the line from the initial resources to the allocation does not cut either of the indifference curves passing through the allocation. It is thus the only allocation which cannot be improved upon in the way described.

Note what we have done. We replicate ad infinitum (ad nauseam if you will) our Ada and Bill economy. In so doing we know that eventually we will have n Adas and n Bills, with n sufficiently large to remove any non–competitive allocation in the original core. Recall again that we can always look at allocations in the original Edgeworth box since we know that core allocations in these replica economies have the equal treatment property.

The observant reader will have noted something further. The procedure we have just described gives us a way of defining competitive allocations apparently quite different from the definition that we gave earlier.

Characterization. An allocation is competitive for a given economy if and only if it remains in the core for every replication of that economy.

There is a little looseness of language involved which the reader will probably find is more than offset by the occasional insistence on precision in later chapters! When we say "remains in the core" we mean the replication of the allocation, i.e., giving that allocation to every member of each type remains in the core.

The important thing to observe is that this definition in no way involves the idea of prices, yet it is by means of prices that competitive allocations are normally defined. It is a remarkable fact that the Walrasian idea of a solution to the problem of exchange comes to coincide with the Edgeworth solution as an economy is expanded in the way that we have described. Put another way, those allocations which persist as acceptable from the Edgeworth viewpoint are precisely those which Walras singled out as solutions.

We have said previously that the competitive equilibrium is, like Wagner, appropriate for large orchestras. Recalling that the number of possible coalitions in economies with many agents is large we might feel that the core is less plausible in this context. Thus, the core is like the music of Corelli, more suitable for smaller orchestras. If the orchestra is large enough, however, Corelli begins to sound like Wagner!

One might be tempted to make the following argument on the basis of our results. The core is a cooperative solution, no group or individual can improve upon its allocations, therefore it is in some sense democratic or "socially acceptable". The fact that the only allocations which remain socially acceptable turn out to be competitive, adds weight to the idea that the competitive allocation has social merit as a solution. The reader will see the hole in this reasoning very quickly. The objection to the competitive allocation, from a social viewpoint, is that it depends upon the ownership of the initial resources. In other words, "into those that hath shall it be given". Exactly the same objection applies to the core, it is *democratic, given the initial distribution of resources.* The latter may be very unequal and if this is the case, the inequality may persist in the core allocations.

Let us backtrack a little and note what we have shown. We have discussed what happens to the core when economies become large in a very special way, that is are replicated. We have given a geometric argument to show how this happens. This argument, however, is only valid for the two–type, two–good case, but we will give a different argument for the general case in the text. The change in the core with the increase in the size of the economy enabled us to characterize competitive allocations.

Despite our denial of any special social context of this fact we will emphasize yet again its most interesting feature. If one asks under what circumstances would an individual accept prices as given, the answer is, as we have suggested, standard. He will accept prices and act as a price taker when he feels that he can have no effect on those prices; in other words, if he is an insignificant member of the market. What happens when we replicate an economy? The individuals in that economy become insignificant. Thus, the coincidence of competitive allocations and core allocations occurs under precisely those circumstances when competitive behaviour makes sense.

Rephrasing our result we can say, if we take a given economy and replicate it until all the individuals become insignificant, that the only allocations in the core of this enlarged economy are competitive.

6. A Conjuring Trick

A question that preoccupied Walras and many of those who followed him was under what assumptions does a competitive equilibrium exist? The brief answer is that in the sort of economy illustrated by our Ada and Bill example, a competitive equilibrium, that is a competitive allocation and the associated prices, always exists. We will sketch here an argument to show that this is so, an argument sufficiently different from the standard one that it may seem to old hands at mathematical economics something of a rabbit out of a hat. This is not the case, but showing that our argument boils down to the traditional one may occupy a few minutes of even the well–trained reader's time.

The basic result of Chapter 4 is that, for the sort of economies of which our two-person case is an example, the core is never empty. That is, there is an allocation which can be improved upon by no coalition in such an economy. Now think of our replica economies, the two–person, four–person, six–person, etc., sequence. Associated with each of these economies will be a core allocation f_1, f_2, f_3,... In each case consider just the allocations to one person of each type, i.e., the allocation to one Ada and one Bill. Remember that this is legitimate since the f's are core allocations and members of the same type are equally treated. Now it is easily shown that there is a subsequence of this sequence of allocations which converges to something, say, $\overline{f}$. It is also easily shown that $\overline{f}$, given to all n members of each type, is in the core for every n-fold replica economy. Therefore, f is a competitive allocation for the first economy.

To see this argument in terms of our original box consider what we were doing. We took some core allocation in the first economy, i.e., some allocation on the segment of the contract curve between the two indifference curves which passed through the initial endowment point. This was f_1. Then we took an allocation f_2 from the core of the four–man economy, that is from the subset of the original core shown in Figure 1.17b. Then f_3 is taken from the core of the six–man economy and so forth. This sequence of points (or rather a subsequence of it) must converge, of course, and does, to some allocation $\overline{f}$, and this allocation is competitive, thus showing the existence of such an allocation. Using our previous argument we can find the associated prices. We know that the limit of our sequence must be a point on a line from the initial resources just separating the preferred sets of Ada and Bill on the contract curve, i.e., the slope of this line provides the competitive prices for the allocation.

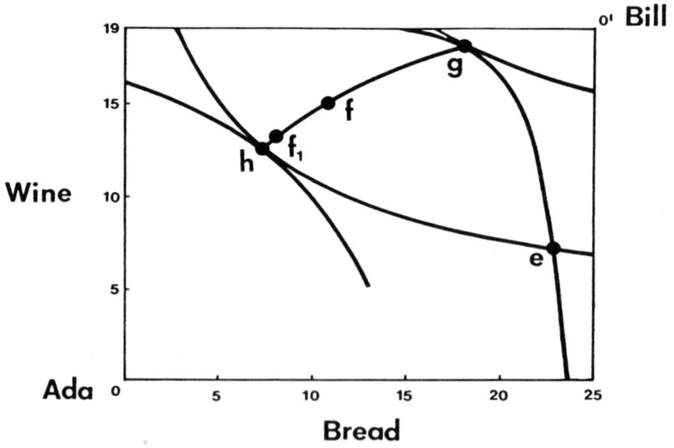

Figure 1.17a: Original core

We will return to the Walrasian theme shortly, but first let us expand the remarks above about insignificance.

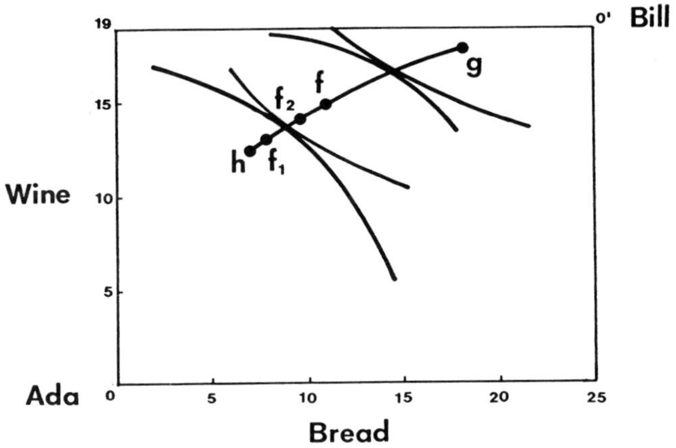

Figure 1.17b: Core of a four–man economy

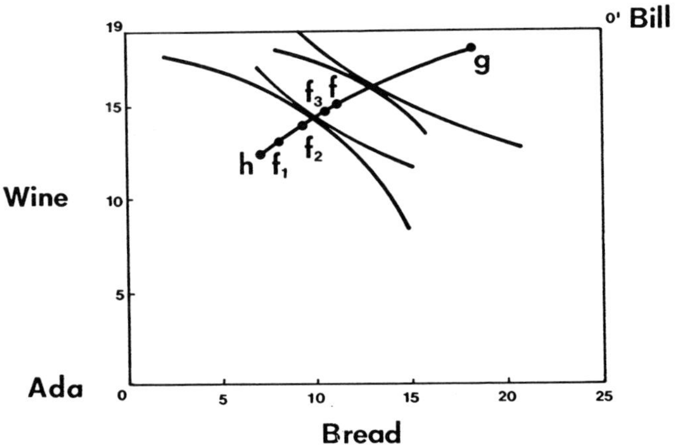

Figure 1.17c: Core of a six–man economy

7. Limit Economies and the Importance of Being Insignificant

We talked about replicating an economy until the individuals in the economy were insignificant. For competitive behaviour (passive behaviour might be a better description) to make sense, individuals must believe themselves to be insignificant. Now, in general, in an economy with a finite number of individuals, the latter will be able to change prices, for example, by altering their own behaviour as we showed in our earlier example. However, we can talk about economies where individuals would actually not have this capacity. Thus, we can define an economy where each individual has literally no weight or influence, where the removal of an individual would change nothing. Such an economy should not be thought of as a description of a possible economy but rather as an idealization in the same way that physicists might think of perfect fluids, rather than of the individual particles of which these fluids are composed. As an example, we might think of the agents in an economy as corresponding to the points on the unit interval. There is, then, a continuum of agents each having no "weight". For such an idealized economy it can be shown that, under rather weak assumptions about the characteristics of individuals, the core and the competitive allocations are the same. Note, of course, that in this sort of economy, as in any other, there may be several equilibrium allocations. We will return to this later. The point is that in these rather rarefied economies we have the equivalence towards which we worked with our replication arguments. The final and perhaps most important remark about these continuum economies is that they may be regarded not just as idealizations but also as limits of a sequence of finite economies. This leads us directly to the next idea.

Once we can talk about a sequence of economies approaching a limit then we talk about the "convergence" of the core to the competitive equilibria in a simple way. Suppose that we remain in the Ada and Bill world for a moment. Now instead of imagining this world expanding by a simple replication, could we answer the following question? As the Ada and Bill world becomes big is it true that core allocations are near to competitive allocations? The Ada and Bill world may not become big in the way that we specified previously. More Bills may be added than Adas and so forth. You could imagine a sequence of increasing economies being generated as follows. Take a deck of cards with all the kings and queens removed. Now draw a card. If it is an odd number, an ace counts as one, a jack as eleven, then add that number of Adas to the economy. If it is even, do the same for the Bills. At any moment in this procedure the proportions of the two types will be fairly arbitrary, but if we do it long enough we will have the proportion of Adas converging to $\frac{25}{55}$ and that of Bills to $\frac{30}{55}$.

Let us take a core allocation for each of these economies and look at the sequence of these. We run into trouble straight away because our "equal treatment" property has disappeared. People of the same type may receive different bundles in a core allocation if there are not equal numbers in each type. We give a simple example of this in the text. How can we get over this difficulty? What we can do is to ask how far is an individual's allocation from the nearest competitive allocation for him? Now consider the individual with the greatest such distance and let us refer to this as "the distance of the core of the nth economy from its competitive allocations". Now with some restrictions, for example that the "limiting frequencies" that we have just described are positive, as was the case in our example, and that the equilibrium price system for the limit economy be unique then the "distance" that we have defined goes to zero as the economies become large. This again captures Edgeworth's original idea. The important thing to see here is that our results confirm the impression that the limit or continuum economy does have something important to tell us about large but finite economies. We have continuity, in the sense that what is true in the limit is almost true in very large economies.

8. Back to Walras

Up to this point the existence of the Walrasian theme, that is, of prices which decentralize the allocation of goods, has only been shown by using the core and for many readers this must seem a little bizarre. The mainstream of mathematical economics has focused firmly on the problem of demonstrating the existence of competitive equilibria and it is only recently that Edgeworth's approach has encroached upon the scene.

Let us then revert to the traditional approach and see how one might set about establishing existence without even a glance over the shoulder at game theory. To do this we will concentrate on the demand of the individuals in the economy.

Recall that the choice of an individual a at given prices is the bundle that he most prefers within the budget set, and we referred to this as $\varphi(a,p)$. This is illustrated for Ada in Figure 1.18. The excess demand

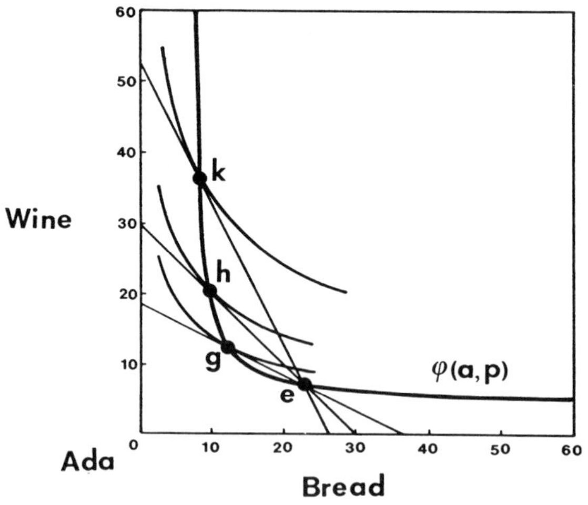

Figure 1.18

$z(a,p)$ is the difference between the demand and the initial resources $e(a)$ as we have already said, i.e.,

$$z(a,p) = \varphi(a,p) - e(a) .$$

Now with our assumptions several things are true. Firstly $z(a,p)$ is continuous. Secondly $z(a,p)$ is unchanged if we multiply the prices of both goods by some number. Thirdly the consumers will always spend all their income on goods by the greed assumption. Now the second of these observations means that we can normalise, i.e., choose the level of prices. So let us here set $p_1 + p_2 = 1$. In addition the third remark shows us that desired expenditure will equal income at each price, that is

$$p_1\varphi_1(a,p) + p_2\varphi_2(a,p) = p_1 e_1(a) + p_2 e_2(a) .$$

But this means nothing more than that the value of the excess demand is zero, a statement which is known as Walras' Law, i.e.,

$$p_1 z_1(a,p) + p_2 z_2(a,p) = 0$$

or with our normalisation

$$p_1 z_1(a,p) + (1 - p_1) z_2(a,p) = 0 .$$

It will be obvious to the reader, after this, that it is enough to look at the excess demand for good 1 to know that for good 2.

We do however have a fourth property of $z(a,p)$ which we obtain from our greed assumption, which is that as the price of one good goes to zero (i.e., that of the other becomes one) then the demand for that good becomes arbitrarily large.

Now exactly the same considerations hold for Bill and Ada together, i.e., for their aggregate excess demand

$$z(p) = z(a,p) + z(b,p) .$$

With all this in mind let us trace out the aggregate excess demand for Ada and Bill. This is done in Figure 1.19.

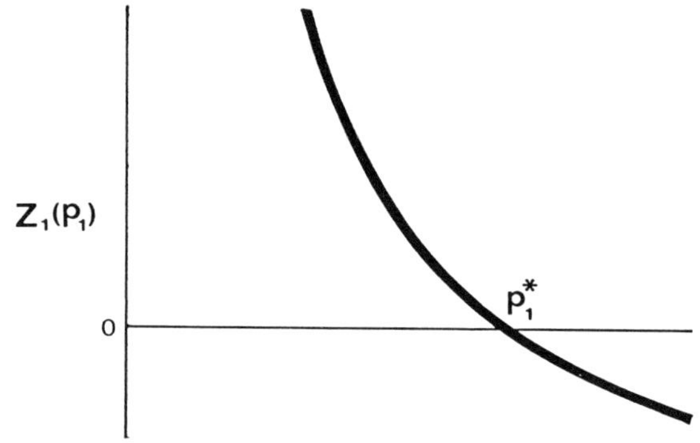

Figure 1.19

That there is an equilibrium price can, of course, be seen but the argument that proves this for such an economy is very simple.

When p_1 is low enough $z_1(p_1)$ must be positive. When p_1 is close to 1, $p_2 = 1 - p_1$ is very low and the excess demand $z_2(p_1)$ for good 2 must be positive. But if the excess demand for good 2 is positive then that for good 1 must be negative by Walras' Law. Now since the excess demand for good 1 is easily shown to be continuous it must in passing from positive to negative become zero for some price. In other words in passing in Figure 1.19 from somewhere above the axis to somewhere below it it must cut the axis. Since this happens for a positive price p_1^*, by Walras' Law again, the excess demand for good 2 must also be zero. Thus p_1^* must be an equilibrium price. This simple "proof" of the existence of an equilibrium can be, of course, and indeed will be, formalised in Chapter 3.

What we have just done is equivalent to the following. In our Edgeworth box for each price find the bundle demanded by Ada. As prices change then bundles trace out a curve that is illustrated in Figure 1.18. Do the same for Bill and observe that, with the assumptions that we have made, there will be some price, in our case p_1^* at which the curves will cross and we will have an equilibrium. This is illustrated in Figure 1.20.

It is evident that if the excess demand function had had jumps our argument would not have held. These jumps cannot occur if we have strongly convex preferences. That is, when preferences are strongly convex then excess demand behaves as a continuous function of prices. This continuity of the excess demand relation is at the heart of the existence proofs in Chapter 3. In our example and in the literature in the Walrasian tradition this assumption of convexity of the individual's preferences is necessary. Indeed, the basis of the arguments used in all the standard proofs of existence is that aggregate behaviour has the continuity properties of individual behaviour. Thus, if individuals are "well behaved" then so will the economy be.

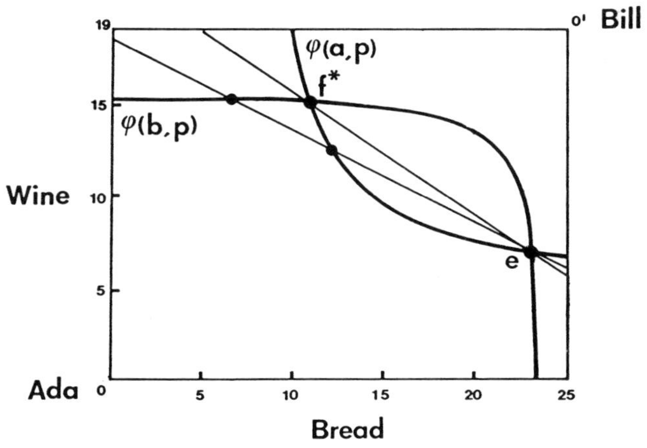

Figure 1.20

9. Less Well Behaved Individuals

Suppose that we had made fewer assumptions about Ada and Bill. In particular, suppose that we had not assumed them to have convex preferences. After all, many people might be indifferent between a main course of steak or one of duck, but there are few who would find a mixture of the two attractive. In our example with bread and wine, preference for extreme bundles would be difficult to justify, but if there are many goods it is easy to see how such choices might arise. In the simple two–good world bread and wine would be needed for survival, but if we extend the range of goods then there will be many consumers who dislike certain mixtures and prefer to eliminate certain commodities from their consumption.

That this presents a problem is clearly seen by changing our example. Suppose that Ada, instead of being the amiable convex person of earlier pages now becomes more extreme. If her preferences now look as in Figure 1.21 and in particular we see that she is indifferent between the

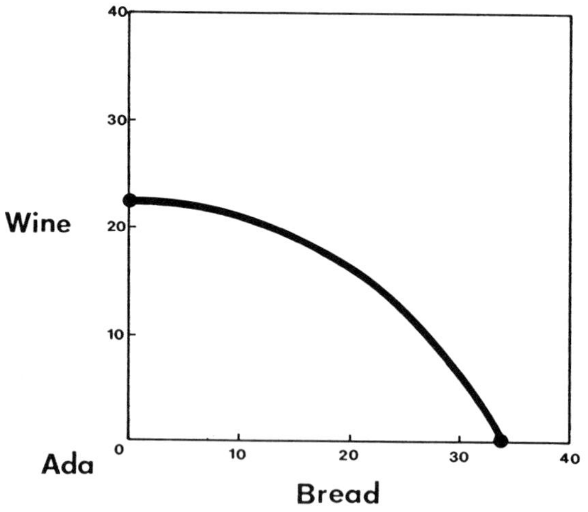

Figure 1.21

two bundles $(0, \frac{67}{3})$ and $(\frac{67}{2}, 0)$. However, far from preferring intermediate bundles any mixture of these two bundles is worse for her. Now as long as a bottle of wine is cheaper than one and a half loaves of bread she will always choose to consume only wine and no bread.

Yet when the price of bread is exactly equal to $\frac{2}{3}$, (i.e., three loaves of bread are worth two bottles of wine), she will choose either $\frac{67}{3}$ bottles of wine or $\frac{67}{2}$ loaves of bread and as bread becomes cheaper she will want only bread. Her demand curve is no longer a nice continuous curve, but when the price of bread is $\frac{2}{3}$, jumps from one side to the opposite side of Bill's demand curve. There is then no equilibrium in this case. The lack of convexity led to a lack of continuity of Ada's demand curve and thus destroyed our hope of finding an equilibrium. Supposing, however, that we had modified Ada's demand somewhat by "convexifying" her demand. Thus we would modify her choice when the price of bread is $\frac{2}{3}$ to include all bundles between $(0, \frac{67}{3})$ and $(\frac{67}{2}, 0)$. This is clearly a distortion of the truth.

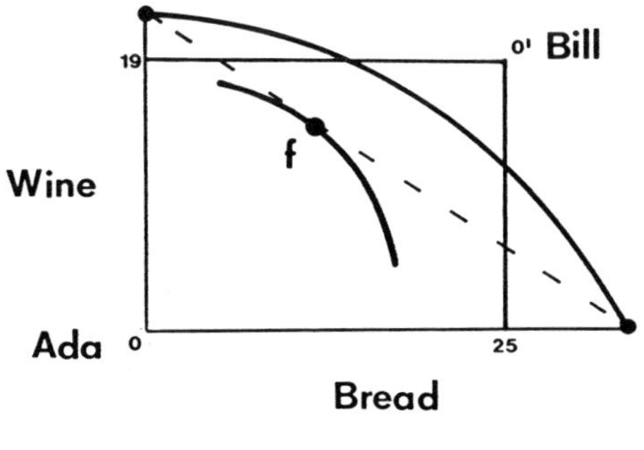

Figure 1.22

But it does give us back an "equilibrium". At equal prices Ada has the whole dotted line from $(0, \frac{67}{3})$ to $(\frac{67}{2}, 0)$ as best choices and one of these $(11, 15)$ gives us an equilibrium (Figure 1.22). Thus we are back in the old situation having artificially added this line to Ada's demand curve.

Now this was a distortion of Ada's preferences. In effect we flattened out her indifference curves until they coincided with the price lines and were thus just convex. However, the real question is how important is this distortion? By changing the demand of individuals in the way we did we restore our ability to use the mathematical results mentioned earlier. Thus, we may prove the existence of "equilibria". How close to real equilibria are these objects?

To see the answer consider increasing the number of Adas. Now add their offers at each price. The problem occurred when the bread price was $\frac{2}{3}$. Consider first the case of two Adas: at such a price the demands of the two look as in Figure 1.23.

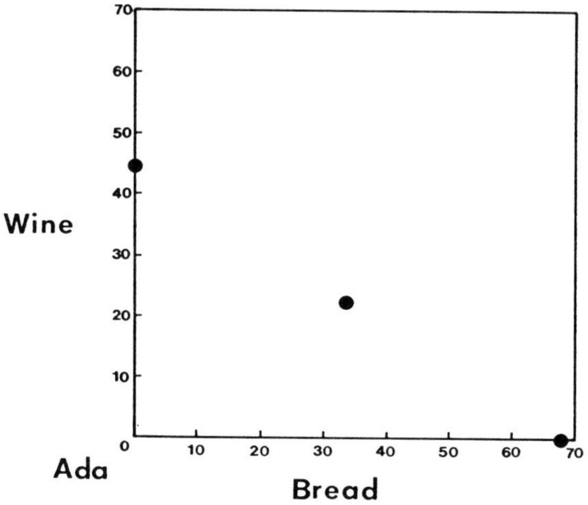

Figure 1.23

Clearly, with two Adas and two Bills our problem is still not solved. If one Ada takes $(\frac{67}{2}, 0)$ and the other $(0, \frac{67}{3})$, as best bundle for them at the price $\frac{2}{3}$, and each Bill chooses $(14, 4)$ then we do not have an equilibrium but we are in some sense "nearer" to an equilibrium. In this case, adding one Ada was not enough to generate a point on the offer curve which exactly coincided with one on the two Bills' demand curve. Now, if we had had four Adas the picture would have been as in Figure 1.24. It is clear that the points are gradually filling out the gaps, thus reducing the discontinuity of the aggregate offer curve. The reader may care to check that in an economy with 48 Adas and 25 Bills there is an equilibrium.

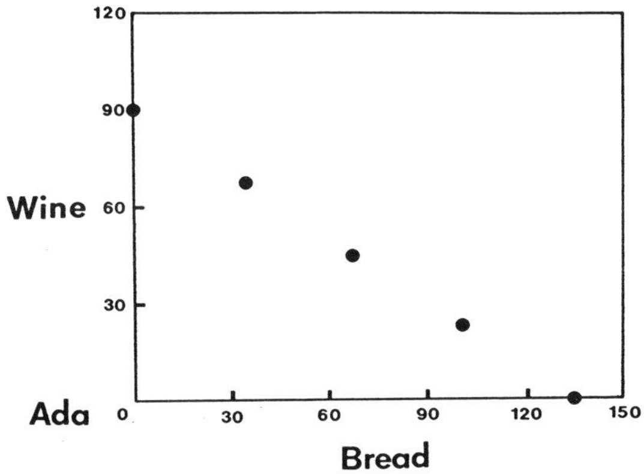

Figure 1.24

What we can and do show in Chapter 3 is that if all individuals can have non–convex preferences then we can find an "equilibrium" by "convexifying" their demand. Furthermore, if there are many individuals almost all of them will receive something in their original unmodified demand set at the "equilibrium" prices. Thus, in a large economy, nonconvexity is relatively unimportant. Individual discontinuity is not inconsistent with aggregate continuity.

Now, having assured ourselves that in the setting that we have constructed and in even more general ones Walras' theme will be played, we pass on to a natural question.

10. What Other Features Does Walras' Theme Have?

We have developed at some length the idea of a competitive equilibrium. Recall how we should think of such a situation. If the price p_1^* in our example were announced and Ada and Bill made their choices accordingly, their demands would just exhaust the available quantities of the two goods. Furthermore there would be no reason for any departure from that position. Yet two natural questions can now be asked. Is the equilibrium price unique in our sort of economy? Furthermore would a natural adjustment process lead us from a non–equilibrium price towards an equilibrium? We will see, in a moment, that the answers to these questions depend upon the nature of the aggregate excess demand function of our economy. To be able to give positive answers to our questions we will need to know more about $z(p)$ than the basic properties that we have just mentioned. Do the assumptions that we have made in constructing our simple economy imply any such properties? The answer, unfortunately, is no! In our simple example remember that we managed to show the existence of an equilibrium price. To do this we made essential use of what happened when p_1 went to either zero or one. If we ignore, briefly, what happens at these extremes we can in fact make the following rather remarkable statement. If we are given any continuous function $f(p_1)$ then for prices p_1 between ϵ and $1-\epsilon$, where ϵ is a positive number which our reader is free to choose, we can find two individuals whose aggregate excess demand $z_1(p_1)$ for good 1 is exactly $f(p_1)$. Furthermore these two individuals have preferences and initial endowments that satisfy all the conditions that we specified for Ada and Bill. Thus we know no more than our basic properties about $z(p)$. The observant reader will notice that we have used our properties in the same way as when we showed the existence of competitive prices. Firstly we require that the function which is a candidate to be an excess demand function of a two–person economy should be continuous. Secondly we normalised prices which we can do because we required that the function in question should have the property that it be the same if we multiply both prices by some positive number. Thirdly once we have specified $z_1(p)$ which is equal to $f(p)$ we have of course by Walras' Law automatically specified $z_2(p)$. However now, by confining our attention to prices between ϵ and $1-\epsilon$ we have avoided the restrictions imposed by what happens as p_1 goes to zero or one. Thus it may well be the case that for no p_1 between ϵ and $1-\epsilon$ we have $f(p_1)=0$ or on the other hand this may happen for several p_1.

Let us now see geometrically why it is true that any continuous $f(p_1)$ can be an aggregate excess demand function. Let us suppose that $f(p_1)$ looks as in Figure 1.25, and suppose that we choose $\epsilon = \frac{1}{5}$. Thus we consider $f(p_1)$ for prices p_1 between $\frac{1}{5}$ and $\frac{4}{5}$. Firstly the reader will have noticed that $f(p_1)$ could not be an aggregate excess demand function for a two–man economy for all prices. Yet we will show how we can construct an economy which has exactly $f(p_1)$ as its excess demand for good 1. Now recall that $f(p_1)$ will represent for each price p_1 the amount of good 1 demanded over and above the total amount of good 1 available in the economy, i.e., $e_1(a)+e_1(b)$.

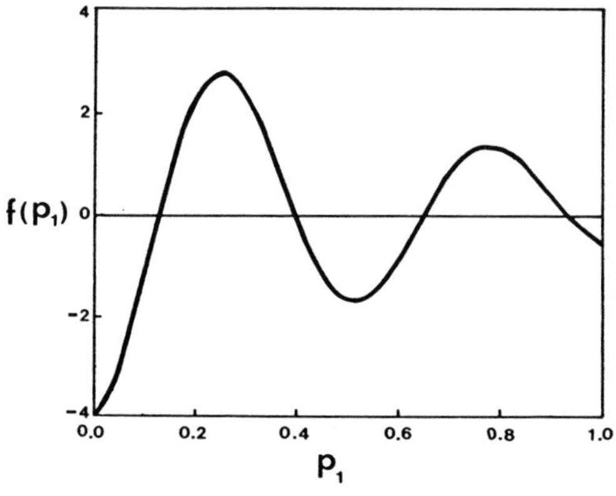

Figure 1.25

The first observation is this. If we "scale down" $f(p_1)$ for the relevant prices and then manage to construct an economy this will suffice. Suppose that we divide $f(p)$ by n, and then construct two individuals who have an aggregate excess demand $z_1(p_1) = \frac{1}{n}f(p_1)$ for prices between $\frac{1}{5}$ and $\frac{4}{5}$. Now we simply "blow up" the economy n times and it will have $f(p_1)$ as its aggregate excess demand for good 1. In other words we blow up the initial endowments n times and the indifference curves in the same way. Thus, if in the economy we construct, individual a prefers x to y, then we simply construct an individual who prefers nx to ny. So suppose that we divide the f given in Figure 1.25 by some large n. It will now look as in Figure 1.26.

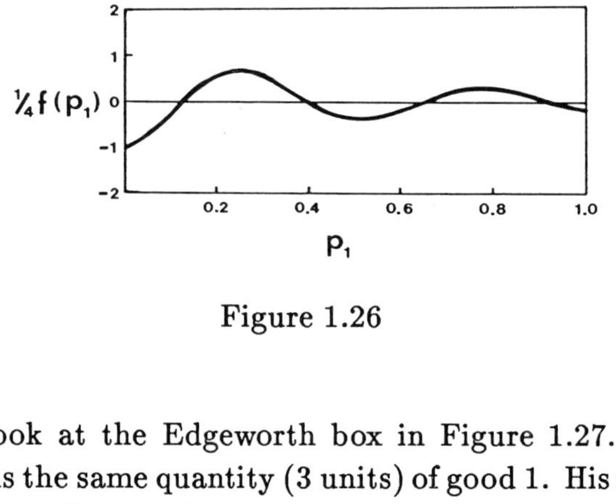

Figure 1.26

Now we look at the Edgeworth box in Figure 1.27. Individual b always demands the same quantity (3 units) of good 1. His demand curve is just the vertical line in the diagram. Now the other curve has been drawn so that at each price the amount demanded by a will, when added to b's unit, just exceed or be below 3 at each price p_1 by $f(p_1)$. Thus when the wavy line is to the right of the vertical line there is positive excess demand for good 1 and when it is to the left there is negative excess demand, or rather excess supply. Now the reader will have little difficulty persuading himself that he can put indifference curves in the box for b so that he has the vertical line as his demand curve and then he can do the same for a and generate the wavy line. We have done this for three prices in Figure 1.28.

Hence the reader should be convinced that we have constructed an economy with $\frac{1}{n}f(p_1)$ as its aggregate excess demand for good 1 for prices between $\frac{1}{5}$ and $\frac{4}{5}$ and hence by blowing up the box we would have an economy with $f(p_1)$ as its aggregate excess demand.

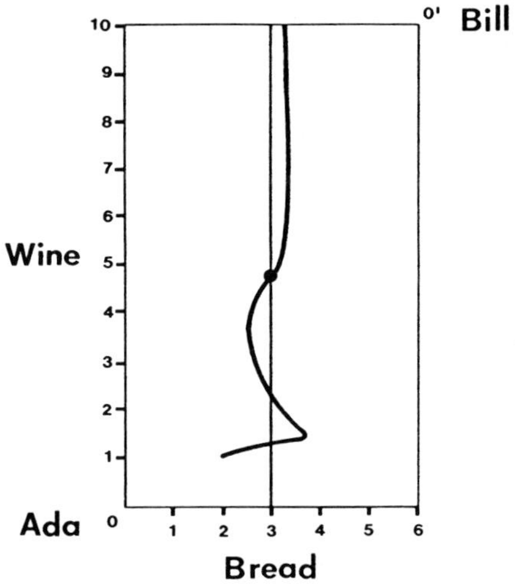

Figure 1.27

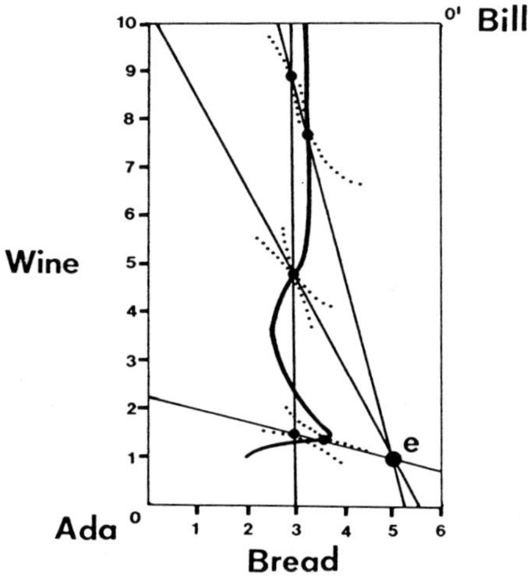

Figure 1.28

11. What Hope for Uniqueness?

The reader may well now feel that our "proof" of the existence of competitive prices in the preview section offers small comfort and be a little discouraged at this point, since the fact that excess demand functions may have more or less any form except near zero prices offers no real hope, as we shall see in Chapter 6, for uniqueness or for stability. Thinking back to the previous section it is easy to see that we could have, for example, an infinite number of equilibria as in Figure 1.29.

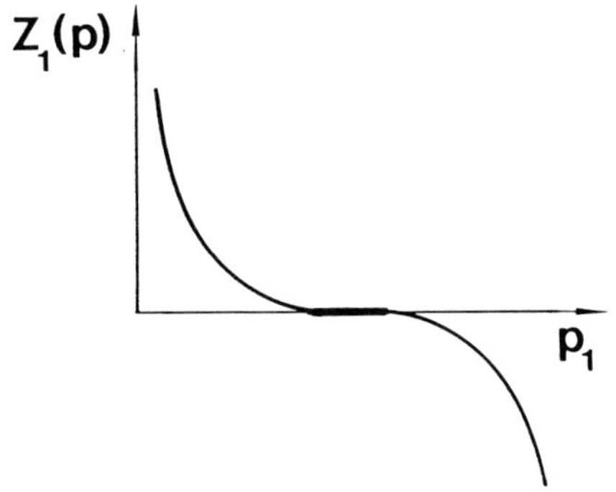

Figure 1.29

In an Edgeworth box this would correspond to the situation in Figure 1.30, for example.

In this example if Bill and Ada start at e then every redistribution on the contract curve from g to h is a competitive equilibrium. Note, however, that moving e a little would remove all these equilibria except at most one. In fact, others might appear, but it is possible to show that for "almost all" initial endowment positions there are only a finite number of equilibria.

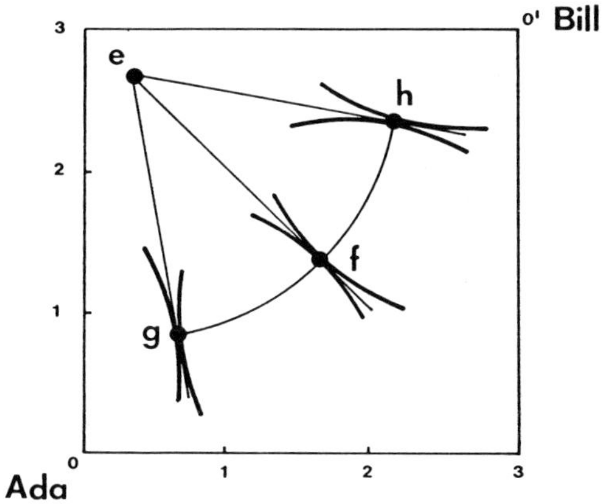

Figure 1.30

If we go back to the previous figure, if we moved the excess demand curve a little all but one of the equilibria would disappear. In fact, if we require a little more than we have explicitly said, that is that consumers have "smooth" indifference curves, as indeed we have, usually, drawn them, then we know that the excess demand curve must, in general, look as in Figure 1.31.

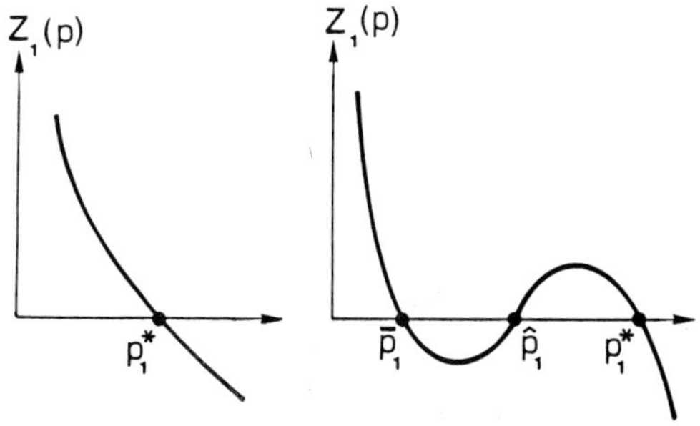

Figure 1.31

The astute reader will notice that this must mean that equilibrium prices are finite in number, separated from each other and indeed he will observe, by drawing diagrams himself, that in general the number of them must be odd.

Now, while it is clear that we cannot hope for just one equilibrium, "global uniqueness", there is, in general, "local uniqueness".

12. Stability

If we examine the previous figure we might ask the following question. If, when there is positive excess demand for a good we increase the price of that good and if negative we decrease it, for example by an amount proportional to the excess demand. Will we arrive at an equilibrium? In the two–good case this must be true. Indeed the argument that we used to prove the existence of equilibrium will suffice. In this special case if we can ever get the excess demand for one good to zero then the other good must also have zero excess demand, we have found an equilibrium and there will be no further adjustment. In other words the process that we have just described, the so–called Walrasian tâtonnement process, will converge. Thus, there is at least one stable equilibrium in the sense that if our economy starts with prices near enough to this equilibrium then the tâtonnement will converge to those prices.

The reader should check this for p^* in the previous figure. Now it is easy to see that $\hat{p}$ is not stable in this sense. No matter how near we are to $\hat{p}$ the adjustment process will take us away to $\overline{p}$ or to p^*. Put another way, if the equilibrium price $\hat{p}$ were slightly disturbed the economy would not come back to that equilibrium. Thus in our special two-good case we may have both locally stable and unstable equilibria but there will be at least one which is locally stable.

However, as will become clear in Chapter 6, as soon as we leave the two-good case this is no longer true. Indeed, we will show a famous example where there is a unique but unstable equilibrium. The lesson is that without restrictions on the form of the aggregate excess demand function we cannot hope for stability of our adjustment process. Yet, as we have seen, even the strong assumptions we have made on individuals will provide no such restrictions.

13. To What Avail?

The reader who now tackles this book should bear the following in mind. What he learns is at the heart of modern economic theory. Almost all of the economic literature, theoretical and applied, turns around models in which the nature of "the equilibrium" is discussed and analysed. Although these models may be more elaborate in some ways, perhaps less general in other ways, their common ancestor is the sort of model we develop here. Thus a knowledge of what is in this book is fundamental for an understanding of modern economics. The reader should be impressed by the generality of the conditions under which we can prove that equilibrium exists, but perhaps a little depressed that we cannot go much further. Maybe, however, there is among our readers, one who will be able to develop a model on a less "individualistic" basis than the one that we construct and as a result progress much further. This would be a break with a tradition of several centuries and such traditions die hard. When a book describing such a theory is written the reader can be sure of one thing. It will not start with Ada and Bill!

Chapter 2

Exchange Economies

1. Introduction

Having heard the major themes played briefly we shall now build up the fully orchestrated score. For this we must construct a formal version of the model discussed in Chapter 1. Recall that the basic problem discussed was that of barter. Production plays no role in our considerations. We might justify this in two ways. First, we may merely regard the pure exchange problem as a simplified abstraction and as a first approach to the more general problem with production. Alternatively, we can think of the exchange economy as being a subsection of a much larger economy which does involve production activities. Consider, for example, an agricultural economy, where families produce at home on small farms and then go to market to barter with what they have produced. The reader may object that such a separation is not at all evident in the economy with which he is familiar. However dissatisfied with our simplification such a reader may be, he will have to admit that if we cannot solve, in a reasonably satisfactory way, the exchange problem, then there is not much hope for the solution of the more general one. Of course, a Marxist who believes that production and the control of means of production are the essential features of an economy will regard our whole approach as aberrant and will view this separation into production and exchange activities as unacceptable. If the reader accepts the point of view implied by such an attitude that the allocation of goods according to the demand for them, is at best, is a side issue, then he should pick up another book. However, we might just observe that exchange does seem to be an important activity in most economies, whether or not production does take place.

Our problem then boils down to the following. A group of individuals possessing bundles of goods wishes to redistribute these goods amongst themselves with a view to improving their welfare. We will be concerned with "satisfactory" solutions to this very basic problem. Before proceeding to a closer examination of solutions to this exchange problem we will have to specify more precisely the nature of the model with which we work.

We have used two fundamental concepts so far, the *commodities* and the *agents* who possess and exchange them. We must now discuss in detail the characteristics which we attribute to these two features of our model. To establish results we will have to make assumptions, and frequently these assumptions will be stronger than really necessary. This we do to reduce the weight of the mathematics required and to focus attention on the essential nature of the results and the method of proof. The reader who is prepared to pay the high price often exacted for full generality may indulge himself by following up the references. At each stage we will try to make a clear distinction between essential and technical assumptions. Where this distinction appears arbitrary to the reader, he should bear in mind that it is usually based on a more advanced analysis than that given here.

2. The Commodity Space

A commodity is anything which may be used or consumed. It may be a physical good such as bread or a service such as the use of some object. In our model, recall again that we will be concerned only with the exchange of commodities which exist already and no production takes place. Thus, for us, labour is not a legitimate commodity, since it may be "converted" into various goods or services. This would introduce the idea of production and a productive technology, which we wish to exclude. In passing, we mention that, of course, if labour is consumed directly then it is admissible. Thus, we allow the oldest profession in the world to exist.

A commodity must then be completely homogeneous, i.e., one unit of it must be completely indistinguishable from another in all respects. "In all respects" means not only in terms of its physical characteristics, but also in terms of where it is located in time and space. A bar of chocolate now is different from a bar of chocolate to be received in a year's time, as any child will know. Corn in Kansas is different from the same species of corn in Illinois, particularly if you live in Kansas. Thus, a commodity is fully described by its physical characteristics and the time and place at which it is available.

We assume that there is only a finite number ℓ of commodities. Note that this does not impose any real restriction, since all that we are assuming is that the agents in an economy are only capable of distinguishing between a finite number of commodities. Quantities of commodities are given by non–negative real numbers. We assume, in particular, that the quantity which may be available or exchanged can be any such number. This is the first significant point on which the reader's credibility is tested, since we are all aware of the existence of commodities which may not be split up without losing their character. However, infinite divisibility will be used extensively in most of what follows, since it allows us to make use of a branch of mathematics called Analysis. We will, nevertheless, mention later a case where it is dropped.

We consider then a "bundle" of commodities as ℓ non–negative real numbers. Indexing the commodities from 1 to ℓ we may then describe such a bundle as a vector $x = (x^1, x^2, \ldots, x^\ell)$ in ℓ–dimensional Euclidean space. This is simply the natural ℓ–dimensional generalization of the two–dimensional discussion of chapter 1. Thus, in summary:

the commodity space	is given by R^ℓ
a commodity bundle	is is given by $x = (x^1, x^2, \ldots, x^\ell)$, an element of $\mathbb{R}^\ell_+$.

3. Agents' Characteristics

The reader will undoubtedly have observed that an economic agent, as defined here, has a rather limited character. His features are simply that he possesess a commodity bundle, his *initial resources*, and is supposed to make choices. His choices are based on his *preferences* which extend over a subset of the commodity space called his *consumption set.* For our purposes, an agent is completely characterized by three elements, his consumption set, his preferences and his initial resources. Let us look at each of these aspects of our skeletal agents.

3.1. Consumption Set

What does an economic agent contemplate when he makes his plans? In our simple exchange model he will look at commodity bundles which have only non–negative components, since negative amounts of commodities make no sense. In fact, suppose that the agent has to obtain, by exchange, his needs for the next day, then he will confine his attention to those bundles which will permit him to survive until the next exchange takes place.

To see this in a simple diagram consider two commodities, rice and tea, and that a man needs half a pound of rice and one pint of tea to survive from one day to the next. Thus, he will only meaningfully be able to consider bundles containing not less than this, as in Figure 2.1. A man's real subsistence level would then provide a lower bound to his consumption set.

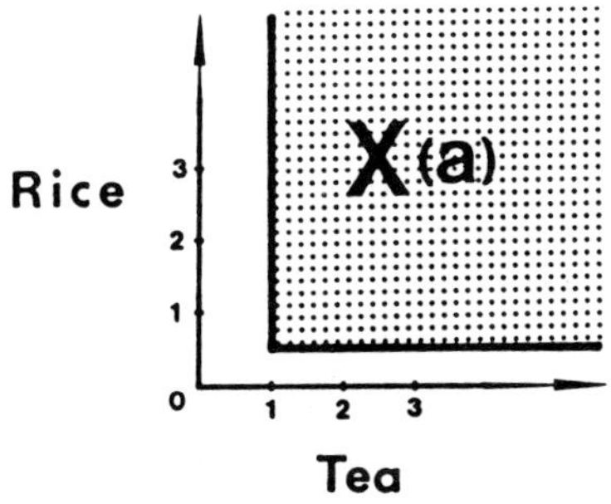

Figure 2.1

He will thus be interested in $X(a) \subset R^{\ell}_{+}$. In fact, $X(a)$ may really be a very restricted subset of R^{ℓ}_{+} and this would cause no problems, but we will make the simplifying assumption in what follows, that $X(a) = R^{\ell}_{+}$ for every agent a.

A possible *consumption plan* for the agent a is then any commodity bundle in his consumption set, i.e., $x \in R^{\ell}_{+}$. So far then, we have

the consumption set $X(a)$	is the positive orthant of R^{ℓ}_{+},
a consumption plan x	is an element of R^{ℓ}_{+}.

3.2. Preferences

The fundamental characteristics of an agent in the sort of economy considered here are his "tastes" or "preferences". All our earlier discussion turned on Ada's and Bill's preferences. When considering two bundles in his consumption set, as we have seen, an agent is able to make one of the following statements: "I prefer x to y", "I prefer y to x", or "I am indifferent between x and y". The operational significance of this is that when faced with two bundles and allowed to choose freely, agents will choose that which they prefer. In defining these preferences we will assume and continue to exact a certain degree of consistency and we will also discuss several additional, technically convenient, restrictions.

Let us examine in more detail the basic concept involved which is the relation "is preferred or indifferent to", for which we write $\succsim$[1] , that is x is preferred or indifferent to y is written $x \succsim y$. From this basic relation which we take to be *complete* , that is which permits comparison of any two bundles in X, we can derive two subsidiary relations as follows:

(a) x is *indifferent* to y (written $x \sim y$) if $x \succsim y$ and $y \succsim x$.

(b) x is strictly preferred to y (written $x \succ y$) if $x \succsim y$ and y is not preferred or indifferent to x (written $y \not\succsim x$).

We could work only with the strictly preferred relation and still obtain most of our results, but this would add some technical complications. The same holds for the assumption of completeness. A man in Bonn, for example, would find it hard to compare bundles of basic foods delivered in Peking and Tokyo, or in Hamburg and Berlin for that matter. Nevertheless, to simplify the analysis we will assume the $\succsim$ relation to be complete.

---

[1] Although we will be referring to preferences etc., of a particular individual a, we will drop the reference to that agent where this will cause no confusion.

Throughout this discussion it is important that the reader does not lose sight of our goal. *We discuss preferences not because of their intrinsic interest, but because they lie behind the choices that agents make.* The choices made in different circumstances are what interest us. It is clear that, in general, an agent will make his choice from a whole set of alternatives. If the preference relation that we consider is to lead to consistent choices over the whole set we have to endow it with more structure. Our goal is to discuss the *best choice* for an agent in a given set of alternatives C, i.e., to find an element $x \in C$ such that $x \succsim y$ for all $y \in C$ (see Proposition 2.1. below).

Suppose that an agent can compare every pair of elements in a given set. How do we know that there will be a best choice for him in that set? Consider the preferences illustrated in Figure 2.2 where the arrows have the obvious interpretation.

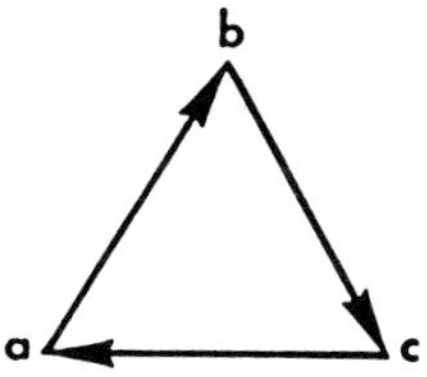

Figure 2.2

Clearly, there is no best choice among the three alternatives a, b and c. To rule out this sort of problem we need to impose certain requirements of consistency on the preference relations that we consider.

The first such condition that we shall require of the preference relation is that it should be *transitive*, i.e., whenever $x \succsim y$ and $y \succsim z$ then $x \succsim z$. Obviously, if the preference relation $\succsim$ is transitive then in any finite set of alternatives there is a best element. Transitivity would seem to be a very basic requirement, but it is possible to consider cases where it might be violated.

Example 2.1. Consider an agent who is always in one of three different moods. In each mood he orders three alternatives as follows:

mood 1: $x \succ_1 y \succ_1 z$,

mood 2: $z \succ_2 x \succ_2 y$,

mood 3: $y \succ_3 z \succ_3 x$,

Now define his basic preference relation as follows: x is preferred to y if it is preferred in the majority of moods. This gives

$$x \succ y, \quad y \succ z \quad \text{but } z \succ x \ ,$$

i.e., intransitivity.

However, at the individual level it has been observed that while people do make intransitive choices, when this is pointed out to them they tend to regard this as a mistake and to rectify their choice appropriately. Inconsistency in behaviour does not necessarily reflect underlying inconsistent preferences.[2)] As Jacob Marschak has remarked, individuals frequently make arithmetical errors and yet do not deny the laws of arithmetic. In the same way as the individual corrects an arithmetical mistake he will also correct a "mistake" in his choice. It should be noted in passing that transitivity of $\succsim$ implies the transitivity of $\succ$ and of $\sim$. As with other assumptions transitivity can be dispensed with, at the cost of adding another assumption as the reader will see at the end of this section.

The second requirement of consistency is of a more technical nature but will play an important role in what follows. We require that the relation $\succsim$ be *continuous*, that is that if x is strictly preferred to y, all bundles "sufficiently close" to x are strictly preferred to all bundles "sufficiently close" to y. More formally, but as we show below, equivalently, we require that the sets $\{x | x \succsim y\}$ and $\{x | y \succsim x\}$ be closed for all y in X.

---

2) The perceptive reader will note, of course, that if preference and choice are related in the way we describe, such "mistakes" could not occur. We are dealing with a model in which "well behaved" individuals choose with grim inevitability what they prefer!

Example 2.2. The classic example of a plausible preference relation which is not continuous is the so-called lexicographic order. Consider a world in which the only commodities are whisky and bread, and an agent with alcoholic leanings who has the following preferences. If a bundle x contains more whisky than a bundle y then x is preferred to y. If the quantities of whisky are equal in two bundles, the agent prefers that which has more bread. To see why this ordering is not continuous we recall that for a continuous relation the set less preferred than a point must be closed. That is

$$\{x \in X \mid y \succsim x\} \text{ is closed for all } y \text{ in } X.$$

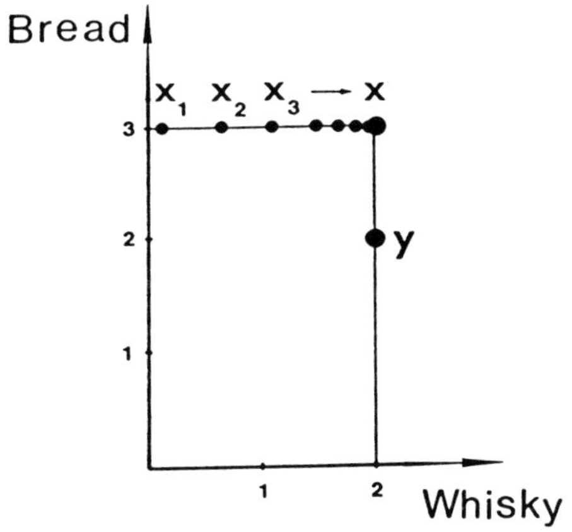

Figure 2.3

Now in Figure 2.3 consider the sequence of bundles $x_1, x_2 \ldots,$ where $x_n = (2 - \frac{1}{n}, 3)$. The bundle $y = (2, 2)$ is preferred to each of the bundles x_n, since each contains less whisky than y, yet the limit bundle of the sequence $x = (2, 3)$ has the same amount of whisky and more bread than y and therefore is preferred to y. Thus, the set to which y is preferred is not closed and the relation is not continuous.

Up to this point we have presumed on the reader's intuition and have only talked about the properties of the preference relation without specifying precisely what such a relation is. A little thought will reveal that a relation is defined by which elements of a set are in relation to which others and how the elements which are in relation are ordered. Thus, if we specify all the ordered pairs (x, y) of commodity bundles in X, such that x is preferred or indifferent to y, we define the relation "is preferred or indifferent to". Hence, a *binary relation*[3] on X is nothing other than a set of ordered pairs, i.e., a subset of $X \times X$.

Definition 2.1. A binary relation, i.e., a subset $\succsim \subset X \times X$ is called a *preference relation* if it has the following properties:

(i)	*Reflexivity:*	$x \succsim x$ for all $x \in X$.
(ii)	*Completeness:*	$x \succsim y$ or $y \succsim x$ for every $x, y \in X,\ x \neq y$
(iii)	*Transitivity:*	whenever $x \succsim y$ and $y \succsim z$ then $x \succsim z$.
(iv)	*Continuity:*	the sets $\{x \mid y \succsim x\}$ and $\{x \mid x \succsim y\}$ are closed for all y in X.

The set of ordered pairs which defines the relation is also called, somewhat tautologically, the *graph* of this relation. The graph is difficult to visualize, since we are constrained to orders on the real line if we are to be able to give diagrams.

---

[3] We will use the more appealing notation $x \succsim y$ for $(x, y) \in \succsim$.

Example 2.3. Consider preferences on the real line given by the following relation: $x \succ y$ if $x > y + 1$ and then $x \sim y$ if $y - 1 \leq x \leq y + 1$. Figure 2.4 (a) is a graph of the strictly preferred relation and Figure 2.4 (b) a graph of the preferred relation.

The reader should observe that this relation does not conform to our assumptions since the relation $\sim$ is not transitive.

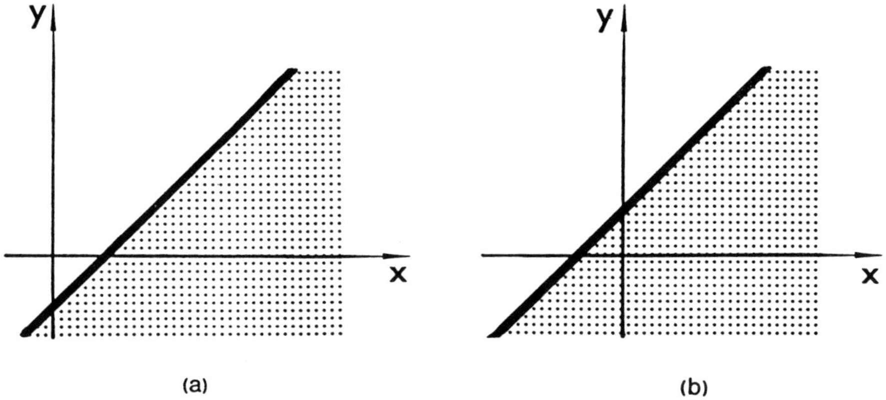

Figure 2.4: (a) Graph of $x \succ y$, and (b) graph of $x \succsim y$.

It is important to view a preference relation as a subset of $X \times X$ since later on we will sometimes wish to talk about whether people have "similar" preferences and this will amount to discussing whether two sets are "similar". As we observed earlier, our goal in discussing preferences is to determine the best choice in a given set of alternatives. Now, as we remarked, transitivity guarantees that there is a best element in every *finite* set of alternatives. We will show furthermore that transitivity, together with continuity, ensures that there is a best element in a larger class of alternatives, namely in all *compact* (shorthand, in our framework, for closed and bounded) sets.

Proposition 2.1. Let C be a non–empty compact subset of X and let $\succsim$ be a continuous transitive complete preference relation on X. Then there exists a best element $\hat{x}$ in C (i.e., $\hat{x} \succsim x$ for all $x \in C$) and the set $C_{\succsim}$ of all best elements is compact.

Proof. This is a special case of Theorem A.III.3. in the Mathematical Appendix. However it is so basic to all that follows that we give a direct argument.

For every $z \in C$ consider the "not worse than z" set $\{x \in C | x \succsim z\} = C_z$. By continuity of the preference relation the set C_z is closed. The set $C_{\succsim}$ of best elements in C is then $\bigcap_{z \in C} C_z = C_{\succsim}$. As an intersection of closed sets the set $C_{\succsim}$ is clearly closed and hence compact. It remains to show that it is non–empty. For this we first observe that for any *finite* set $z_1, \dots, z_q$ of points in C we have $\bigcap_{n=1}^{q} C_{z_n} \neq \emptyset$. Indeed, by transitivity of $\succsim$ there is obviously a best element in the finite set $\{z_1, \dots, z_q\}$, say z_q. But then $C_{z_q} \subset C_{z_n}$ for all $n = 1, \dots, q$. Hence, $C_{z_q} = \bigcap_{n=1}^{q} C_{z_n}$ and this set is non–empty since $z_q \in C_{z_q}$. Now we use a well–known property of compact sets (Mathematical Appendix I., Proposition AI.5 (iv)): the intersection of *any* collection of closed subsets of a compact set is non–empty if the intersection of *every finite* part of the collection is non–empty. But the last property is what we have just established. Therefore, the intersection $\bigcap_{z \in C} = C_{\succsim}$ is non–empty and this completes the proof of the proposition.

Q.E.D.

When discussing the graph of a preference relation it is convenient to use an alternative definition of continuity. In addition we have already mentioned a very intuitive definition which simply says that if x is strictly preferred to y then everything sufficiently close to x is strictly preferred to everything sufficiently close to y. Proposition 2.2. shows that these alternative definitions are in fact equivalent.

Proposition 2.2. Let $\succsim$ be a reflexive, complete, transitive binary relation on a set $X \subset R^{\ell}$. Then the following three statements are equivalent:

(i) $\succsim$ is continuous.

(ii) The graph of $\succsim$ is a closed subset in $X \times X$.

(iii) If $x \succ y$ then there exist neighbourhoods U_x and U_y of x and y respectively such that $x' \succ y'$ for every $x' \in U_x \cap X$ and $y' \in U_y \cap X$.

Proof. It is easy to show that (i) and (ii) are equivalent and that (iii) implies (i). We only show that (i) implies (iii). Let $x \succ y$. If there exists a vector $z \in X$ with $x \succ z \succ y$ then we take $U_x = \{a \in X \mid a \succ z\}$ and $U_y = \{b \in X \mid z \succ b\}$. We have $x \in U_x$ and the set U_x is open since U_x is the complement of the closed set $\{a \in X \mid z \succsim a\}$. This follows from the completeness of the relation. The same argument applies for U_y.

Consider now the case where the set $\{z \in X \mid x \succ z \succ y\}$ is empty. Then we define $U_x = \{a \in X \mid a \succsim x\}$ and $U_y = \{b \in X \mid y \succsim b\}$. Again, $x \in U_x$ and $y \in U_y$. The two sets U_x and U_y are closed by the definition of continuity. But U_x is the complement of U_y, and hence it is open. The same holds for U_y. This completes the proof.

Q.E.D.

The properties of transitivity and continuity just discussed are basic to the analytic approach that we use. We repeat that from now on whenever we refer to a preference relation $\succsim$ it will be a reflexive, complete, transitive and continuous binary relation. The set of all such preference relations defined on the positive orthant $\mathbb{R}^{\ell}_{+}$ is denoted by $\mathcal{P}$. However, there are other conditions on preferences which we will use but which are not, in general, so essential to the theory that we should include them in the actual definition of preferences.

The idea that commodities are desirable to individuals and that the well–being of the latter may always be improved upon has intuitive appeal. To this end we introduce the following definition.

Definition 2.2. A preference relation $\succsim \in \mathcal{P}$ is *monotonic* if $x \succ y$ for every x, y in $\mathbb{R}^{\ell}_{+}$ with $x \geq y$ and $x \neq y$.

This is a strong assumption in that it says that no matter what one's level of consumption, a bundle with slightly more of anything is preferred to what one has. This amounts to saying that individuals are greedy and when we come to study the choices that individuals make, the significance of such an assumption will become clear. From now on, we will usually be working with monotonic preferences and unless otherwise stated we will define our basic concepts in terms of monotonic relations. The set of all monotonic preferences is written $\mathcal{P}_{mo}$. In addition to the basic assumptions that we have made about the preferences of an agent, we will frequently wish to impose further restrictions, i.e., to demand further properties of the relations. Each time we use one of these restrictions we will be considering a subset of $\mathcal{P}$ and in general we will indicate this by adding a subscript to $\mathcal{P}$.

Before leaving the topic of preferences we shall consider one further type of restriction that may be placed on a preference relation. This is the idea, familiar from diagrams in textbooks, that a preference relation should be convex.

Definition 2.3. A preference relation $\succsim$ on X is *convex* if for every $x \in X$ the set $\{y \in X \mid y \succsim x\}$ is convex.

Definition 2.4. A preference relation $\succsim$ on X is *strongly convex* if $x, y \in X$ with $x \sim y$ and $x \neq y$ implies that $\lambda x + (1-\lambda)y \succ y$ for every λ, $0 < \lambda < 1$.

The intuitive notion involved is that individuals prefer bundles in which commodities are fairly evenly distributed to those which are concentrated on a few goods. However this idea has little appeal if the unit of time considered in the definition of a commodity is very short. In this case it is not difficult to think of examples in which evenly distributed bundles are less attractive at some moment than more extreme bundles. An individual indifferent between a glass of Beaujolais and a glass of Sauterne is unlikely to prefer a mixture of the two. If, however, we view the period involved as somewhat longer, he may well prefer to have both Beaujolais and Sauterne in his cellar, as opposed to concentrating on one or the other. The three parts of Figure 2.5 illustrate indifference curves of preferences with varying degrees of convexity.

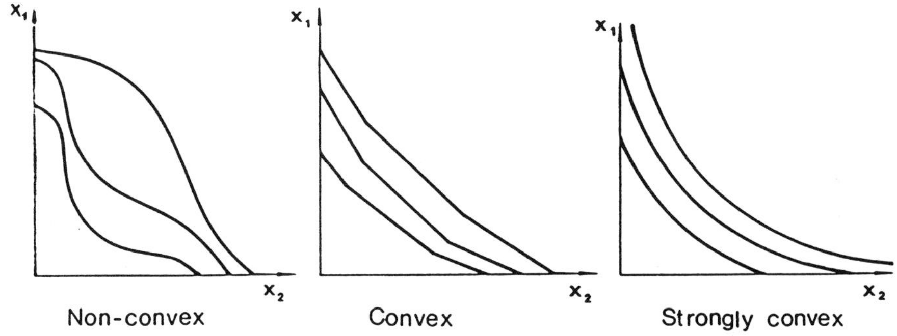

Figure 2.5

The convenience from a technical viewpoint of strong convexity will become apparent as we proceed and we will frequently make use of it. The set of all convex (resp. strongly convex) preference relations is written $\mathcal{P}_{co}$ (resp. $\mathcal{P}_{sco}$).

We have chosen preferences to be complete and transitive since by Proposition 2.1. they have best elements on compact sets. However we can dispense with completeness and furthermore *either* convexity *or* transitivity will suffice to ensure the existence of a maximal element. This assertion is proved in the Mathematical Appendix III.

3.3. Utility Functions

Perhaps the most familiar object in micro–economics is the utility function, a function which assigns numbers to bundles in such a way that a bundle receives a higher number than another if, and only if, the former is preferred to the latter. For some purposes it is convenient to work with "utilities" instead of the actual bundles associated with these utilities. Hence, it is worth indicating how, given some conditions on preferences, we may find a *continuous* function $u : X \to \mathbb{R}$ which represents these preferences in the following sense.

Definition 2.5. A *utility function* for $\succsim$ is a continuous function $u : X \to \mathbb{R}$ with the property that $u(x) \geq u(y)$ if and only if $x \succsim y$.

The construction of a utility function that we will explain first, requires stronger conditions on the preferences and consumption set than are necessary.

Let $X = \mathbb{R}^{\ell}_{+}$, then for any monotonic preference relation $\mathcal{P}_{mo}$ consider the following function u:

$$u(x) := max\{\xi \mid \xi \cdot \mathbf{1} \precsim x\},$$

where $\mathbf{1}$ is the ℓ vector of 1's.

Alternatively, we could define $u(x)$ as the number such that $u(x) \cdot \mathbf{1} \sim x$. With two commodities it is easy to see what this means. In Figure 2.6 we have an indifference curve of the relation $\succsim$ for a bundle x lying on this curve. $u(x)$ is determined by the point where the 45° line from the origin cuts this indifference curve. We have still to show that $u(x)$ constructed in this way is in fact a utility function.

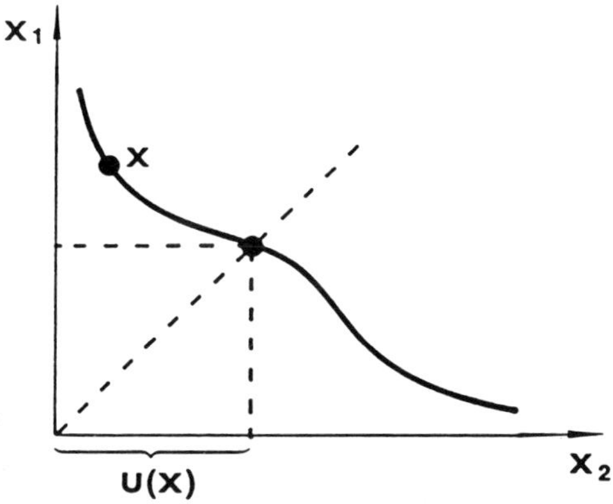

Figure 2.6

Proposition 2.3. For a monotonic preference relation $\succsim$ on $\mathbb{R}^{\ell}_{+}$, the function $u : \mathbb{R}^{\ell}_{+} \to \mathbb{R}$ as defined above, is a utility function.

Proof. Firstly we wish to show that $u(x) \geq u(y)$ if and only if $x \succsim y$. This follows easily once we have shown that

$$x \sim u(x) \cdot \mathbf{1}.$$

By definition $u(x) \cdot \mathbf{1} \precsim x$. Suppose that $u(x) \cdot \mathbf{1} \prec x$. Then by continuity there is a positive δ such that $(u(x) + \delta) \cdot \mathbf{1} \prec x$ a contradiction to $u(x)$ being a maximum.

To show the continuity of u it suffices to show that the set $u^{-1}([\alpha, \beta])$ is closed for every interval $[\alpha, \beta]$ (see Proposition 18. of Appendix I.6). Consider Figure 2.7 and observe that the inverse image of the interval $[\alpha, \beta]$ is the shaded strip which is given formally by

$$\{y \in \mathbb{R}^{\ell}_{+} | y \succsim \alpha \cdot \mathbf{1}\} \bigcap \{x \in \mathbb{R}^{\ell}_{+} | x \precsim \beta \cdot \mathbf{1}\}.$$

As each of these sets is closed, by the continuity of the preference relation $\succsim$, their intersection is also closed.

Q.E.D.

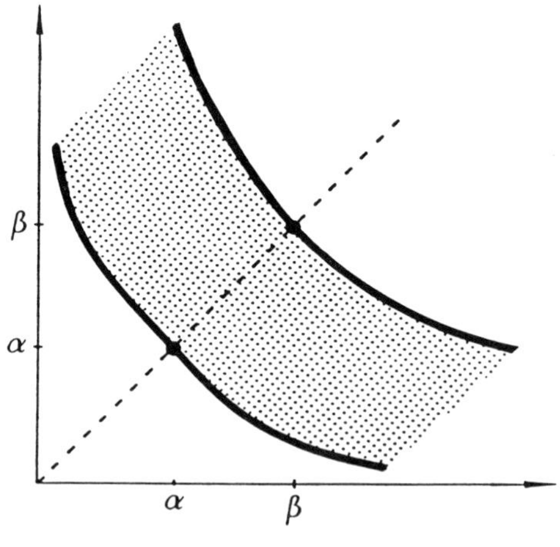

Figure 2.7

The above definition of $u(x)$ made use of monotonicity. However there is a more general result available which is

Theorem 2.1. Let $\succsim$ be any preference relation on an arbitrary subset X of $\mathbb{R}^\ell$. Then there exists a utility function for $\succsim$.

The above result shows that it is more or less a matter of taste whether one uses a preference relation $\succsim$ on X or a utility function $u : X \to \mathbb{R}$. In the literature, in particular in earlier writings, the utility function was not only taken as the "primitive concept", but these utility functions were also assumed to have very specific properties. In particular, the assumptions most frequently made were those of *differentiability, concavity* or *additivity.*

However, these assumptions are not invariant with respect to an increasing transformation (i.e., if u represents given preferences the $f \circ u$ also represents these preferences provided f is a strictly increasing function, e.g. $(u(x))^3$ or $e^{u(x)}$.) Thus, for example, while $f \circ u$ is a perfectly acceptable utility function it might not be concave whilst u itself may be. Thus we are faced with the following question. Can we characterize those classes of preference relations which can be represented by utility functions with specific properties? That is, can we say of a preference relation that if it falls into some class of such relations, then among the many utility functions that represent it, there is at least one with the property required? In other words, is this property intrinsic to that relation? We discuss this in detail in the Appendix of this chapter.

3.4. Initial Endowments

Having now described, at some length, the preference of an individual and having emphasized that this was directed to considering his choices, we now need to discuss what he owns. After all, it is this that gives him the means of exchange and enables him to realize his choices. We assume that all agents have something of some commodity. Thus, the initial resources of an individual are given by a bundle in $\mathbb{R}^{\ell}_{+}$. An agent is thus, in summary, characterized by the following:

(a)	*consumption set:*	$X \subset \mathbb{R}^{\ell}_{+}$
(b)	*preferences:*	$\succsim \in \mathcal{P}$
(c)	*initial resources:*	$e \in \mathbb{R}^{\ell}_{+}$

4. An Exchange Economy and its Core

A particular economy or trading group will naturally then be given by a specification of the actual preferences and endowments of the individuals involved. The characteristics of an individual in such an economy are given by a point in $\mathcal{P} \times \mathbb{R}^{\ell}_{+}$, the space of preferences and endowments. An economy will be completely described by the assignment of a point in $\mathcal{P} \times \mathbb{R}^{\ell}_{+}$ to each agent in A. Thus, an economy is really a mapping from the set A of agents into the space $\mathcal{P} \times \mathbb{R}^{\ell}_{+}$ of characteristics.

Definition 2.6. An *exchange economy* $\mathcal{E} : A \to \mathcal{P} \times \mathbb{R}^{\ell}_{+}$ is a mapping from the set of agents A into the space of agents' characteristics, $\mathcal{P} \times \mathbb{R}^{\ell}_{+}$, where the total endowments $\sum_{a \in A} e(a)$ are strictly positive.

This we will often shorten to $a \mapsto (\succsim_a,\ e(a))$ if it is clear which mapping $\mathcal{E}$ is involved. It is perhaps easiest to think of a basic set of agents A who only constitute a trading group or exchange economy when they have had their characteristics filled in. Thus, we only give economic identity to Ada and Bill when we give them preferences and initial endowments. The particular way in which characteristics are assigned to individuals is what constitutes a particular economy.

The problem with which the individuals in the economy are faced is, as we know, that of how to redistribute their resources. For this the various possible ways of redistributing the initial bundles have to be considered. We define now an allocation as an assignment of bundles to individuals and we will wish to focus our attention on those allocations which are, in fact, redistributions. In other words, in the two–man economy, points in the Edgeworth box.

Definition 2.7. An *allocation* for an economy $\mathcal{E}$ is a mapping f from A into $\mathbb{R}^{\ell}_{+}$. A *redistribution*, (*feasible allocation*), or *state* of the economy $\mathcal{E}$ is an allocation f for $\mathcal{E}$ with

$$\sum_{a \in A} f(a) = \sum_{a \in A} e(a) \ ,$$

From now on we will write $\sum_{a \in A} e(a)$ as $e(A)$ and similarly for f, "par abus de notation".

Conceptually we can look at the problem of distinguishing between allocations in two ways. Either we establish a criterion and find the set of "best" allocations according to that requirement, or alternatively, we proceed by eliminating those allocations which are, in some way, unsatisfactory. In fact, these two approaches are formally equivalent. However, we will be working in the spirit of the latter approach, that is we will be looking at sets of redistributions which cannot be eliminated by some criterion. The reader will observe the re–emergence of the Edgeworthian theme.

What is the very minimal requirement of a redistribution for it to be economically acceptable? It is surely that it should be *efficient.* Efficient, here, meaning that no individual can be made better off than in some allocation f without someone else also being made worse off. Any redistribution which does not meet this requirement might reasonably be considered unsatisfactory. In our earlier example these efficient redistributions were those on the contract curve in the Edgeworth box. The set of efficient redistributions consists, in the general case then, of those which satisfy the following definition. [4)]

Definition 2.8. A redistribution f for an economy $\mathcal{E}$ is *Pareto efficient*, or *Pareto optimal*, if there is no redistribution g for $\mathcal{E}$ such that $g(a) \succsim_a f(a)$ for all a in A, and $g(a) \succ_a f(a)$ for at least one agent a in A.

While this requirement has intuitive appeal it seems too general to be satisfactory on its own. For example, if all commodities are desirable the redistribution which gives all the goods to one individual is clearly efficient but hardly satisfactory. To avoid the latter case the notion of "individually rational" Pareto optima is sometimes introduced. The idea is that for f to meet this requirement it should have the property that, for all a in A, $f(a) \succsim_a e(a)$.

That is, one should not accept any redistribution which is unfavourable for some individual. To elaborate on an earlier point, it is interesting to note that this requirement is a source of dispute since it adds to the Pareto condition the feature of ownership. To say that a redistribution should be Pareto efficient is a statement that is not conditioned by the initial holdings of individuals. To demand that it should

[4)] With monotonicity of preferences this is equivalent to a simpler definition where it is stipulated that there should exist no redistribution g with $g(a) \succ_a f(a)$ for all $a \in A$.

be also individually rational includes now the notion of the initial distribution. If the latter were extremely unequal it might be argued that since extreme inequality is not desirable we should not accept individually rational redistributions since these would inevitably maintain this inequality. The initial distribution will, as it did in our simple example, play a basic role in what follows. Thus, once we move beyond the simple criterion of "efficiency", the reader should bear this in mind. This discussion will be pursued later.

The two notions mentioned of what constitutes a satisfactory redistribution have a similar nature. In the case of efficiency one is saying that if the whole economy can improve upon a given redistribution then the latter will not be acceptable. In the case of "individually rational" Pareto optima we require that neither the whole group of agents nor any individual should be able to improve upon f. We use "improve upon", as in Chapter 1, to mean redistribute initial resources in order to achieve something preferred to f. For an individual alone this reduces to requiring that $f(a)$ should be preferred to $e(a)$.

Now, more generally, suppose that instead of rejecting those redistributions that can be improved upon, either by all agents together or by individuals alone, we consider those redistributions which cannot be improved upon by any subset, or "coalition", of individuals. We have used the term "coalition" in an intuitive way in Chapter 1 and it is made precise in the natural way in the following definition

Definition 2.9. A *coalition* E is a non–empty subset of A. The set of all coalitions is denoted $\mathcal{A}$.

In other words, we make *no restrictions* as to the coalition that can form. There is no reason why one should not, *a priori*, decide that as a result of communication difficulties, or cost, some coalitions could not organize themselves to improve upon an allocation. On the other hand, certain individuals may, from the outset, join in unbreakable coalitions. Nevertheless, for want of good reasons for such *a priori* restrictions we will consider all coalitions as possible. Now we can bring back our first theme in this more general framework. As before, the set of allocations which can be improved upon by no coalition, we call the *core*. More precisely we have the following definitions.

Definition 2.10. A coalition S in $\mathcal{A}$ can *improve upon* an allocation f for $\mathcal{E}$ if there exists an allocation g for $\mathcal{E}$ such that:

(i) $g(a) \succ_a f(a)$ for all a in S

and

(ii) $\sum_{a \in S} g(a) = \sum_{a \in S} e(a)$.

Definition 2.11. The *core* of an economy $\mathcal{E}$, denoted $C(\mathcal{E})$, is the set of all redistributions for $\mathcal{E}$ that can be improved upon by no coalition in $\mathcal{A}$.

We put the core forward in Chapter 1 as a candidate for an acceptable set of redistributions without very much justification. To remedy this we should make some observations as to its interpretation. Indeed, this theme has so often been misinterpreted that it is necessary to clarify some of its important features at the outset.

In the first place, it is essential to note that the coalitions operate in a very restricted way. They may only eliminate allocations which they themselves may improve upon: the term for "improve upon" widely used in the literature is "block", but it is precisely because of the misunderstandings that have arisen in discussing the core that we drop this term. The idea that a coalition may block a redistribution might suggest the notion of the function exercised, for example, by a trade union in our society. The bargaining power employed in deciding which redistributions are acceptable is, in this case, quite different from that involved in the core. The power of a union is that the withdrawal of its labour may have a substantial impact on the welfare of those who are not members. The power of a coalition with a monopoly of some essential good is involved in the threat to the welfare of others if they, the monopolists, refuse to exchange it. This sort of power is not reflected in the core and the reader should view with circumspection facile interpretations of coalitions as modern pressure groups.

The core, as a plausible equilibrium concept for an exchange economy, has already been discussed at length but let us recall its origins. Edgeworth, in his *Mathematical Psychics* (1881) introduced the concepts of improving and core under the terms "recontracting" and "contract curve". The fundamental contribution of Edgeworth received little attention and was not further developed for almost 80 years, and it was through game theory that it came to light again.

In 1953 Shapley and Gillies analysed solutions for games in characteristic function forms with transferable utility. In this connection they formulated a new solution concept for such games which they called the *core*. The connection between the Edgeworth contract curve of an exchange economy and the core of a game was perceived by Shubik (1959) who developed and partly extended Edgeworth's ideas in the framework of game theory with transferable utility.

Inspired by these important contributions Scarf (1967) presented a stimulating analysis of the core and competitive equilibria for general exchange economies without the assumption of transferable utility. We will come back to the game theoretic approach in Chapter 4 but for the moment let us reemphasize the essential feature of the core of an exchange economy.

The allocations suggested as reasonable solutions to the exchange problem are based on a very simple idea. They cannot be improved upon by certain coalitions. For the Pareto optima the only coalition in question is the whole set of individuals. For the individually rational Pareto optima the coalitions are the individual agents and the whole set. For the core, any subset of agents may be a coalition. That the core is contained in the individually rational Pareto optima, and these in turn in the set of all Pareto optimal, is obvious. In this sense the core is the most exacting of these concepts and we will concentrate our attention on it.

We have argued up to this point that the core has, for a given economy, certain advantages as a solution concept. In particular, we suggested that for some exchange situations the core provided a meaningful solution where prices and competitive outcomes made little sense.

Nevertheless the competitive solution plays a basic role in economics and will feature largely in what follows. To develop it we must introduce some basic notions.

5. Prices and Demand: The Competitive Model

As the reader will recall, when an individual chooses, he does so under constrains, and what constrains his choice is the value, in exchange of his resources, that is, his income. However, to talk about value or income we must have prices, to weight the various commodities.

5.1. Prices

A price for the i–th commodity is a real number p^i, and the price vector for all commodities is then $(p^1, \ldots, p^\ell) = p \in \mathbb{R}^\ell$. If all commodities are desirable and scarce then all prices will be positive, i.e., p is an element of the interior of $\mathbb{R}^\ell_+$. Prices serve to describe the rate at which goods can be exchanged. Thus p^i/p^j gives the amount of good j that may be exchanged for one unit of good i. If no gifts or loans are envisaged then two bundles $x = (x^1, \ldots, x^\ell)$ and $y = (y^1, \ldots, y^\ell)$ can be exchanged for each other if

$$\sum_{i=1}^{\ell} p^i x^i = \sum_{i=1}^{\ell} p^i y^i ,$$

written $p \cdot x = p \cdot y$. Prices are more than simple barter rates: if we look, for example, at the prices for the same quantity of a commodity delivered at two different dates then the difference defines the interest or discount rate over time.

Understanding what prices are does not require much of the reader. However, he may well feel inclined to ask where those prices come from, how they are established or who in particular determines them? These questions are not answered in this book nor are they answered satisfactorily elsewhere for that matter. Throughout those parts of the book where prices play a role the reader should view them as being determined in some arbitrary manner and then accepted as given by the agents. For consumers this is perhaps not unreasonable, particularly in a large economy. Though we may well feel that collectively demand is effective in determining prices, few of us are capable of changing prices that actually obtain. In other words, acceptance of prices is plausible in large economies where individuals feel themselves to be insignificant. Prices then are simply given by $p \in \mathbb{R}^\ell$.

5.2. Budget Set

When an individual makes his choice given a price system p he is constrained to choose bundles whose exchange value is no more than that of his initial resources. This means that he is choosing in a subset of $\mathbb{R}^\ell_+$. He chooses what he can afford, his expenditure does not exceed his income. Students, in particular, will find this at first sight a highly unrealistic situation. However, they can think of themselves as exchanging resources that they will have in the future against current consumption. At least, this must be what their creditors believe! An individual's budget set will then depend upon the prevailing price system and his resources.

Definition 2.12. For an agent a with initial resources e the budget set $\beta(p, e)$ at prices p, is given by

$$\beta(p, e) = \{x \in \mathbb{R}^{\ell}_{+} \mid p \cdot x \leq p \cdot e\} .$$

Note that the budget set is non–empty and compact if $p \gg 0$ and $e \geq 0$. In Figure 2.8 we see a budget set for an agent who has initial resources of bread and wine. From here on we will always refer to $p \cdot e$ as the individual's *income*. This will clearly depend upon the prices obtaining.

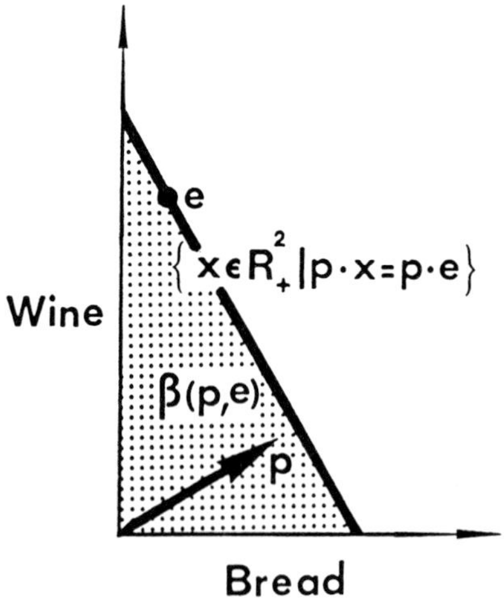

Figure 2.8

5.3. Demand

We finally arrive at our goal for this section which is to describe what an agent does. He chooses the best bundle available to him in his budget set. There may be several best bundles in which case what he *demands* is any one of these bundles and we describe his *demand* set as the set of best bundles. He is indifferent between any of the bundles in that set. We should perhaps, at this point, hoist a small danger signal. The individual is presumed to choose the best bundle available to him. If we have strong convexity this bundle will be unique and there is no problem. Suppose, however, that there are different best bundles, how does the individual choose between them? The most plausible answer would be "at random", but in general this will not overcome the difficulty. So the reader should bear in mind that certain results will be based upon the individual choosing an "appropriate" bundle in his demand set.

Definition 2.13. For an agent a with preference relation $\succsim$ and initial resources e, the demand set $\varphi(\succsim, e, p)$ at prices p is given by the set of best elements in his budget set $\beta(p, e)$, i.e.,

$$\varphi(\succsim, e, p) = \{x \in \beta(p, e) \mid x \succsim y \text{ for all } y \in \beta(p, e)\} .$$

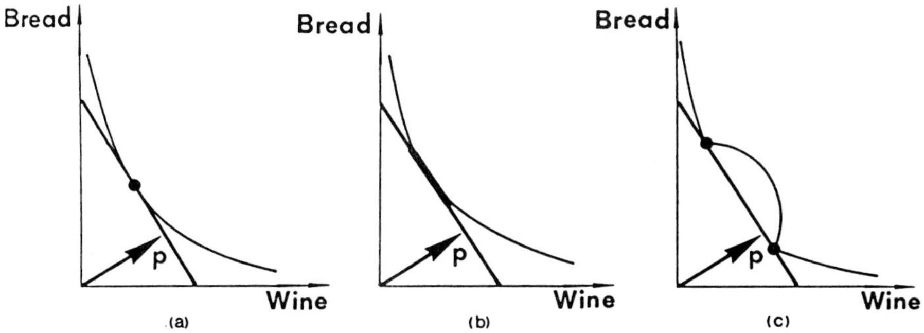

Figure 2.9

Demand sets for individuals with the same resources but different preferences are shown in Figure 2.9. In Figure 2.9 (a) the demand set is a unique point, reflecting the strong convexity of the preferences, in Figure 2.9 (b) it is a set but convex, reflecting the convexity of the preferences, and in Figure 2.9 (c) the set is not even convex.

It follows from Proposition 2.1. that the demand set $\varphi(\succsim, e, p)$ is never empty provided $e \geq 0$ and $p \gg 0$. Later, in Section 2 of Chapter 3 we will consider how the demand set varies as initial resources and prices change. It is clear that demand will not change if all prices are multiplied by a positive number since the budget set does not change. As a result we can "normalise" prices for example by taking $\sum p^i = 1$ or by setting the price of some commodity equal to one. It is clear that the situation depicted in Figure 2.9 (a) is the most convenient from the analytic point of view, since we would be dealing with a single point for each price and bundle of initial resources, that is with a *function*. In the other cases we are dealing with a set of vectors for each price–resource pair, that is with a set valued mapping or *correspondence*. Strong convexity, as we will show in the Appendix, is not a much stronger assumption than convexity. Therefore if this was the only step we wished to make it would not be worth dealing with correspondences. However, even if we keep convexity assumptions, as soon as we drop either completeness or transitivity we have to consider maximal elements rather than the best elements in order to define demand, and hence we are obliged to deal with demand correspondences. It is also convenient for technical reasons as we shall see, for example in the proof of Theorem 3.1. to use correspondences.

Now let us summarize.

5.4. Competitive Model

We have then as the primitive concepts of our model:

(1) *the commodity space* $\mathbb{R}^{\ell}_{+}$;

(2) *a set* A *of individuals each of whom has the following characteristics:*

  (a) *consumption set* $X = \mathbb{R}^{\ell}_{+}$,

  (b) *preferences* $\succsim \in \mathcal{P}$,

  (c) *initial resources* $e \in \mathbb{R}^{\ell}_{+}$;

(3) *a price system* $p \in \mathbb{R}^{\ell}_{+}$.

From these we derive two concepts indicating what an agent can choose and, given this, what he wants to choose. Namely

(4) *the budget set*

$$\beta(p, e) = \{x \in \mathbb{R}^{\ell}_{+} \mid p \cdot x \leq p \cdot e\} \ ;$$

(5) *the demand set*

$$\varphi(\succsim, e, p) = \{x \in \beta(p, e) \mid x \succsim y \text{ for all } y \in \beta(p, e)\} \ .$$

6. Walras Equilibrium

These definitions enable us finally to develop our first theme, that of decentralization by prices, which leads us to introduce the idea of a competitive or Walras equilibrium. Recall that the principle is that there is a given price system. At these prices individuals choose the vector that they most prefer in their budget set. If the total demand equals total supply of all goods at these prices then this is said to be a Walras equilibrium. These prices then decentralize the allocation problem. Thus, we have the following definition.

Definition 2.14. A Walras equilibrium for an economy $\mathcal{E}$ is an allocation f and a price system $p \in \mathbb{R}^\ell$ such that:

(a) $f(a) \in \varphi(\succsim_a, e(a), p)$ for all $a \in A$;

(b) total demand equals total supply, i.e.

$$\sum_{a \in A} f(a) = \sum_{a \in A} e(a).$$

An allocation f for the economy $\mathcal{E}$ for which there exists a price system such that(f, p) is a Walras equilibrium is called a *Walras allocation*. The set of Walras allocations is denoted $W(\mathcal{E})$. Similarly, a price system p for which there exists an allocation f such that (f, p) is a Walras equilibrium for the economy $\mathcal{E}$ is called an *equilibrium price system* for that economy, and the set of such price systems is denoted by $\Pi(\mathcal{E})$.

One of our main aims in this book is to explore and develop the relationship between our two basic themes, that is to say to show the links between the core and the competitive equilibria of economies. It is easily shown that all Walras allocations are in the core but it will require much more work to prove that in large economies core allocations are essentially competitive, that is, can be approximately decentralized by a price system.

Proposition 2.4. $W(\mathcal{E}) \subset C(\mathcal{E})$ for every economy $\mathcal{E}$.

Proof. Consider $f \in W(\mathcal{E})$ but $f \notin C(\mathcal{E})$. Then there is a coalition $S \in \mathcal{A}$ and an allocation g for S such that

(i) $g(a) \succ_a f(a)$ for all a in S

and

(ii) $\sum_{a \in S} g(a) = \sum_{a \in S} e(a)$.

Since f is a Walras allocation, (i) implies that for the equilibrium price vector p associated with f one has

$$p \cdot g(a) > p \cdot e(a) \text{ for all } a \text{ in } S.$$

Hence,

$$p \cdot \sum_{a \in S} g(a) = \sum_{a \in S} p \cdot g(a) > \sum_{a \in S} p \cdot e(a) = p \cdot \sum_{a \in S} e(a) ,$$

a contradiction with (ii).

Q.E.D.

Although Proposition 2.4. follows directly from the definitions that we have given, its economic content is important. Indeed it implies that were a competitive equilibrium to be established and then the price system abandoned, there would be no incentive for any coalition to withdraw from the economy. If ever the first theme is played even by a small ensemble no group of players will be tempted to go off and play a different theme.

The reader will recognize this as being a strengthening of the "First Theorem of Welfare Economics" which says that a Walras allocation is Pareto efficient.

Up to this point we have not discussed the problem of the existence of our solutions. Given Proposition 2.4. we have existence of both solutions for an exchange economy if we can show the existence of Walrasian equilibria. This will be done in Chapter 3.

Appendix to Chapter 2

1. Particular Types of Utility Functions

In Chapter 2 we mentioned that certain rather special types of utility functions are often treated in the literature. We give here a brief discussion of certain of them and references to the appropriate literature.

For the particular properties of u that we have mentioned namely,

(a) additive utility, i.e..

$$u(x_1, x_2, \ldots, x_\ell) = u_1(x_1) + \ldots + u_\ell(x_\ell);$$

(b) differentiable utility;

(c) concave utility, i.e.,

$$u(\lambda x + (1-\lambda)y) \geq \lambda u(x) + (1-\lambda)u(y), \qquad 0 \leq \lambda \leq 1;$$

the question of an intrinsic characterization in terms of preferences has been studied extensively in the literature. Here is a brief guide to some readings:

(a) This problem has been studied by Leontief (1947), Samuelson (1947), Debreu (1964) and others. A good survey of the problem and an extensive reading list can be found in Koopmans (1972).

(b) The basic reference is Debreu (1972). A complete account can be found in Mas–Colell (1985).

(c) Any utility function for a convex preference relation is quasi–concave, i.e., $\{x \in \mathbb{R}^\ell | u(x) \geq k\}$ is convex for all k. Thus, the problem amounts to asking, when is there a strictly increasing transformation f of a quasi-concave function u such that $f \circ u$ is concave? This problem was first discussed by de Finetti, and developed by Fenchel (1953, 1956).

The answer depends upon the "curvature" of the indifference surfaces, a topic which has achieved some prominence in the literature. A full investigation is made by Kannai (1977).

Problems (b) and (c) have a rather simple solution if one is satisfied with an "approximation" of the given preference relation by one which has a differentiable and concave utility representation. Here the key word is "approximation". To make this precise one has to consider a metric (or more generally a topology) on the space $\mathcal{P}$ of all preference relations. In other words, we have to establish a sufficient structure to enable us to say what it means for one preference relation to be a "close approximation" of another.

2. The Space $\mathcal{P}$ of Preferences

We have defined an economy as a mapping $\mathcal{E}$ of a finite set into the space $\mathcal{P}\times\mathbb{R}^{\ell}_{+}$ of agents' characteristics. It should be clear that any notion of equilibrium based on this description of an economy, for example the core $C(\mathcal{E})$, should depend in a continuous way on the parameters defining the economy. In our case the appropriate parameters are the preferences and endowments of the participating agents. Thus, for us any meaningful solution concept should depend in a continuous way on small changes in preferences and endowments. This is, indeed, an absolutely fundamental requirement, since even supposing that we believe, in principle, that we can obtain micro-data, such data could never be perfectly accurate. We would obviously wish that any small errors in observation would have corresponding small effects on the computed solutions.

The precise meaning of a "small change" in endowments is obvious since endowments are in $\mathbb{R}^{\ell}$ and we are well aware of a precise definition of "small changes" in $\mathbb{R}^{\ell}$. However, what would be the precise meaning of intuitive statements such as "*a small change* in preferences" or alternatively "a sequence $\succsim_n$ of preference relations *converges* to a preference relation $\succsim$"? To make this precise we have to introduce a *metric* on the set of preferences and, of course, the choice of any particular metric has to have an acceptable economic motivation.

For the purpose of this section – the approximation of a given preference relation by preference relations having particularly nice properties – it suffices to give a precise meaning to the statement "$\succsim_n \to \succsim$". It will become clear in the following section that this concept of convergence is, from the economic point of view, an appropriate one. For example, we will show in Chapter 3 that the demand function (if defined) will be a continuous function of preferences and prices.

Definition 2.15. A sequence $(\succsim_n)$ of preferences in $\mathcal{P}_{mo}$ is said to be *convergent* to a preference relation $\succsim$ in $\mathcal{P}_{mo}$ if for every $x, y \in \mathbb{R}^\ell_+$ with $x \succ y$ and for every sequence (x_n) converging to x and every sequence (y_n) converging to y there exists an integer $\overline{n}$ such that

$$x_n \succ_n y_n \quad \text{for every} \quad n \geq \overline{n} .$$

For example, if the preferences $\succsim_n$ and $\succsim$ in $\mathcal{P}_{mo}$ are represented by utility functions u_n and u respectively, then $(\succsim_n) \to \succsim$ if and only if $u_n(x_n) \to u(x)$ for every $x \in \mathbb{R}^\ell_+$ and every sequence (x_n) converging to x.

Example 2.4. An obvious example in a two–good situation is that where the utility function u is Cobb–Douglas, i.e., of the form $u(x, y) = x^\alpha y^{1-\alpha}$ with $0 \leq \alpha \leq 1$. A convergent sequence of preferences would be represented by the sequence of utility functions

$$(u_{\alpha_n}(x, y) = x^{\alpha_n} y^{1-\alpha_n}), \qquad \alpha_n \to \alpha .$$

For the interested reader we might mention that one can define a metric d on $\mathcal{P}$ such that the metric space $(\mathcal{P}, d)$ becomes a separable metric space, and a sequence $(\succsim_n)$ converges in the above sense to $\succsim$ in $\mathcal{P}_{mo}$ if and only if $d(\succsim_n, \succsim) \to 0$. For details and the properties of the space $(\mathcal{P}, d)$ we refer to Hildenbrand (1974, Chapter 1.2).

Proposition 2.5 (approximation of convex preferences by strictly concave utilities). Let $\succsim$ be a convex and monotonic preference relation on $\mathbb{R}^{\ell}_{+}$. Then there exists a sequence $(\succsim_n)$ of strictly convex preference relations in $\mathcal{P}_{mo}$ which converges to the given $\succsim$. Furthermore, every preference relation $\succsim_n$has a strictly concave utility function $u_n : \mathbb{R}^{\ell}_{+} \to \mathbb{R}$.

The proof can be found in Kannai (1977).

Remark. In fact, one can show a good deal more. One can show that one can approximate every convex and monotonic preference relation by preferences which admit a utility function which is differentiable infinitely often (even analytic). Further, the demand function derived from these "smooth" preferences is a differentiable (even analytic) function in prices. For our purposes these results are not needed and anyway the proofs would require considerably more mathematical techniques. However, the interested reader may consult Mas–Colell (1985) and Kannai (1974).

Chapter 3

Existence of Competitive Equilibrium

1. Introduction

We will now take up our first theme, that of Walras. Here we recall that we speak of a situation which has two essential features. Firstly, *prices are announced* in some way, for example by a central agent or auctioneer. Secondly, individuals are *price–takers*, that is, they have no influence on prices and therefore take them as given. This case occupies a central role in economics. Much of the economic literature is preoccupied with the idea that market economies tend naturally to a "resting point" or equilibrium and so much time is spent in discussing the properties of such equilibria that we must ask, like the child about the emperor's clothes, do they exist? The fact that it is much discussed is no proof of the existence of equilibria, indeed our theme might be like that in Elgar's "Enigma Variations", the fact that nobody knows whether there is a main theme has not stopped the music being played.

Yet for us the existence of equilibria is the most fundamental test of the consistency of the competitive model and we shall give several proofs of existence.

We start by establishing certain properties of individual and total demand, in particular, properties of continuity. We shall then study the case of an economy in which agents have strongly convex preferences and where they, in consequence, have *demand functions.* This case, of course, gives a direct result for those economists who prefer not to start with utility maximisation but to treat demand functions as the "primitive concept" of the model.

Our basic mathematical tool is the "fixed point theorem" of Brouwer and its generalisation to correspondences by Kakutani.

We shall relax the assumption of strong convexity to that of convexity alone and will then give a proof for the case in which we have now demand correspondences rather than functions. This includes naturally demand functions as a special case. This paves the way for the case in which we drop convexity completely. Some reflection will show that convexity is a restrictive hypothesis. However, it plays an essential role in the fixed point theorems which are used to prove existence. In fact, we can replace the assumption of convexity of preferences by another one, that of a large number of individuals. In the case of an economy with a finite number of individuals we obtain a weaker result, that there are allocations which are "nearly competitive". In the extreme case where there are infinitely many individuals we obtain again the full equilibrium result.

At the risk of being repetitive, we come back again to one of the basic lessons of our first chapter. This is the fundamental importance of large numbers of agents in equilibrium analysis. In fact, the effect of large numbers as far as the total demand set is concerned is a "convexifying" one, as will become clear in the proof of our result. One could then ask, why should we be happier with one assumption, that of many agents, rather than another, convexity of preferences? The answer should, by now, be very clear. Since the competitive solution has as its basic behavioural justification the insignificance of the individual, it does not make very much sense to discuss it out of this context.

2. Individual Demand

We now turn to the problem of how an individual's demand changes in the face of changes in his environment, or that part of his environment formed by prices and his initial resources. What we would like is that individuals should not react violently to small changes in these data. They should not, in the face of a small change in prices or income, radically alter their choice of commodity bundle. The reason for requiring such coherent, or more precisely "continuous" behaviour is clear. If this is true for the individual then it will also be true for the whole economy, and this is what really interests us. The reader may object that discontinuous individual behaviour may not be at odds with continuous behaviour of the whole economy. This is surely true, but then we would have to adopt a very different approach. We would have to specify the distribution of individual characteristics that would lead to continuous behaviour of the whole economy. This is a difficult problem which has not yet a fully satisfactory solution. Here we follow the traditional approach and content ourselves with building continuity at the level of the economy as a whole from continuity at the individual level.

Our first task will therefore be to show that demand sets do indeed behave continuously. To prove the results that follow some knowledge of the continuity of correspondences will be needed, and for this the reader is referred to the mathematical appendices. To establish continuity of demand, we need to know that the budget set changes continuously. It is clear that we could not hope to establish continuity of the demand set if, for some small change of prices or resources, the set from which choices are made changes radically.

Recalling from Chapter 2 the definition of the budget set correspondence as

$$\beta(e,p) = \{x \in X \mid p \cdot x \leq p \cdot e\} ,$$

what we wish to know is whether the correspondence β is continuous. A simple example will show that this is not necessarily the case.

Example 3.1. Consider an individual with $e = (1,0)$ and now consider a sequence of prices $p_n = (\frac{1}{n}, 1)$ converging to $p = (0,1)$. As we see in Figure 3.1 the budget set is compact for each n, contracts continuously and then in the limit we have $\beta(e,p) = [0,\infty)$.

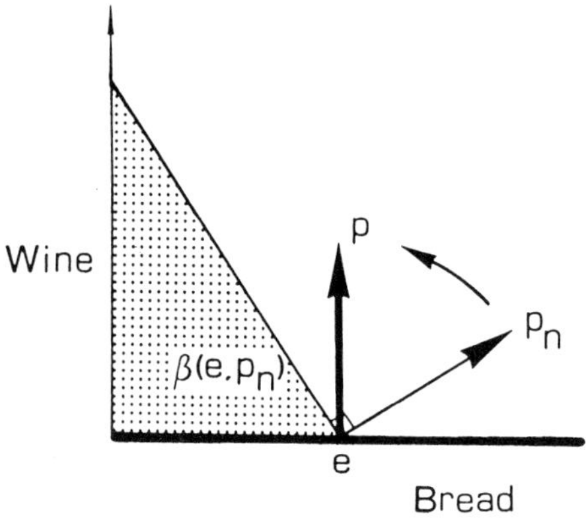

Figure 3.1

How might we avoid this problem? It is clear that the budget set presented no difficulties as long as it was given by positive prices, but as one of our prices became zero the discontinuity occurred. This happened because the agent was unable to profit from the falling price of bread since he only possessed bread. So his income dropped to zero. However, at this point he could obtain arbitrarily large quantities of bread since it costs nothing. To avoid this situation occurring we need the income $p \cdot e(a)$ to be greater than the cheapest possible consumption bundle, i.e.,

$$p \cdot e(a) > inf_{x \in X}\ p \cdot x \ .$$

Now, however, as we observed earlier, if we confine our attention to strictly positive prices and assume $X = \mathbb{R}^{\ell}_{+}$ the problem will never arise, since every agent, by assumption, has a positive quantity of some commodity and thus his income will be such that

$$p \cdot e > 0 = inf_{x \in \mathbb{R}^{\ell}_{+}} \, p \cdot x \; .$$

In fact, we will, in what follows, consider the price set as confined to strictly positive prices and will show later that this is sufficient. Furthermore, we will assume that the consumption set is $X = \mathbb{R}^{\ell}_{+}$. Now, the basic results that we need are summarized in the following proposition.

Proposition 3.1. Let $(\precsim, e) \in \mathcal{P} \times \mathbb{R}^{\ell}_{+}$. Then the following holds:

(1) The demand set $\varphi(\precsim, e, p)$ is non–empty and compact for every $p \gg 0$.

(2) The demand correspondence $\varphi(\precsim, e, \cdot)$ is homogeneous of degree zero in prices (i.e., for every $p \gg 0$ and $\lambda > 0$ one has $\varphi(\precsim, e, p) = \varphi(\precsim, e, \lambda p)$.

(3) The demand correspondence $\varphi(\precsim, e, \cdot)$ is upper hemi–continuous at every $p \gg 0$.

(4) If the preference relation $\precsim$ is monotonic and if the sequence (p_n) of strictly positive price vectors converges to a price vector p which is not strictly positive and $p \cdot e > 0$, then 'demand tends to infinity', i.e.,

$$inf\{|x| \in \mathbb{R} \mid x \in \varphi(\precsim, e, p_n)\} \underset{n}{\longrightarrow} \infty \; .$$

(5) If the preference relation $\precsim$ is convex then the demand set $\varphi(\precsim, e, p)$ is convex.

(6) If the preference relation $\precsim$ is strongly convex then $\varphi(\precsim, e, \cdot)$ is a continuous function in $p \gg 0$.

Proof.

(1) If $p \gg 0$ and $e \geq 0$ then the budget set $\beta(e,p) = \{x \in \mathbb{R}^\ell_+ \mid p \cdot x \leq p \cdot e\}$ is clearly non–empty, bounded and closed, hence compact. Since the preference relation is continuous it follows therefore from Proposition 2.1. that $\varphi(\precsim, e, p)$ is non–empty and compact.

(2) This follows immediately from the definition of the demand set.

(3) To show that $\varphi(\precsim, e, \cdot)$ is upper hemi–continuous, written u.h.c. at $p \gg 0$, we have, by Theorem AIII.1. in Mathematical Appendix AIII., to show that for every sequence (p_n) converging to p and for $x_n \in \varphi(\precsim, e, p_n)$ there is a converging subsequence of (x_n) whose limit belongs to $\varphi(\precsim, e, p)$. Since $p \gg 0$ we have $p_n \gg 0$ for n large enough. Let

$$\pi = inf\{p_n^h \mid h = 1, \ldots, \ell,\ n \geq \overline{n}\} .$$

Clearly, $\pi > 0$. Since $x_n \in \beta(e, p_n)$ we have

$$0 \leq x_n^h \leq \frac{p_n \cdot e}{\pi} \qquad (h = 1, \ldots, \ell).$$

Hence, the sequence (x_n) is bounded and therefore there is a convergent subsequence which we will also write $(x_n) \to \hat{x}$. Clearly, $\hat{x} \in \beta(e,p)$, since $p_n \cdot x_n \leq p_n \cdot e$ and $p_n \to p$ implies $p \cdot \hat{x} \leq p \cdot e$. Clearly, in the trivial case $e = 0$ and hence $p \cdot e = 0$ the vector 0 is the only element in the budget set and hence the best element. Now, however, assume that y is such that $p \cdot y < p \cdot e$, then for n large enough we have $p_n \cdot y < p_n \cdot e$. Since $x_n \in \varphi(\precsim, e, p_n)$ it follows that $x_n \succsim y$. Yet the preference relation is continuous and the sequence (x_n) converges to $\hat{x}$, hence it follows that $\hat{x} \succsim y$. Thus, we have shown that every vector y which costs less than $p \cdot e$

is not better than $\hat{x}$. On the other hand, suppose that $e \neq 0$ and y is such that $p \cdot y = p \cdot e$. Since $p \cdot e > 0$ then we can find a sequence (x_n) converging to y with $p \cdot x_n < p \cdot e$. Hence, by the above, $x_n \precsim \hat{x}$ and by continuity of $\precsim$ we obtain $y \precsim \hat{x}$.

(4) Assume property (4) is false. Thus, there is a bounded set $B \subset \mathbb{R}^{\ell}_{+}$ such that $\varphi(\precsim, e, p_n) \cap B \neq 0$ for infinitely many n, say for all n, in some subset of the positive integers, i.e., for $n \in Q \subset N$. Let $z_n \in \varphi(\precsim, e, p_n) \cap B$, $n \in Q$. The sequence (z_n) is bounded. Hence, there is a convergent subsequence, written, again for convenience, $(z_n) \to \hat{z}$. We now show in the same way as in the proof of (3), using the assumption $p \cdot e > 0$, that $\hat{z} \in \varphi(\precsim, e, p)$. But this is a contradiction, since the set $\varphi(\precsim, e, p) = \emptyset$. This is clear since at least one price is zero and every commodity is desired. Hence, there can be no best element in the budget set.

(5) Clearly,

$$\varphi(\precsim, e, p) = \bigcap_{z \in \beta(e,p)} \{x \in \beta(e,p) \mid x \succsim z\} \ .$$

By the definition of convex preferences the set $\{x \in \mathbb{R}^{\ell}_{+} \mid x \succsim z\}$ is convex. Since the budget set $\beta(e,p)$ is convex, it follows that the set $\{x \in \beta(e,p) \mid x \succsim z\}$ is convex, and consequently the intersection of all these sets, that is, the demand set $\varphi(\precsim, e, p)$ is itself convex.

(6) Let x and y be in $\varphi(\precsim, e, p)$ with $x \neq y$. Clearly, $x \sim y$. Thus, by the assumption of strong convexity we have $\frac{1}{2}(x + y) \succ x$, but since $\frac{1}{2}(x + y) \in \beta(e,p)$, this is a contradiction to $x \in \varphi(\precsim, e, p)$. Therefore, the demand correspondence is actually a function. But for a function u.h.c. means continuity, as explained in Mathematical Appendix A.III.2.

Q.E.D.

Remark. In Proposition 3.1. we assumed that the price system $p \gg 0$, since this guaranteed that the demand set was non–empty. Of course, it may happen in some instances that the demand set is non–empty even when $p \geq 0$ and some price $p^h = 0$. For example, this is the case when the consumption set X is compact or the preferences allow for satiation. Then the demand correspondence $\varphi(\precsim, e, \cdot)$ is still u.h.c. at p provided the income $p \cdot e > 0$. Compare the proof of Proposition 3.1. (3).

3. Total Demand

From these results for individual demand it is a trivial step, with the aid of the basic mathematical results in Mathematical Appendix AIII., to show that the same properties carry over to total demand. Armed with these results, we will be able to proceed to the two proofs of existence. For the total demand of the economy then we have the following proposition.

Proposition 3.2. Let $\mathcal{E} : A \to \mathcal{P}_{mo} \times \mathbb{R}^{\ell}_{+}$ be an exchange economy. Then the total demand correspondence

$$\Phi(p) := \sum_{a \in A} \varphi(\mathcal{E}(a), p), \qquad p \gg 0$$

has the following properties:

(1) Φ is homogeneous of degree zero [i.e., for every $p \gg 0$ and $\lambda > 0$ one has $\Phi(\lambda p) = \Phi(p)$].

(2) (Walras' identity). For every price vector $p \gg 0$ and $x \in \Phi(p)$ one has $p \cdot x = p \cdot e(A)$.

(3) The correspondence Φ is compact–valued and u.h.c. at every $p \gg 0$.

(4) If the sequence (p_n) of strictly positive price vectors converges to p which is not strictly positive, then 'total demand tends to infinity', i.e.,

$$inf\{|x| \in \mathbb{R} \mid x \in \Phi(p_n)\} \underset{n}{\longrightarrow} \infty\ .$$

(5) If the preferences $\precsim_a$ are convex for every a in A then the demand set $\Phi(p)$ is convex.

(6) If the preferences $\precsim_a$ are strongly convex for every a in A then Φ is a continuous function at every $p \gg 0$.

Proof. All these properties for the total demand correspondence follow immediately from the associated properties of the individual demand correspondence. For this we need only that the sum of compact–valued and u.h.c. correspondences be again compact–valued and u.h.c., for which see Mathematical Appendix AIII., Proposition 3. Since in the definition of an exchange economy, we assumed $e(A) \gg 0$ there is at least one agent with a positive income and therefore (4) follows from Proposition 3.1.

Q.E.D.

4. Existence of Equilibria: Strongly Convex Preferences

In this section we make the assumption that all preference relations are strongly convex. The consequence of this simplifying assumption is that each individual a has a *demand function*[1] $\varphi(a, \cdot)$, i.e., at each price system p there is a single best commodity bundle $\varphi(a,p)$ as in Figure 3.2. Consequently, the total demand of an economy is also a function of the prevailing price system.

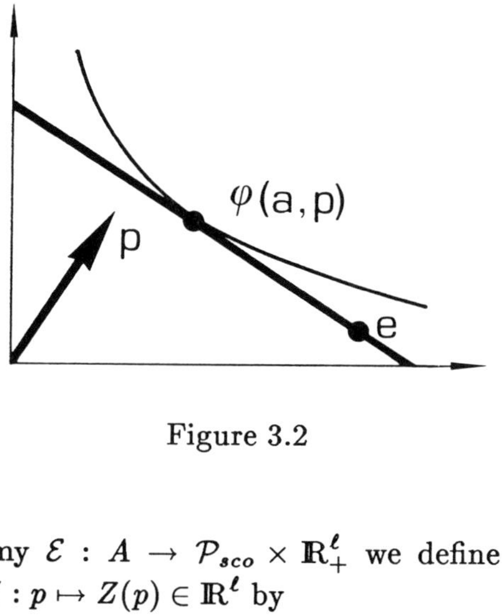

Figure 3.2

For an economy $\mathcal{E} : A \to \mathcal{P}_{sco} \times \mathbb{R}^{\ell}_{+}$ we define the total *excess demand function* $Z : p \mapsto Z(p) \in \mathbb{R}^{\ell}$ by

$$Z(p) = \sum_{a \in A} \varphi(a,p) - \sum_{a \in A} e(a) \, .$$

Our Definition 2.14. of an equilibrium price system can now be restated as follows: *A price vector p^* is an equilibrium price if and only if $Z(p^*) = 0$.*

---

[1] For convenience, we shall often write $\varphi(a,p)$ instead of $\varphi(\precsim_a, e(a), p)$.

Hence, showing the existence of a competitive equilibrium for an economy $\mathcal{E}$ amounts to solving this system of ℓ equations in ℓ unknowns:

$$\begin{aligned} Z^1(p^1,p^2,\ldots,p^\ell) &= 0 \\ \vdots \quad &\ \vdots \quad \vdots \\ Z^\ell(p^1,p^2,\ldots,p^\ell) &= 0 \end{aligned}$$

Furthermore, to make economic sense, we are looking for a *positive* solution $p^1 > 0,\ldots,p^\ell > 0$, or at least for a non–negative one $p^1 \geq 0, \ldots, p^\ell \geq 0$.

The reader will easily be able to find very special cases in which such a system of equations can be solved explicitly.

To see this consider the following

Example 3.2. (economies with Cobb–Douglas utilities). Assume that every agent of the economy $\mathcal{E} : A \to \mathcal{P}\times\mathbb{R}^\ell_+$ has a preference relation $\succsim_a$ which is defined by a Cobb–Douglas utility function, i.e.,

$$u_a(\xi_1,\ldots,\xi_\ell) = \xi_1^{\alpha_a^1} \cdot \xi_2^{\alpha_a^2} \cdot \ldots \cdot \xi_\ell^{\alpha_a^\ell} ,$$

where $\alpha_a^h > 0$ and $\sum_{h=1}^{\ell} \alpha_a^h = 1$. It follows that the individual demand functions are given by

$$\varphi(\precsim_a, e(a), p) = \left(\frac{\alpha_a^1 \cdot p \cdot e(a)}{p^1}, \ldots, \frac{\alpha_a^\ell \cdot p \cdot e(a)}{p^\ell} \right) .$$

Hence the market demand function is

$$\Phi(p) = \left(\frac{\sum_{h=1}^{\ell} p^h \cdot \sum_{a\in A} \alpha_a^1 e^h(a)}{p^1}, \ldots, \frac{\sum_{h=1}^{\ell} p^h \cdot \sum_{a\in A} \alpha_a^\ell e^h(a)}{p^\ell} \right) .$$

If we set $b_{kj} = \sum_{a\in A} \alpha_a^k e^j(a)$ then it is clear that p^* is an equilibrium price system if p^* is a positive solution of the system of *linear equations:*

$$\begin{bmatrix} b_{11} - e^1(A) & b_{12} & \dots & b_{1\ell} \\ b_{21} & b_{22} - e^2(A) & \dots & b_{2\ell} \\ \vdots & \vdots & \vdots & \vdots \\ b_{\ell 1} & b_{\ell 2} & \dots & b_{\ell\ell} - e^\ell(A) \end{bmatrix} \begin{bmatrix} p^1 \\ p^2 \\ \vdots \\ p^\ell \end{bmatrix} = \begin{bmatrix} 0 \\ 0 \\ \vdots \\ 0 \end{bmatrix} .$$

Since all off–diagonal elements of the coefficient matrix are positive and the column sums are zero, by a standard result in linear algebra there exists a non–trivial solution $p^* \gg 0$.

In this example we were able to compute the equilibrium prices explicitly. This is true even though the system is not fully numerically specified (we were free to choose the coefficients α_a^h), because we obtained a system of linear equations.

However, this example has a special property which alone, even though it does not permit explicit computation of the equilibrium, does allow a simple direct proof of the existence of such an equilibrium.

This property is that of what is known as "gross substitutability". For every commodity h the market demand function $\Phi_h(p)$ for this commodity is strictly increasing in all prices other than p_h. Thus for differentiable demand, as in the above example, the property can be simply written as

$$\partial_{p_j} \Phi_h(p) > 0, \qquad h \neq j \ .$$

The reader will realize that, even in the simple exchange economies with which we deal, this assumption is restrictive. Moreover it is a condition which is given on market demand functions; no general property of individual preferences is known which implies it for individual and hence for market demand functions.

Nevertheless as the following proposition shows, it greatly simplifies the proof of existence.

Proposition 3.3. For every exchange economy $\mathcal{E} : A \to \mathcal{P}_{\substack{mo\\sco}} \times \mathbb{R}^{\ell}_{+}$ whose total demand function $\Phi(p)$ satisfies "gross substitutability", there exists an equilibrium price vector $p^* \gg 0$.

Proof. Consider the function $g(p) = max_h \, Z_h(p)$, i.e., the amount of that good for which the excess demand is maximal. Now consider the following problem:

$$\min_{p \gg 0} g(p) \; .$$

We will show that the minimum is reached at some $p^* \gg 0$ and that $g(p^*) = 0$, and hence, by Walras' identity, all excess demands are zero. Thus we have an equilibrium.

Consider the price $\overline{p} = (\frac{1}{\ell}, \frac{1}{\ell}, \ldots, \frac{1}{\ell})$. Now define the following non-empty set:

$$M = \{p \in \Delta \mid p \gg 0 \quad \text{and} \quad g(p) \leq 2g(\overline{p})\} \; ,$$

where $\Delta = \{p \in \mathbb{R}^{\ell}_{+} \mid \sum p^h = 1\}$. From Proposition 3.2. properties (4) and (6) it follows that M is compact. Therefore g has a minimum on M, say at p^* which is in the interior of M unless $g(p^*) = g(\overline{p}) = 0$, in which case we have an equilibrium. Suppose that $g(p^*) > 0$. This implies by Walras' identity that there is a commodity h such that

$$Z_h(p^*) < 0 \; .$$

Decrease now the price of this commodity p^*_h by a sufficiently small amount and get the price vector $\hat{p}$ and still leave $Z_h(\hat{p}) < 0$. By gross substitutability we obtain $g(\hat{p}) < g(p^*)$.
Since $g(\frac{\hat{p}}{|\hat{p}|}) = g(\hat{p})$ we have a contradiction to the definition of p^* as minimizing $g(p)$ in M.

Q.E.D.

If we now turn to the general case, our problem is far from an easy one. We shall see in Chapter 6 that as the problem is formulated, total excess demand may be virtually any continuous function. The only structural properties that we can guarantee are the Walras' identity, homogeneity and the boundary behaviour. Other than this, we have no restrictions and, in particular, no information about the functional form of the total excess demand function.

Yet despite this lack of structure, by using more powerful mathematical tools we can still show that an equilibrium does exist. This is important since competitive equilibrium plays a central role in economic theory. How has this problem of the existence of such an equilibrium typically been treated? A well–known item in the folklore of economics is the so–called "law of supply and demand" (or in more poetic terms, the "invisible hand of Adam Smith" ...) which suggests that market economies will, effectively, adjust so as to be in equilibrium. That this works in "partial analysis" where we study a single market seems evident if one thinks of the simple "cross" diagram of supply and demand curves. The reasoning involved in the partial case is carried over by economists to the general case where we have a whole system of interdependent markets.

First, then, if we have a system $Z(p)$ which describes the excess demand equations of an economy there should, at least, be a solution p^* of the system of equations $Z(p) = 0$. Furthermore, one would like that this equilibrium should be a resting point of an economically plausible *price adjustment process.* Nevertheless, to model such an adjustment process in a realistic way is extremely difficult and till now nobody has succeeded in doing it satisfactorily. The reason for this is clear: If agents can trade at non–equilibrium prices, individual plans are not consistent. We would then have to specify who can trade and how much may be exchanged. In addition, we would have to specify who changes prices and by what rules.

The way in which economists have got round these problems is to use an ingenious idea of Walras, the so–called "tâtonnement" process. Walras envisaged a situation in which a central auctioneer or "crieur" announces prices and then modifies them progressively until equilibrium is achieved. No trade whatsoever takes place before equilibrium is attained.

How does the auctioneer modify prices? First he announces any strictly positive price vector $p(1)$ and then responds to market demand in the following way. Suppose that the total excess demand is not equal to zero for all goods. Then he simply increases the price $p^h(1)$ of each commodity h whose demand exceeds the supply and decreases the prices of those commodities whose supply exceeds demand. This leads to a new price vector $p(2) = p(1) + H(Z(p(1)))$, where $H^h(Z(p))$ has the same sign as $Z^h(p)$. That is the price vector $p(1)$ is changed to the price vector $p(2)$ in function of the excess demand at $p(1)$. Having obtained the new price vector $p(2)$ if still $Z(p(2)) \neq 0$ then the auctioneer repeats the procedure and generates a vector $p(3)$ and so on. The sequence $(p(n))_{n=1,2,\ldots}$ of price vectors will, according to the folklore, converge to an equilibrium price vector. Clearly the price change rule should have then two properties. Firstly that $p + H(Z(p))$ be strictly positive and secondly that $H(Z(p)) = 0$ implies $Z(p) = 0$. Economists have frequently thought of a rule which changes prices proportionally to excess demand. This could be expressed for each good h as

$$p^h(2) = p^h(1) + \lambda Z^h(p(1)) \ , \qquad \lambda > 0 \ .$$

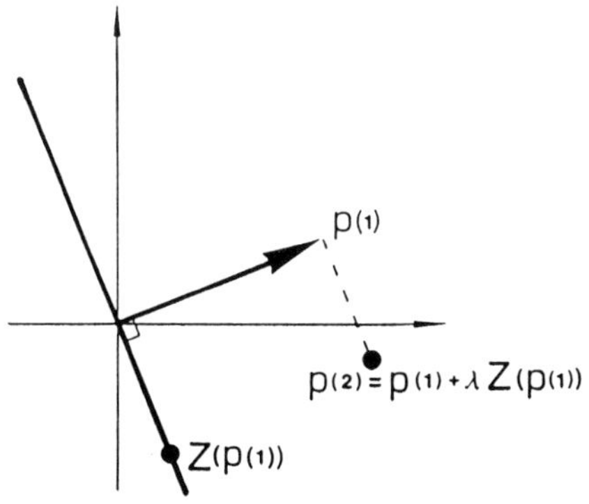

Figure 3.3

This is, of course, too simple. We have to be sure that λ is chosen so that the new price vector at any step is sure to be positive. Unless λ is chosen appropriately depending on p and $Z(p)$ this may not be the case. This is clear for example in Figure 3.3.

We could, of course, for each good take

$$p^h(2) = max\left[0, p^h(1) + \lambda Z^h(p(1))\right] .$$

But this would not overcome the problem since excess demand is not defined for zero prices. This sort of difficulty can be overcome as we show in Chapter 6 by working in continuous time.

In fact, if we consider the following example we can see that prices do, indeed, converge if we choose the adjustment speed appropriately.

Example 3.3. Consider the excess demand function

$$Z(p) = \begin{bmatrix} \dfrac{-p_1 - 2p_2 + p_3}{p_1 + p_2} + \dfrac{-2p_1 + p_2 - p_3}{p_1 + p_3} \\[2mm] \dfrac{+p_1 - p_2 - 2p_3}{p_2 + p_3} + \dfrac{-p_1 - 2p_2 + p_3}{p_1 + p_2} \\[2mm] \dfrac{-2p_1 + p_2 - p_3}{p_1 + p_3} + \dfrac{+p_1 - p_2 - 2p_3}{p_2 + p_3} \end{bmatrix}$$

which can be derived from an exchange economy with three goods and three consumers. We will come back to this example in more detail in Chapter 6. Taking $\lambda = 0.0004$ and starting from $p_0 = (0.08, 0.75, 0.17)$ we see, in Figure 3.4, how prices converge in the price simplex to the equilibrium price vector $p^* = (\frac{1}{3}, \frac{1}{3}, \frac{1}{3}) \in \Delta$.

Nevertheless, appealing as this type of approach may be, there is a problem. If we now modify our example by changing the distribution of initial endowments we obtain a new excess demand function

$$Z(p) = \begin{bmatrix} -\dfrac{p_2}{p_1 + p_2} + \dfrac{p_3}{p_1 + p_3} \\[2mm] -\dfrac{p_3}{p_2 + p_3} + \dfrac{p_1}{p_2 + p_1} \\[2mm] -\dfrac{p_1}{p_1 + p_3} + \dfrac{p_2}{p_3 + p_2} \end{bmatrix}$$

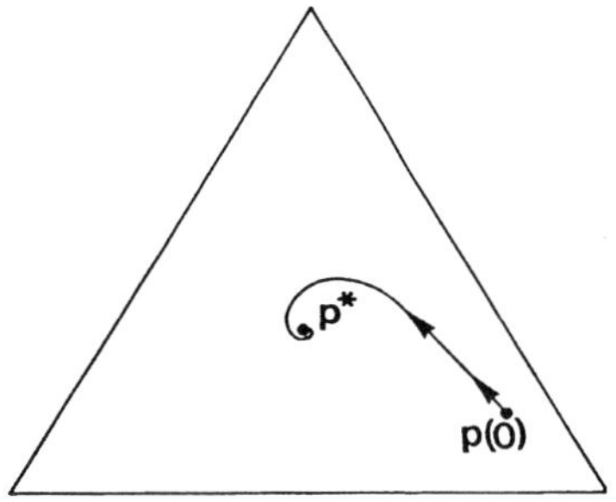

Figure 3.4

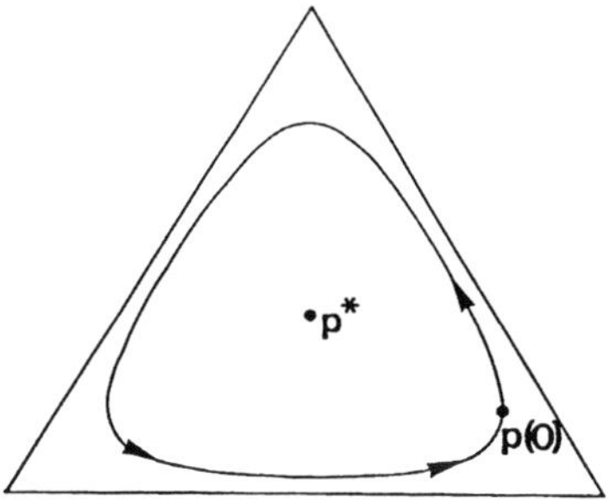

Figure 3.5

As we see in Figure 3.5, starting from the same price vector p_0 the process no longer converges to its equilibrium price vector which is still $p^* = (\frac{1}{3}, \frac{1}{3}, \frac{1}{3})$. The discovery of this possibility by Scarf (1960), whose example this is, was more than a little disturbing. It was all the more so since the example that Scarf constructed does not contain any pathological features. The surprise created by discoveries such as Scarf's is easily explained. Much of economic analysis has been done in terms of two–dimensional diagrams. In the case under discussion it happens that the adjustment process described does converge if there are only two commodities. This illustrates the danger of intuitive arguments based on two–dimensional geometrical reasoning. It may lead to unfulfilled and unfulfillable hopes!

In retrospect, the possibility of non–convergence is not surprising at all since, as we said earlier, the system of equations $Z(p) = 0$ contains very little structure. Think for a moment of two goods, cars and gasoline. Suppose prices were such that cars were in excess demand and gasoline in excess supply. Normal behaviour for the auctioneer would be to raise the price of cars and lower that of gasoline. But doing the former only pushes down the demand for gasoline, while the latter adjustment increases the demand for cars! The sort of complementarity which leads to these difficulties is ruled out for example by the assumption of gross substitutability, which we used above, in the standard literature on the stability of adjustment processes. We will come back in Chapter 6 to discuss these problems in more detail.

Some readers may, by now, have had their interest in our second theme dissipated. They may feel that the equilibrium concept is without interest. We should, however, remind them that we said earlier that the equilibrium concepts discussed in this book are essentially static in character. Once the economy is in equilibrium, then we gave good reasons as to why it should remain there. The definition alone does not contain any indication as to how an economy might get there. This is clearly reflected by the fact that even though an adjustment process may not converge, nevertheless a *fixed point* p^* of it exists. This would give us an equilibrium, since for such a fixed point p^* we obviously have to make no further adjustment.

If we confine ourselves to a fixed point of the adjustment process then this process, as such, has no real intrinsic economic content. We can then arbitrarily choose a process to suit our purpose. The only criterion is its mathematical convenience.

For example consider the following adjustment rule

$$p \mapsto \mathcal{A}(p) \quad \text{where} \quad \mathcal{A}^h(p) = \frac{p^h + max(0, Z^h(p))}{1 + \sum_i max(0, Z^i(p))} .$$

One can easily show that a fixed point p^* of this mapping, $p^* = \mathcal{A}(p^*)$ if it exists, has the following property

$$Z^h(p^*) \leq 0 \qquad \text{for all } h$$

and $Z^h(p^*) = 0$ if $p^*_h > 0$.

Assume on the contrary that there is a commodity h with

$$Z^h(p^*) > 0$$

then there is at least one commodity k with $Z^k(p^*) \leq 0$. Then

$$p^{*k} = \frac{p^{*k} + 0}{1 + \sum_h max(0, Z^h(p^*))} \neq p^{*k} \ .$$

Thus we have shown $Z(p^*) \leq 0$. By Walras' identity if $p^{*h} > 0$ then $Z^h(p^*) = 0$. If in addition $p^* \gg 0$ than we have $Z^h(p^*) = 0$ for all h and hence an equilibrium.

To show the existence of such a fixed point we need $\mathcal{A}$ to be defined on the whole price simplex Δ. But excess demand functions derived from the agents' characteristics that we have specified are not defined on the boundary of Δ since individual consumption sets are unbounded and preferences are monotonic. If we now truncate the consumption sets of every individual, and assume that individual initial endowments are strictly positive then we can show as in Proposition 3.1. that individual excess demand functions and hence total excess demand are continuous on the whole price simplex. This motivates the following

Proposition 3.4. Let $Z : \Delta \to \mathbb{R}^\ell$ be an "excess demand" function with properties (1), (2) and (6) of Proposition 3.2., then there exists $p^* \in \Delta$ such that $Z(p^*) \leq 0$ and $Z^h(p^*) = 0$ if $p^{*h} > 0$.

Proof. Define the price adjustment rule $\mathcal{A}$ as above and apply Brouwer's fixed point theorem (see Mathematical Appendix IV.) to find p^*.

Q.E.D.

If we now return to exchange economies as we originally defined them we wish to prove the following

Theorem 3.1. Let $\mathcal{E} : A \to \mathcal{P}_{\substack{mo \\ sco}} \times \mathbb{R}_+^\ell$ be an economy. Then there exists an equilibrium price vector $p^* \gg 0$.

First Proof. We could use the above proposition by truncating the individual consumption sets in such a way that each of these still contains the initial endowments which have to be strictly positive. Then we can show that the p^* obtained above is actually strictly positive and is an equilibrium of the original economy.

However, a simple direct argument using Kakutani's generalization of Brouwer's Theorem (see Mathematical Appendix IV.) is to extend the adjustment rule $\mathcal{A}$ to the boundary $\partial\Delta$ as follows.

For $p \in \partial\Delta$, let $\mathcal{A}(p) = \{q \in \Delta \mid q^h = 0 \text{ if } p^h > 0\}$. Properties (4) and (6) of Proposition 3.2. imply that the correspondence $\mathcal{A}$ is convex valued, and the graph of this correspondence is closed.

To see this, consider a sequence $p_n \to p$ where p is in $\partial\Delta$. For example $p = (0, 0, p^3, \ldots, p^\ell)$ where $p^3 \ldots p^\ell$ are positive. Now $|Z(p_n)| \to \infty$ and the coordinates $Z^3(p_n) \ldots Z^\ell(p_n)$ remain bounded. Therefore for each of the coordinates $h = 3, \ldots, \ell$ $\mathcal{A}^h(p_n)$ converges to zero. Therefore every limit point of the sequence $\mathcal{A}(p_n)$ belongs to $\mathcal{A}(p)$. This proves that the graph is closed. Therefore by Kakutani's fixed point theorem there exists a fixed point p^*, i.e., $p^* \in \mathcal{A}(p)$. Obviously $p^* \gg 0$ from the definition of $\mathcal{A}(p)$ on the boundary. Hence p^* is an equilibrium.

Q.E.D.

We now give an alternative proof of Theorem 3.1. which involves an extreme adjustment process, the value of that commodity for which excess demand is greatest is made as high as possible. This radical adjustment process has little intuitive appeal but leads us directly to a constructive argument. This proof of Theorem 3.1. is due to Debreu (1975b).

Second Proof. Consider the total excess demand function $Z : int\Delta \to \mathbb{R}^\ell,\quad p \mapsto Z(p) \in \mathbb{R}^\ell$, which is continuous and fulfills Walras' identity. For every $p \gg 0$ let

$$\Lambda(p) = \{h \in \{1,\ldots,\ell\} \mid Z^h(p) = \max_{i=1,\ldots,\ell} Z^i(p)\}\ ,$$

i.e., a list of those commodities which have the greatest excess demand. The idea is simple. Given p with $Z(p) \neq 0$, we will make commodity $h \notin \Lambda(p)$ very cheap in order to increase its demand. Formally

$$p \mapsto \mu(p) = \{q \in \Delta \mid q^h = 0 \text{ if } h \notin \Lambda(p)\},$$

i.e., $\mu(p)$ is a facet of Δ spanned by the vectors e_h where $h \in \Lambda(p)$ and where e_h is the h–th unit vector.

Example 3.4. Let $p = (\frac{1}{3}, \frac{1}{3}, \frac{1}{3})$. If $Z(p) = (-4, 2, 2)$ then
$\Lambda(p) = \{2,3\}$ and $\mu(p) = \{(0, p^2, p^3) \mid p^2 + p^3 = 1\ ,\ p^2, p^3 \geq 0\}$.
If $Z(p) = (2, 1, -3)$ then $\Lambda(p) = \{1\}$ and $\mu(p) = \{(1, 0, 0,)\}$.
If $Z(p) = (0, 0, 0)$ then $\Lambda(p) = \{1, 2, 3\}$ and $\mu(p) = \Delta$.

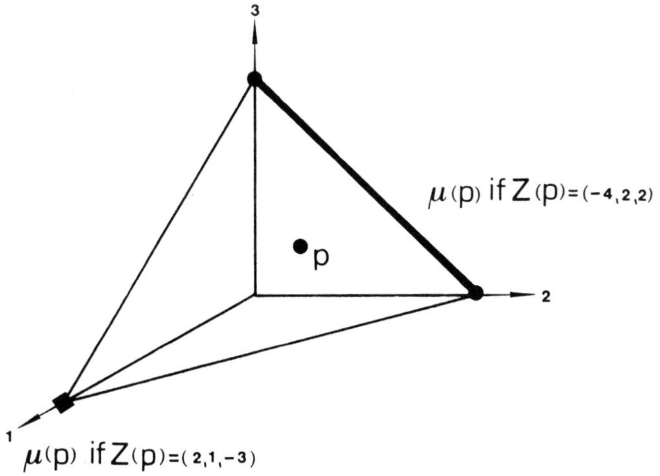

Figure 3.6

The correspondences Λ and μ are not defined on the boundary of the price simplex. Thus if $p \in \partial\Delta$ let

$$\Lambda(p) = \{h \mid p^h = 0\} \quad \text{and} \quad \mu(p) = \{q \in \Delta \mid q^h = 0 \text{ if } h \notin \Lambda(p)\}$$

or equivalently, as before, $\mu(p)$ is the convex hull of the unit vectors e^h such that $h \in \Lambda(p)$.

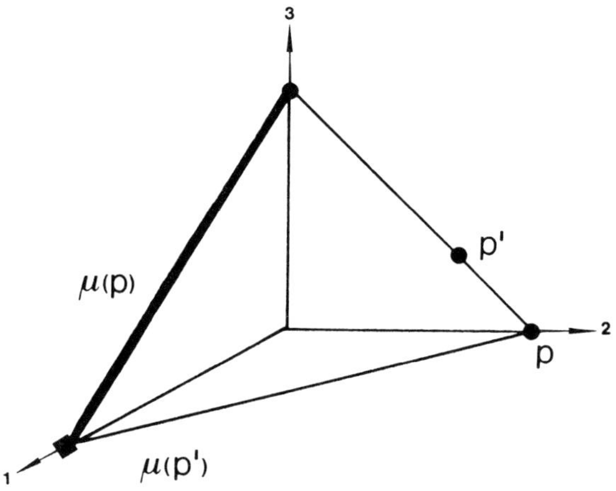

Figure 3.7

An equilibrium price vector p^* (i.e., $Z(p^*) = 0$) is obviously a fixed point of the correspondence μ, since $\Lambda(p^*) = \{1, \ldots, \ell\}$, hence $\mu(p^*) = \Delta$. Conversely, if $p^* \in \mu(p^*)$, then clearly $p^* \gg 0$ and by definition of μ we must have $\Lambda(p^*) = \{1, \ldots, \ell\}$, hence $Z^h(p^*) = \xi$ for all commodities $h = 1, \ldots, \ell$. Hence we obtain from the Walras' identity $p^* \cdot Z(p^*) = 0$ that $Z(p^*) = 0$.

Thus it remains to show that the correspondence μ has a fixed point. For this we apply Kakutani's theorem (see Mathematical Appendix IV). By definition the set $\mu(p)$ is convex and closed. In order to show that the graph of μ is closed we choose converging sequences $p_n \to p, \pi_n \to \pi$ with $\pi_n \in \mu(p_n)$ and show that $\pi \in \mu(p)$. If $p \gg 0$ this follows from the continuity of the excess demand function Z. Indeed, for n large enough we have $\Lambda(p_n) \subset \Lambda(p)$. This inclusion implies $\mu(p_n) \subset \mu(p)$ and hence, $\pi_n \in \mu(p)$ and consequently $\pi \in \mu(p)$ since $\mu(p)$ is closed. If p is not strictly positive we may assume without loss of generality that $p = (0, 0, \ldots, p^{r+1}, \ldots, p^{\ell})$; hence $\Lambda(p) = \{1, 2, \ldots, r\}$. The sequence of excess demands $Z^h(p_n)$ for commodities $h > r$ remains bounded if $n \to \infty$. Since $\| Z(p_n) \| \to \infty$ (see Proposition 3.2.), there is for n large enough a commodity $h_n \leq r$ with greatest excess demand, i.e., $\Lambda(p_n) \subset \{1, 2, \ldots, r\}$. Hence we obtain $\pi_n \in \mu(p_n) \subset \mu(p)$ for n large enough and consequently $lim\, \pi_n = \pi \in \mu(p)$.

We can now apply Kakutani's fixed point theorem (see Mathematical Appendix IV.). Thus there exists a fixed point p^* of μ which is, as shown above, an equilibrium price vector for the economy $\mathcal{E}$.

Q.E.D.

The proof that we have just given guarantees the existence of equilibrium. However, as we remarked, an adjustment process will not necessarily lead us from an arbitrary initial price system to the equilibrium. Is it then possible to find some constructive procedure which will enable us to start with any given price vector and then to trace a path to the equilibrium? The answer to this question has been provided by Scarf. A detailed account of his algorithm for finding equilibrium prices and related work is given in his book (Scarf (1973) or see Scarf (1982)).

We will now sketch the basic ideas involved and in so doing we will follow Debreu (1975b).

Recall that in the proof of Theorem 3.1. we associated with every price vector p, a set of integers $\Lambda(p)$. A price vector p^* clearly is an equilibrium if and only if $\Lambda(p^*) = \{1, 2, \ldots, \ell\}$. Suppose that we could find a subset S in Δ with a small diameter and such that S is "completely labelled" i.e., $\cup_{p\in S}\Lambda(p) = \{1,2,\ldots,\ell\}$, then since the diameter of S is small the variation of the function $Z(p)$ is also small. Further, since every index $\{1,2,\ldots,\ell\}$ is used, the excess demand $Z^h(p)$ must be approximately the same for every commodity h. Therefore, by Walras' identity, the excess demand must be small for every commodity. Thus the smaller the diameter of the set S the smaller the excess demand for each commodity. A price system for which the excess demand for every commodity is small we can describe as an *approximate equilibrium*, even though it may be far from any true equilibrium price system. Thus the approximation is made in terms of the excess demand, and not in terms of proximity in the price simplex to a true equilibrium price vector.

We now explain how we can find such a set S, i.e., a small "completely labelled" set. In every set, $\Lambda(p)$, we choose one integer say $\lambda(p)$. This "labelling λ" must satisfy two conditions. These are, firstly, that the vertices of the price simplex form a set which is fully labelled by λ, i.e., for every h from 1 to ℓ there is exactly one vertex v for which $\lambda(v) = h$. Secondly, no facet is fully labelled (a facet of an ℓ simplex is an $\ell - 1$ simplex). A rule that satisfies these conditions is the following. Choose $\lambda(p)$ arbitrarily for every strictly positive p. For the remaining p do the following. Choose $\lambda(p) \in \Lambda(p)$ such that $\lambda(p) - 1(mod\ \ell) \notin \Lambda(p)$. This means that if $1 < \lambda(p) \leq \ell$, then $\lambda(p) - 1 \notin \Lambda(p)$ and if $\lambda(p) = 1$ then $\ell \notin \Lambda(p)$. We will now use this labelling rule to assign numbers to points "above" Δ and this in turn will enable us to find a completely labelled subset S of Δ.

Let T be the part of $\mathbb{R}^\ell_+$ that is above Δ. We want to divide T in a regular way into ℓ simplices whose vertices have integer coordinates. This is referred to as a "regular triangulation" and is illustrated in Figure 3.8. The construction and description of such a triangulation is very technical and we will not go into the details. The intuitive idea given by the figure will suffice for our purposes.

We now give every point in the integer grid a label $1,2,\ldots,\ell$ as follows. Draw the line from each point to the origin. This line cuts the price simplex at one price p. Take the label $\lambda(p)$ and associate it with the corresponding point in the grid. If we can find far to the north–east in $\mathbb{R}_+^\ell$ an $\ell - 1$ simplex whose vertices are fully labelled, then looking back to the price simplex Δ we must have a small fully labelled subset of Δ. How do we find such a set? Before explaining this we need one definition. Two $\ell - 1$ simplices are said to be *adjacent* if there is an ℓ simplex of which they are both facets.

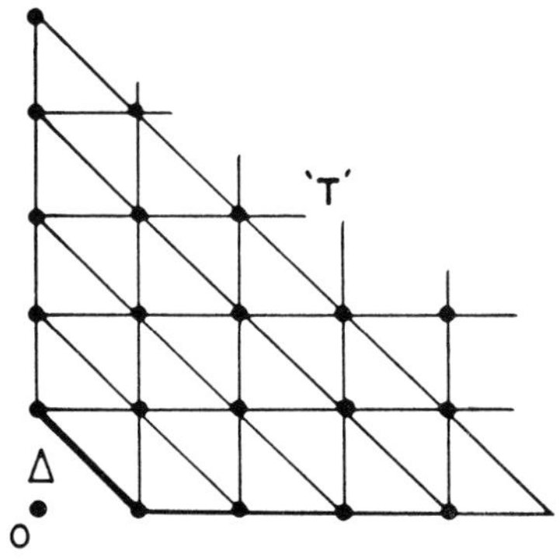

Figure 3.8

Now start with Δ, Δ is a facet of exactly one ℓ simplex. Hence there is exactly one $\ell - 1$ simplex with fully labelled vertices which is adjacent to Δ. Call this Δ_1. Now since Δ_1 cannot belong to the boundary of T there are exactly two ℓ simplices of which Δ_1 is a facet. Hence, there are exactly two $\ell - 1$ simplices with completely labelled vertices adjacent to Δ_1. One of these is Δ so we choose the other, say Δ_2. Now we repeat the procedure, starting with Δ_2 instead of Δ_1 and finding Δ_3 different from Δ_2 and Δ_1. In this way since the procedure does not stop we get a sequence (Δ_i) of $\ell - 1$ simplices, as illustrated in Figure 3.9

Clearly we have to show that this procedure cannot "get stuck" in some finite set of simplices, i.e., visiting each simplex in that set infinitely often. To see that this cannot happen consider the following argument.

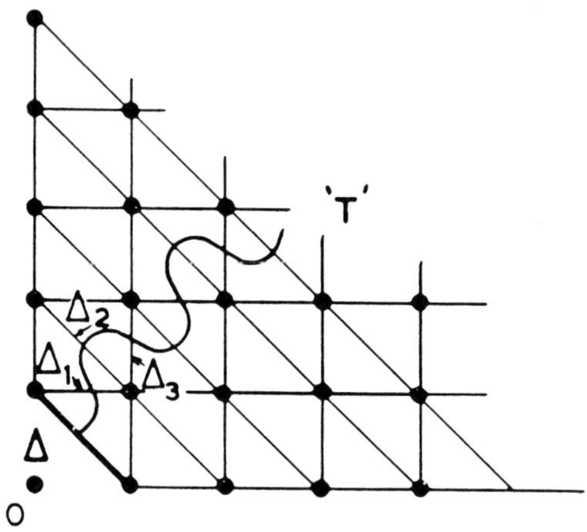

Figure 3.9

You enter a house with a finite number of rooms (ℓ simplices), each room has two doors (fully labelled facets) and you cannot leave a room by the door through which you entered. It is clear, then, that you cannot visit the same room twice and you must leave the house by a different door from that through which you entered. Since we have no fully labelled facets on the boundary we must be taken farther and farther to the north–east in T.

Now consider the "projection" of each Δ_n back onto the price simplex Δ. This gives us a sequence (S_n) of completely labelled subsets of Δ. The farther out Δ_n the smaller the corresponding subset S_n. Hence, we can find what we were looking for, namely a fully labelled subset of Δ as small as we wish.

The reader has obviously realized by now that this gives us a constructive proof of the existence of equilibrium. For, taking a p_n in each S_n, we obtain a sequence of price vectors (p_n), and every limit point p of this sequence is an equilibrium price vector.

The preceding proofs made essential use of a demand *function*. If we abandon strongly convex preferences or if we wish to introduce production, one has typically to face the problem that the excess demand is no longer a function but is multi–valued. We now state and prove the standard existence theorem which covers this more general case.

Remark. It is easy to show that Theorem 3.1. implies that for every economy $\mathcal{E} : A \to \mathcal{P}_{\substack{mo \\ co}} \times \mathbb{R}^{\ell}_{+}$ with $e(A) \gg 0$ there exists a competitive equilibrium. The idea is the same as the one used in the Appendix to Chapter 4. Let $\pi(\mathcal{E})$ denote the set of equilibrium prices for the economy $\mathcal{E}$. Now the correspondence $\mathcal{E} \mapsto \pi(\mathcal{E})$ is closed or more precisely, let $\mathcal{E}_n : A \to \mathcal{P}_{\substack{mo \\ sco}} \times \mathbb{R}^{\ell}_{+}$ be a sequence of economies converging to an economy $\mathcal{E} : A \to \mathcal{P}_{\substack{mo \\ co}} \times \mathbb{R}^{\ell}_{+}$ with $e(A) \gg 0$. (The exact meaning of this is explained in the Appendix to Chapter 4.) If $p_n \in \pi(\mathcal{E}_n)$ every limit point of the sequence (p_n) belongs to $\pi(\mathcal{E})$. Since every economy $\mathcal{E} : A \to \mathcal{P}_{\substack{mo \\ co}} \times \mathbb{R}^{\ell}_{+}$ with $e(A) \gg 0$ can be obtained as a limit of a sequence $(\mathcal{E}_n)$ of economies fulfilling the assumptions of Theorem 3.1. we obtain the required result. We leave the details to the reader, since we shall now give an alternative existence proof which covers this more general situation.

5. Economies without Convex Preferences

Up till now, we have restricted ourselves to the case of strongly convex preferences. In this case the problem boils down to finding a solution of a system of equations. We can, in fact, weaken the strong convexity assumption to one of convexity alone. Indeed, we have already remarked that this can be done by approximating the convex economy by a sequence of strictly convex economies. Alternatively we can modify the mathematical tools that we have used to give similar proofs. We thus pass from functions to convex–valued correspondences. This changes nothing essential in our problem. Formally in this case where the excess demand $Z(p)$ is a correspondence, instead of looking for p^* such that $Z(p^*) = 0$ we look for p^* such that $0 \in Z(p^*)$.

An equilibrium defined in this way is not really decentralized since nothing guarantees that individuals will choose precisely those bundles in their individual net trade set $Z(a,p)$ which will sum up to 0. Although our definition of equilibrium requires only that there should be individual plans compatible with each other, why should individuals choose these particular plans, amongst those that are available?

There is clearly little interest in establishing a proof for the case of convex rather than strictly convex preferences. Nevertheless the method employed for such a proof allows us to make a bigger step and to dispense altogether with the convexity of individual preferences. This shows that the existence result is robust when the convexity assumption is weakened. Thus it is not the convexity of individual preferences which is essential. Recall that we needed this assumption to guarantee that total excess demand should be convex–valued. Is there some alternative way to obtain the convex–valuedness of the sum of individual demand correspondences? We will show later that there is such an alternative. The convexity of the total excess demand correspondence is the key to the problem. Indeed if we now replace $Z(p)$ by its "convexified" version or convex hull *co* $Z(p)$ then we have the following

Theorem 3.2. Let $\mathcal{E} : A \to \mathcal{P}_{mo} \times \mathbb{R}^{\ell}_{+}$ be an economy then there exists $p^* \gg 0$ such that $0 \in co\ Z(p^*)$.

Proof. The proof of the theorem is based on the fundamental lemma which is a direct consequence of Kakutani's fixed point theorem and which is proved in the Mathematical Appendix IV.

Lemma 3.1. Let S be a closed and convex subset of the unit simplex Δ in $\mathbb{R}^\ell$. Assume that the correspondence ψ of S into $\mathbb{R}^\ell$ has the following properties:

(i) ψ is bounded, i.e., there exists a bounded set B in $\mathbb{R}^\ell$ such that $\psi(p) \subset B$ for every $p \in S$;

(ii) the graph of ψ is closed;

(iii) $\psi(p)$ is convex for every $p \in S$;

(iv) for every $p \in S$ we have $p \cdot z \leq 0$ for all $z \in \psi(p)$.

Then there exists $p^* \in S$ and $z^* \in \psi(p^*)$ such that

$$p \cdot z^* \leq 0 \qquad \text{for every} \quad p \in S .$$

Observe that Lemma 3.1. gives us almost the conclusion of Theorem 3.2. if we set $\psi(p) = co\ Z(p)$. This follows from Proposition 3.2. and Proposition AIII.4. in the appendix. Indeed if we knew that the p^* of the lemma were in the interior of S then it would follow that $0 \in \psi(p^*)$. In fact, $p^* \cdot z^* = 0$ and since $p \cdot z^* \leq 0$ for all $p \in S$ we obtain $z^* = 0$. First note that there can be no positive coordinate of z^*, since p^* is in the interior of S and if there was an h with $z^* > 0$ then we can make a small increase in the relative price of this commodity and obtain $\hat{p} \in S$ with $\hat{p} \cdot z^* > 0$, a contradiction. Now since $p^* \gg 0$ by Walras' identity no coordinate of z^* can be negative. Hence $z^* = 0$.

Now we prove the theorem by showing that the above argument does apply since we will show that we can choose S big enough such that p^* is in its interior.

Let K be the set of p in Δ such that there exists a $z \in co\ Z(p)$ with $\sum_h z_h \leq 0$. Observe that K is non–empty, for example $(\frac{1}{\ell}, \ldots, \frac{1}{\ell})$ is in K. It is closed and only contains strictly positive vectors by the boundary condition (Proposition 3.2. (4)).

Now we can choose the set S of strictly positive prices. Let S be closed convex and contain K in its interior. Apply to S the lemma and we obtain $p^* \in S$ and $z^* \in co\ Z(p^*)$ such that $p \cdot Z(p^*) \leq 0$ for every $p \in S$. Now we show that $p^* \in K$ and hence in the interior of S. Since the vector $(\frac{1}{\ell}, \ldots, \frac{1}{\ell})$ is in K, hence in S, and $z^* \in co\ Z(p^*)$ we obtain $\sum z^{*h} \leq 0$. This completes the proof.

Q.E.D.

The reader might, at this point, ask what is the economic significance of Theorem 3.2. A partial answer is provided by the observation that if we consider economies with a "very large" number (a continuum) of agents, total demand or rather, mean demand will be convex even if individuals do not have convex preferences. Furthermore in this case even completeness of preferences can be given up. So in this extreme case, our theorem is appropriate. We will come back later to discuss such an economy.

However, this would be of little interest if in large but finite economies we could say nothing. If we look at the problem of existence what we require is that there should be a positive price vector p^* such that the vector 0 is in $Z(p^*)$. If $Z(p)$ is convex for every p then we know that such a p^* exists. If not, by convexifying $Z(p)$ we can find a p^* such that $0 \in Z(p^*)$. The question is by how much do we distort the original economy by increasing the demand set in this way? What we want to know is how "far away" is the 0 vector from the true aggregate demand $Z(p^*)$? Clearly, if we convexify each of the individual excess demands then we convexify aggregate excess demand. We will give results which show: firstly that the 0 vector in the convexified aggregate excess demand $Z(p^*)$ is the sum of individual vectors which are in the true individual excess demands of all but at most ℓ individuals where ℓ is the number of goods. More formally, we have:

Proposition 3.5[1]. Let $\mathcal{E} : A \to \mathcal{P}_{mo} \times \mathbb{R}^{\ell}_{+}$ be an exchange economy. Then there exists an allocation f and a price system $p^* \gg 0$ with the following properties:

(i) $p^* \cdot f(a) = p^* \cdot e(a)$ for every agent $a \in A$.

(ii) $f(a) \in co\, \varphi(a, p^*)$ for all $a \in A$
and $\#\{a \in A | f(a) \notin \varphi(a, p^*)\} \leq \ell$

(iii) $\sum_{a \in A} f(a) = e(A)$.

This is a straightforward consequence of the following mathematical result.

Lemma (Shapley–Folkman). Let D_i $(i = 1, \ldots, n)$ be non-empty subsets of $\mathbb{R}^{\ell}$ and $z \in co \sum_{i=1}^{n} D_i$. Then there exist vectors $x_i \in co\, D_i$ $(i = 1, \ldots, n)$ such that

$$z = \sum_{i=1}^{n} x_i \qquad \text{and} \qquad \#\{i \mid x_i \notin D_i\} \leq \ell\,.$$

Another way of interpreting the proposition is to say that "on average" the difference between the allocation received and real demand is small, in large economies. We illustrate this here by showing what happens when we sum identical sets. We see clearly that the average of n such sets converges to the convex hull of the average (see Figure 3.10).

[1] To prove Proposition 3.5. we need even less than is assumed. In particular, we do not need the preferences to be *complete*. Completeness or the ability to compare every bundle in the consumption sets might well be regarded as a little implausible, but here at least it is not needed. Dropping completeness and convexity may well lead, in a finite economy, to there being no equilibrium, but there will always be an approximate equilibrium in the sense of the proposition.

However, one might reasonably object that even if ℓ agents are not many, if they received radically different treatment from their real excess demand, then the result is not satisfactory.

In fact we can give a stronger result which shows that if there is an equilibrium price vector p^* with the convexified aggregate excess demand, then there is an allocation at p^* in which at most $\overline{n}$ agents, where $\overline{n}$ is independent of the number of agents in the economy, receive something different from their true demand and moreover *no* agent is far from his true demand.

Theorem 3.3 (existence of approximate equilibrium) Let T be a finite[1)] set of agents' characteristics $T \subset \mathcal{P}_{mo} \times \mathbb{R}^{\ell}_{+}$. Then for every $\epsilon > 0$ and $\delta > 0$ there exists an integer N such that for every economy $\mathcal{E} : A \to T$ with $\frac{1}{\#A} \sum_{a \in A} e(a) \gg \delta$ and $\#A \geq N$ there exists an allocation f and a strictly positive price vector p^* with the following properties:

(i) $\#\{a \in A | f(a) \notin \varphi(a, p^*)\} \leq N$,
i.e., the number of individuals who receive an allocation which is not in their demand set is not greater than N;

(ii) for every agent a such that $f(a) \notin \varphi(a, p^*)$ it follows that $dist\ (f(A), \varphi(a, p^*)) \leq \epsilon$.

The proof of this theorem is given by Hildenbrand, Schmeidler and Zamir (1973). We shall not give it here but the basic idea is quite simple.

By Proposition 3.5. we know that there exists an allocation f with the following properties:

---

1) All that is really needed is that this set should be compact.

(i) $p^* \cdot f(a) = p^* \cdot e(a)$ for every agent $a \in A$

(ii) $f(a) \in co\ \varphi(a,p)$ for all $a \in A$ and $\#\{a \in A | f(a) \notin \varphi(a,p)\} \leq \ell$

(iii) $\sum_{a \in A} f(a) = e(A)$.

Thus at most ℓ agents receive a commodity bundle which is not in their demand sets. How can we modify f to give those agents something "near" (up to ϵ) to their demand set, in such a way that the modified demand is still feasible? To do this we must modify slightly the allocation of individuals other than those who were initially outside their demand sets. Now the amounts of goods involved in these modifications can be shown to be bounded independent of the size of the economy.

Notice that we have now N agents who are only ϵ away from their true demands but of course N may be considerably larger than ℓ.

The reader who is bothered by the fact that the f of the theorem is not in all individuals' demands and hence is not decentralized should note that the theorem directly implies that there is an allocation f in the true demand of all agents such that at the prices p^* of the theorem total excess demand $Z(p^*) \leq N \cdot \epsilon$, hence average excess demand is "small" for large economies.

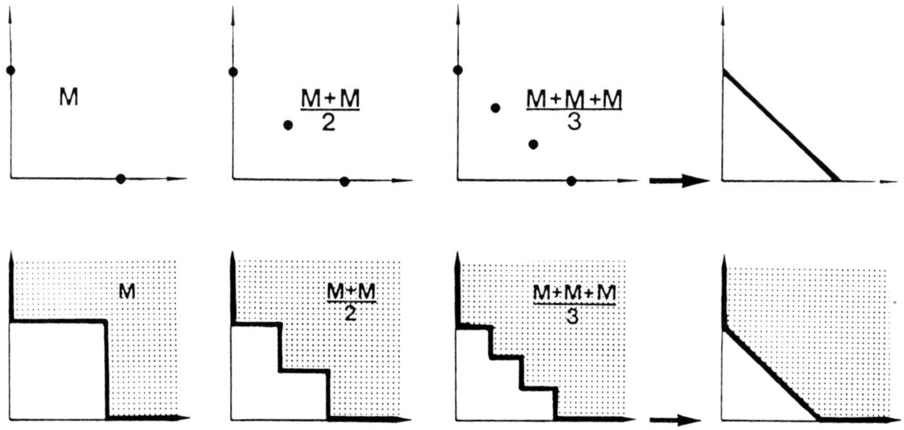

Figure 3.10

6. Conclusion

In concluding this chapter, let us briefly recapitulate what we have shown, and perhaps more importantly, what we have not shown. We have proved the existence of equilibrium in finite "convex economies", and have shown that when we drop the assumption of convexity we still have "approximate equilibria". Furthermore, this approximation is better the larger the economy, and thus the more plausible the assumption of competitive behaviour. So far, so good; we have answers to the very basic but limited question of the existence of competitive equilibria.

However, we pointed out that "stability of equilibria" in the sense that an adjustment process converges to an equilibrium cannot be established in the general framework with which we have dealt up till now.

If we are to show not merely what would be the result after the "invisible hand" had worked, but also that the "invisible hand" does indeed work, then we must assume much more. Indeed the sort of assumptions necessary are very special and of a different type than those on which we have based our analysis up till now, that is assumptions on individual characteristics.

More on this in Chapter 6. The reader should bear in mind for now that while we have shown the Walrasian theme has a certain coherence in a rather general framework, once we require more of it, it can only be played by very specialized ensembles!

Chapter 4

The Core of a Game

1. Introduction

Our cooperative theme, the core, has been left to one side but we will now come back to it. The reader who is interested essentially by economic problems can afford to dispense with the first part of this chapter in which we will examine the core in a more general framework. Recall that the core is a solution to a game and while we are principally interested in rather special, market, games, it is of interest to look at the core of general games. Although this will enrich the background of those interested in this theme, passing over it will not stop the reader from appreciating the music when it is played in our particular context. Starting from an economy let us develop a game and examine its counterpart.

Let $\mathcal{E} : A \to \mathcal{P} \times \mathbb{R}^{\ell}_{+}$ be an economy and let u_a be a utility function representing the preferences of agent a. Working with a utility function rather than preferences is simply a matter of convenience and, as the diligent reader is well aware, does not alter our assumptions in any way. We choose the utility function for each agent at the outset and it remains fixed throughout the analysis. Furthermore, it should be noted that the way in which we use utility functions will not, in any way, involve the "comparison of utilities among agents".

Now if f is any allocation for the economy $\mathcal{E}$ we denote by $u \circ f$ the associated *utility allocation*, i.e., $(u \circ f)(a) = u(f(a))$. Note that utility allocations for the economy will be vectors in $\mathbb{R}^N$, where $N = \#A$ and each individual is identified with one coordinate.

Looking at a particular coalition S we now ask, what utility allocation can they themselves achieve? By this we mean those utility allocations where the coordinates for S are less than or equal to the utilities that the members of S could achieve by redistributing their goods amongst themselves.

Formally, we define

$$V(S) := \left\{ x \in \mathbb{R}^N \;\middle|\; \begin{array}{c} \text{there exists an allocation } f \text{ for } \mathcal{E} \text{ such that} \\ (u \circ f)(a) \geq x_a \ \forall a \in S \text{ and } f(S) = e(S) \end{array} \right\}.$$

The reader should bear in mind that $V(S)$ is a subset of R^N even though only the coordinates associated with the individuals in S are relevant. This implies, for example, that if x is in $V(S)$ and $y \in \mathbb{R}^N$ is such that $x_a = y_a$ for $a \in S$ then y must belong to $V(S)$. It is important to observe that x may be in $V(S)$ but may not in fact be feasible. However, there must be an allocation which is feasible for the coalition S and gives at least x_a in utility to each member a of S.

Figure 4.1 illustrates $V(S)$ for a two–person coalition. The sets $V(S)$ need not be convex.

We will denote by F those utility allocations which are actually feasible for the coalition of all agents, i.e.,

$$F := \left\{ x \in \mathbb{R}^N \;\middle|\; \begin{array}{c} \text{there exists a feasible allocation } f \text{ for } \mathcal{E} \\ \text{such that } u(f(a)) = x_a \text{ for every } a \in A \end{array} \right\}.$$

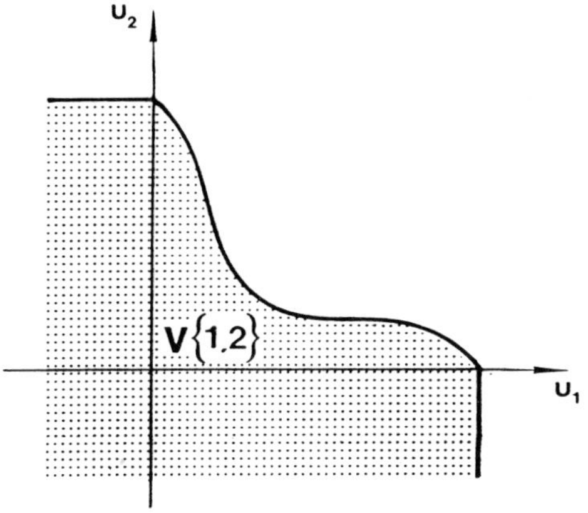

Figure 4.1

The fact that for our purposes we have derived the sets $V(S)$ and F from an exchange economy gives them a certain structure. In particular, they have the following properties, some of which will be essential in what follows:

(i) $V(S)$ are non–empty, closed subsets of $\mathbb{R}^N$.

(ii) $V(S)$ are comprehensive, i.e., if $x \in V(S)$ and $y \leq x$ then $y \in V(S)$.

(iii) F is closed and is related to $V(A)$ by the following: For every $x \in V(A)$ there exists $y \in F$ with $x \leq y$.

(iv) If $x \in V(S)$ and $x_a = y_a$ for all $a \in S$ then $y \in V(S)$.

It is natural to consider for a coalition S the subset of $V(S)$ where each agent is at least as well off as with his initial allocation. The set of *individually rational allocations* in $V(S)$ we will call $Q(S)$. More formally,

$$Q(S) := \{x \in V(S) \text{ such that } x \notin \mathit{int}\ V(\{a\}) \text{ for all } a \text{ in } S\} .$$

With this definition we may specify the following property:

(v) $Q(S)$ is not empty and is bounded from above with respect to the subspace $\mathbb{R}^S$. That is, there exists a number M such that $x_a \leq M$ for all $a \in S$ and all $x \in Q(S)$.

If we choose the utility function u_a, and we are free to do this, so that

$$u_a(e(a)) = 0 \text{ for every } a \in A ,$$

then $V(\{a\})$ has the form $\{x \in \mathbb{R}^N \mid x_a \leq 0\}$ and condition (v) says simply that $V(S) \cap \mathbb{R}_+^N$ is non–empty and bounded relative to $\mathbb{R}_+^S$.

We have, to this point, based our definitions of the sets $V(S)$ and F on an underlying exchange economy. This was done to provide an interpretation of these concepts. However, if we wish to define a game in general we now no longer need all of the structure provided by an exchange economy. We simply start with abstract sets $V(S)$, $S \subset A$, and F in $\mathbb{R}^N$ and impose conditions (i)–(v) on them. This motivates the following definition.

Definition 4.1. An N–person game (A, F, V) is given by:

(1) a set A of players with $\#A = N \geq 2$;

(2) a set F of feasible outcomes $F \subset \mathbb{R}^N$;

(3) a correspondence V of $\mathcal{A}$ into $\mathbb{R}^N$, describing the guaranteed utility allocations of each coalition, where $\mathcal{A}$ is the set of all non–empty subsets of A.

The sets F and $V(S)$ have properties (i)– (v).

The reader should bear in mind the fact that this definition encompasses many games other than the "exchange game" already discussed.

Example 4.1 (a lady with a trunk). Three men are available to carry a heavy trunk for a lady who is prepared to pay \$1 for the service. Any two of them can carry it but none can manage it on his own. Each has a utility function such that money is utility, i.e., $u(x) = x$. The question is who will carry the trunk and what will their pay–off be? This situation may be formulated as a game. Each individual can guarantee himself only zero dollars $V(\{i\}) = \{u|\ u \in \mathbb{R}^3 \text{ such that } u_i \leq 0\}$.

$$V(\{i,j\}) = \{u \in \mathbb{R}^3 \mid u_i + u_j \leq 1\}$$

for any two–man coalition. F, the set of feasible outcomes $= \{u \in \mathbb{R}^3$ such that $u_1 + u_2 + u_3 = 1\}$. The reader may care to try to find a core allocation for this game which is rather different from a market game.

It should be clear how the concept of the core carries over from an exchange economy to any $N-$person game. In fact, historically, our second major theme, that of cooperative improvement, although originally composed by Edgeworth (1881) was only rediscovered through the development of game theory. To present the core in the game context we must first give the following definition.

Definition 4.2. A coalition S can *improve upon* a utility allocation y if there is $x \in V(S)$ with $x_a > y_a$ for all $a \in S$, i.e., $y \in$ *int* $V(S)$.

This leads directly to

Definition 4.3. The *core* C of a game (A, F, V), is the set of feasible outcomes $x \in F$ which can be improved upon by no coalition S in $\mathcal{A}$, i.e.,

$$C(A,F,V) = F \setminus \bigcup_{S \in \mathcal{A}} \mathit{int}\ V(S)\ .$$

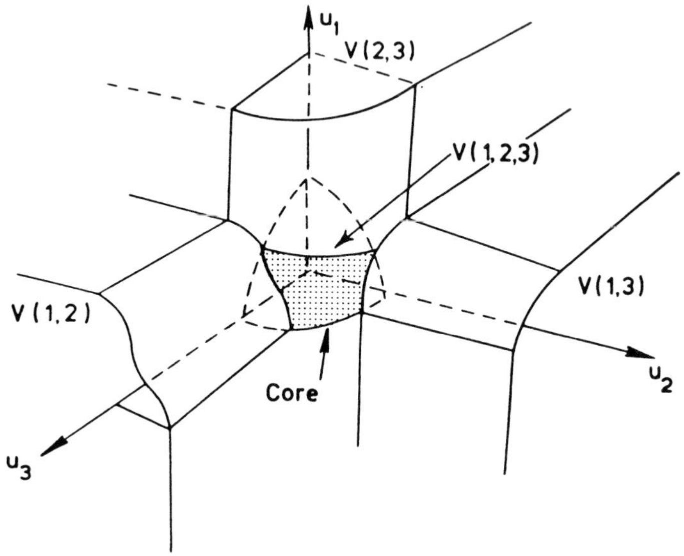

Figure 4.2

Figure 4.2 shows the sets $V(S)$ for each of the three two–man coalitions in a three–person game as well as F which is the part of the sphere in the positive orthant and the core which is the shaded surface.

2. Balancedness

We come now to a fundamental question, that of the existence of core allocations. If we cannot be sure that such allocations exist then the merit of the core as a solution might seem limited. The definition of a game given so far and the conditions imposed do not, indeed, ensure that the core is not empty. For this another property is required. We will then show that the game given by the exchange problem with *convex* preferences does, in fact, have this additional property. Hence, for our problem the solution concept provided by the core is not an empty one. The definition that we have given of a game (A, F, V), gives us insufficient information as it stands. The information that we have is too fragmentary. We cannot conclude from the knowledge that x is in $V(S)$ for a collection of proper subsets of A, that x is also in $V(A)$. We cannot piece together information about feasible outcomes for coalitions to find an outcome for all players. For example, suppose that we have a partition $S_1 \ldots S_q$ of A, can we conclude that if $x \in V(S_i)$ for all i, then $x \in V(A)$? Clearly, in the case of an exchange economy we could do this, although in general we cannot. However, unfortunately for the proof of our main result, we will need to combine the information from collections of sets that are more general than partitions.

We will need a concept which, though it has no intuitive economic interpretation, will be essential to all that follows in this chapter. The reader will find that it will pay well to absorb these definitions at the outset to avoid the temptation to treat them as empty formalism. It is important to be in a balanced frame of mind for this section! This requirement is not only of our readers, in fact it will become clear that precisely what we shall require of games is that they should be *balanced.* In a balanced game it is assumed that for every family $\mathcal{B}$ of coalitions of a certain type (a *balanced family*) we may conclude from the fact that $x \in V(S)$ for all the S in $\mathcal{B}$ that $x \in V(A)$. Consider a family $\mathcal{B}$ of subsets of A and let $\mathcal{B}_a = \{S \in \mathcal{B} \mid a \in S\}$, i.e., we take a collection of coalitions and denote by $\mathcal{B}_a$ all the coalitions in $\mathcal{B}$ to which the agent a belongs. Now we have the following definition.

Definition 4.4. A family $\mathcal{B}$ of subsets in A is *balanced* if there exist non–negative "weights" w_S for S in $\mathcal{B}$ with

$$\textstyle\sum_{S \in \mathcal{B}_a} w_S = 1 \quad \text{for all } a \text{ in } A.$$

Take, for example, all two–player coalitions in a three–person game, i.e., $\{1,2\},\{1,3\},\{2,3\}$. These are balanced by the weights $\frac{1}{2}$. More generally, look at all the two–person coalitions in an $N-$person game and these will be balanced by the weights $w_S = \frac{1}{(N-1)}$, since every player will belong to exactly $N-1$ two-person coalitions. It is also clear that the collection of all $q-$person coalitions in an $N-$person game, with $q \leq N$, is balanced since every individual will belong to the same number of coalitions.

However, balanced sets are not confined to this category. Any partition of A will be a balanced set with weights $w_S = 1$. Less obvious families may also be balanced. In a four–person game consider the following family: $\mathcal{B} = \{\{1,4\},\{1,2\},\{1,3\},\{2,3,4\}\}$. This is balanced by the weights $\frac{1}{3},\frac{1}{3},\frac{1}{3},\frac{2}{3}$, respectively. It is unfortunate that there is no really intuitive means of recognizing a balanced family of sets.

However, we can present a geometric interpretation which may be of some help. Take, for example, the unit vectors $\mathbf{1}_1, \ldots, 1_N$ in $\mathbb{R}^N$. For every S in A define Δ^S as the convex hull of the points $\{\mathbf{1}_a | a \in S\}$. Denote by m_S their centre of gravity and thus the centre of gravity to Δ^S. Then $\mathcal{B}$, a collection of subsets S, is balanced if and only if m_A lies in the convex hull of $\{m_S : S \in \mathcal{B}\}$.

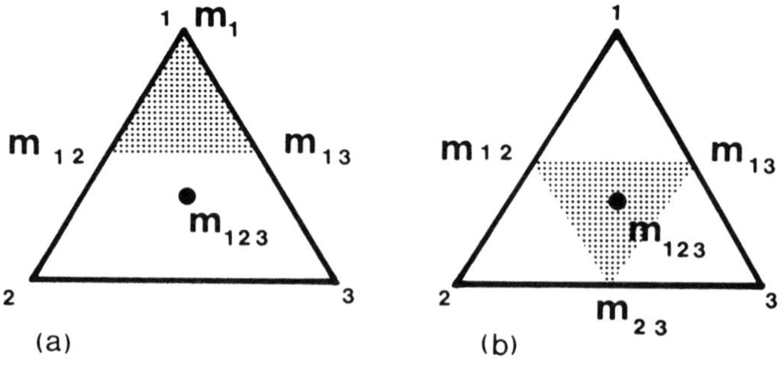

Figure 4.3

Figure 4.3 shows non–balanced and a balanced family of sets. In Figure 4.3 (a) we consider the set $\{\{1\},\{1,2\},\{1,3\}\}$ which is not balanced and in Figure 4.3 (b) the set $\{\{1,2\},\{1,3\},\{2,3\}\}$ which is balanced. The notion of a balanced family of sets leads to the following very important definition.

Definition 4.5. A game (A, F, V) is *balanced* if, for every balanced family $\mathcal{B}$ of coalitions, $\bigcap_{S\in\mathcal{B}} V(S) \subseteq V(A)$.

Now, with all this, we are ready to state our main theorem which was first proved by Scarf (1967).

Theorem 4.1. The core of a balanced game (A, F, V) is not empty.

To proceed directly to the proof of this, the major theorem of this section, would interrupt the basic flow of our argument. So we relegate the proof to a separate section (which we suggest should only be read by those with a particular interest in this topic) and show first that convex exchange economies belong to this class of games.

Proposition 4.1. An "exchange game" (A, F, V) derived from a convex economy $\mathcal{E} : A \to \mathcal{P}_{co} \times \mathbb{R}^{\ell}_{+}$ is balanced.

Proof. If $\mathcal{B}$ is a balanced family of coalitions with weights w_S, $S \in \mathcal{B}$, and $x \in \bigcap_{S\in\mathcal{B}} V(S)$ then we must show that $x \in V(A)$. Now, in an exchange game, $F \subseteq V(A)$.

Since $x \in V(S)$, we can find a redistribution of the total resources of the coalition S, say $f^S(a)$, where $\sum_{a\in S} f^S(a) = \sum_{a\in S} e(a)$ with $u_a(f^S(a)) \geq x(a)$ for all a in S. Now define the allocation

$$f(a) = \sum_{S\in\mathcal{B}_a} w_S f^S(a) \ .$$

Thus, $f(a)$ is a convex combination of the vectors $f^S(a)$, $S \in \mathcal{B}_a$. By the convexity of preferences and hence the quasi–concavity of the associated utility functions, we therefore have $u_a(f(a)) \geq x(a)$, for all a in A. We have only to show that f is a redistribution of $\mathcal{E}$. But we have

$$\begin{aligned}\sum_{a\in A} f(a) &= \sum_{a\in A}\sum_{S\in\mathcal{B}_a} w_S f^S(a) = \sum_{S\in\mathcal{B}} w_S\Big(\sum_{a\in S} f^S(a)\Big)\\ &= \sum_{S\in\mathcal{B}} w_S\Big(\sum_{a\in S} e(a)\Big) = \sum_{a\in A} e(a)\Big(\sum_{S\in\mathcal{B}_a} w_S\Big) = \sum_{a\in A} e(a) \ .\end{aligned}$$

Hence, x is in $V(A)$.

Q.E.D.

The reader should note that Proposition 4.1. requires only that the consumption sets X are convex. Of course, for the game to be well defined we also need the consumption sets to be closed and contain the initial endowments. Now, in conjunction with the basic theorem we can prove the following proposition.

Proposition 4.2. The core of a convex economy $\mathcal{E} : A \to \mathcal{P}_{co} \times \mathbb{R}^\ell_+$ is non–empty and compact.

Proof. Consider the "exchange game" defined by $\mathcal{E}$. This game is balanced and therefore by the main theorem its core is non–empty. This in turn implies that $C(\mathcal{E})$ is non–empty. Next, we show that $C(\mathcal{E})$ is compact. Clearly $C(\mathcal{E})$ is bounded, since $0 \leq f(a) \leq e(A)$. We must now show that $C(\mathcal{E})$ is closed.

Let $(f^q)(q = 1, \ldots)$ be in $C(\mathcal{E})$, $f^q(a) \to f(a)$ for all a in A, and assume that $f \notin C(\mathcal{E})$. Hence, there is a coalition $S \subset A$ and a redistribution g such that $g(a) \succ_a f(a)$ for all a in S, and $g(S) = e(S)$. Hence, for q large enough we have, by continuity of the preferences, that for every a in S, $g(a) \succ_a f^q(a)$ and $g(S) = e(S)$, that is S can improve upon f^q, a contradiction.

Q.E.D.

Before we proceed to the proof of our basic theorem (4.1.) we will need a mathematical result. The core is defined as an *intersection of a collection* of closed sets. Theorems which guarantee that the intersection of a collection of closed sets is non–empty are proved in combinatorial topology. A prototype of such a theorem is the Knaster–Kuratowski–Mazurkiewicz (1926) result. However, we need a generalization of that theorem (from now on referred to as K-K-M). The basic idea is the following. We consider a simplex Δ^A, i.e., the convex hull of $N = \#A$

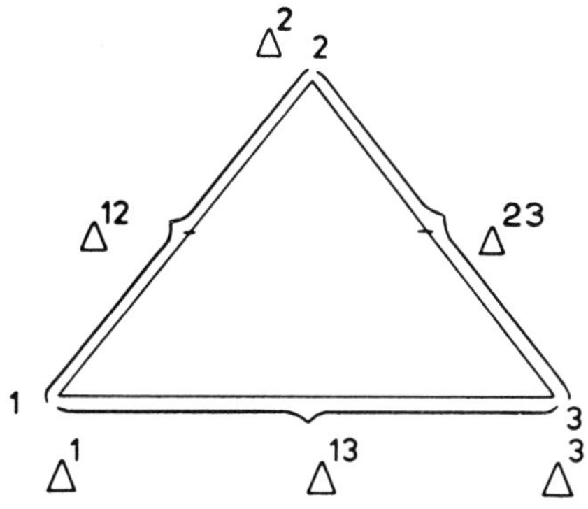

Figure 4.4

independent vectors α_a and the associated "faces" Δ^S each of which is the convex hull of the set $\{\alpha_a | a \in S\}$, $S \subset A$. The most familiar example is the unit simplex when all the α_a are unit vectors. In Figure 4.4 the $N-1$ simplex is the triangle and the Δ^S are the sides and vertices. With this picture in mind, consider the following theorem.

Theorem 4.2. (K-K-M-S)[1] If $\{C_S | S \in \mathcal{A}\}$ is a family of closed subsets of the simplex Δ^A such that for each $T \subset A$, $\Delta^T \subseteq \bigcup_{S \subset T} C_S$ then there exists a balanced family $\mathcal{B}$ of subsets of A such that $\bigcap_{S \in \mathcal{B}} C_S \neq \emptyset$.

We will not give a proof of this result but it is perhaps worth considering an example to see what is involved. In Figure 4.5 we have, as before, a two-simplex. Again a vertex is associated with each individual element $\{1\}$, $\{2\}$, or $\{3\}$, the face of each two element set is the appropriate side $[1,2]$, $[1,3]$ or $[2,3]$ and the whole triangle is the face for the whole set.

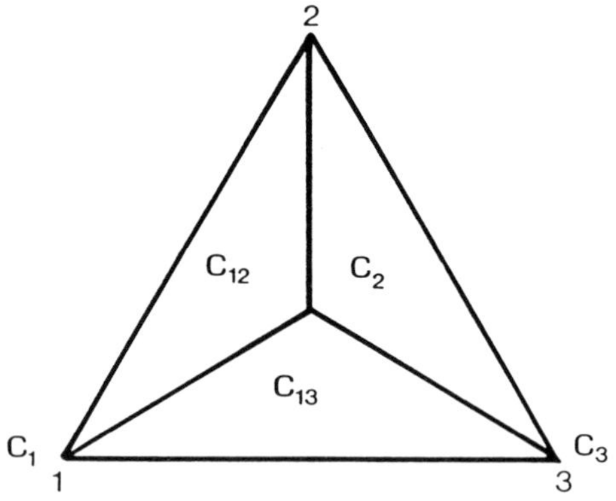

Figure 4.5

[1] The theorem given by Shapley (1972) and referred to by him as K-K-M-S is, in fact, more general than the version we give here.

Now we must have closed subsets associated with each coalition with the property that the union of all sets associated with the subsets S of any given coalition must contain the face, associated with T. Let $C_{123} = \emptyset$, otherwise, since the simplex on its own is a trivially balanced 'family' of sets, we would have to proceed no further. In Figure 4.5 the sets C_S are as labelled and $C_{23} = \emptyset$. Each of the vertices is covered by C_1, C_2, and C_3. The side $[2,3]$ is covered by C_2 and hence by $C_2 \cup C_3$, and so forth. The balanced family of sets whose corresponding subsets $C_S \subset \Delta^A$ have a non–empty intersection as guaranteed by the theorem is $\{\{1,3\},\ \{2\}\}$.

Proof of Theorem 4.1. This proof is taken from Shapley (1972). As explained before, we may assume that the game (A, F, V) is normalized so that we have

$$V(\{a\}) = \{x \in \mathbb{R}^N | x_a \leq 0\} \ .$$

Then the set $V(S) \cap \mathbb{R}^N_+$ is non–empty and bounded relative to $\mathbb{R}^S_+$ since, by property (v), the sets $Q(S)$ of individually rational allocations in $V(S)$ are non–empty and bounded in $\mathbb{R}^S$. Thus, we may find an integer M such that for all S in $\mathcal{A}$, we have

$$\text{if } \ x \in Q(S) \ \text{ then } \ x_a \leq M \ \text{ for all } a \in S \ . \tag{4.1}$$

Define $g_a = -NM\mathbf{1}_a$, $a \in A$, where $\mathbf{1}_a$ is the a–th unit vector in $\mathbb{R}^N$. Now define the simplex Δ^A required for the use of the K-K-M-S theorem as the convex hull of the g_a and the associated "faces" Δ^S as the convex hull of the set $\{g_a | a \in S\}$.

Now, having specified the simplex, we must define the appropriate sets C_S. Define a function τ of $\mathbb{R}^N$ into R by

$$\tau(x) = max\{t |\ x + t \cdot \ \mathbf{1} \in \bigcup_{S \in \mathcal{A}} V(S)\}$$

where $\mathbf{1} = \sum_{a \in A} \mathbf{1}_a$. In Figure 4.6 the situation for a two–player game is illustrated. Note that $\tau(x)$ is finite since the intersection of $V(S)$ with $\mathbb{R}_+^N$ is non–empty and bounded relative to $\mathbb{R}_+^S$ and by the definition of the sets $V(\{a\})$. Further, the reader who has persisted to this point will be able to show that τ is a continuous function since the sets $V(S)$ although not convex have property (ii). We can now define the set C_S by

$$C_S = \{x \in \Delta^A |\ x + \tau(x) \cdot \mathbf{1} \in V(S)\}\ .$$

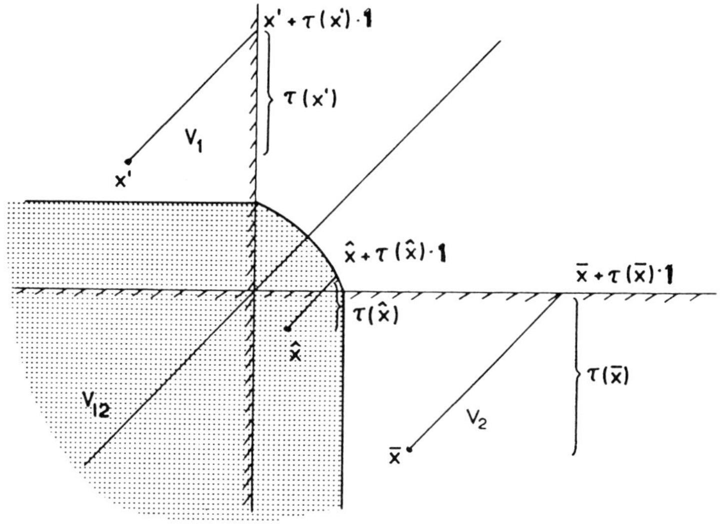

Figure 4.6

The maximum on the line $x + (\cdot) \cdot \mathbf{1}$ is achieved when the line crosses the boundary of the "last" of the $V(S)$. When it reaches this boundary $x + \tau(x) \cdot \mathbf{1}$ can no longer be improved upon, and the particular coalition whose boundary is crossed is that which was able to ensure for its members "most" on this line. Figure 4.7 shows examples of three points, $\hat{x}$ which belongs to C_{12}, $\tilde{x}$ to C_1 and x' to C_2.

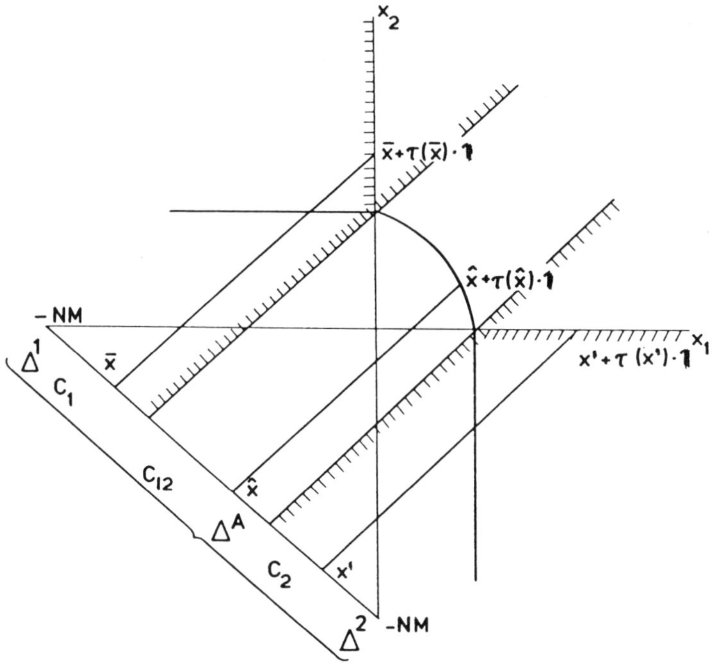

Figure 4.7

Note that the set C_{12} in this example is non–empty and hence the K-K-M-S theorem is trivially satisfied. In general, if C_A is non–empty the theorem holds directly. Hence, if there is any one point where the coalition of the whole can do 'most' for its members then we have a trivial balanced family of sets with non–empty intersection. This reveals why an alternative assumption to balancedness, requiring that there be at least one allocation which can only be improved upon by the coalition of the whole, leads to a non–empty core. The C_S are closed by the continuity of τ and the closedness of $V(S)$. We must now show that

$$\Delta^T \subseteq \bigcup_{S \subseteq T} C_S \quad \text{for every } T \text{ in } \mathcal{A}. \tag{4.2}$$

A glance at Figure 4.7 shows that this condition is obviously satisfied in this case as $\Delta^1 \subset C^1$, $\Delta^2 \subset C^2$ and $\Delta^A \subseteq C_1 \cup C_2 \cup C_{12}$. Recall that every x in Δ^T belongs to at least one set C_S. Therefore, if we can show that

$$x \in C_S \cap \Delta^T \text{ implies } S \subseteq T ,$$

the required property (4.2.) holds. Thus, let $x \in C_S \cap \Delta^T$ and assume $T \neq A$ and hence $\#T < N$. Now as $x \in \Delta^T$ then $\sum_{a \subset T} x_a = -NM$. But then there is at least one $\bar{a} \in T$ such that

$$x_{\bar{a}} \leq -NM/\#T < -M .$$

Hence, the individual $\bar{a}$ alone ensures by the definition of $\tau(x)$ that

$$\tau(x) > M . \tag{4.3}$$

Now since $x \in C_S$, by definition of the set C_S we have $x + \tau(x) \cdot \mathbf{1}$ is in $V(S)$ but not in any one of the *int* $V(R)$, $R \in \mathcal{A}$. Specifically, $x + \tau(x) \cdot \mathbf{1}$ is not in any of the *int* $V\{a\}$, $a \in S$. Thus, $x + \tau(x) \cdot \mathbf{1} \in Q(S)$. So, by (4.1), $x_a + \tau(x) \leq M$, for all a in S. This, together with (4.3), implies that $x_a < 0$ for all $a \in S$. But $x \in \Delta^T$ implies $x_a = 0$ for $a \notin T$. Consequently, $S \subseteq T$ and (4.2) is satisfied.

Now we have essentially finished for, by the K-K-M-S theorem, there exists a balanced family $\mathcal{B}$ of coalitions and a vector $\hat{x} \in \mathbb{R}^N$ such that $\hat{x} \in C_S$ for all S in $\mathcal{B}$. Now let $\hat{y} = \hat{x} + \tau(\hat{x})\mathbf{1}$, then $\hat{y}$ belongs to $\bigcap_{S \in \mathcal{B}} V(S)$ but not to $\bigcup_{S \in \mathcal{A}} int\ V(S)$. Since the game is balanced we have, by definition, that $\hat{y} \in V(A)$. Therefore, by property (iii) there is a point $\hat{z} \geq \hat{y}$ in F, not in $\bigcup_{S \in \mathcal{A}}$ *int* $V(S)$ and hence in its core.

Q.E.D.

In Figure 4.7 it is clear that all the points of the curve with $\hat{x} + \tau(\hat{x})$ are in the core and that the associated balanced family of sets consists of the single coalition $(1, 2)$.

3. Some Non–classical Exchange Economies

Having arrived at the basic result that the cores of balanced games, and hence of convex market games, are never empty, the reader may now well ask, why this concentration on the core? We have already pointed out the significance of this, our first theme, but the reader may still enquire as to why this was introduced as well as the more traditional second theme, that involved in the "competitive solution". Let us re–emphasize some of the reasons. Perhaps the most obvious advantage of the core in a finite economy is that if the normal assumptions necessary to guarantee the existence of a competitive equilibrium are relaxed then the core may still exist although there may be no competitive solution.

Example 4.2. Consider an economy with two goods x and y, and two individuals a and b. Each of the two individuals has preferences which are represented by

$$U_a(x_a, y_a) = x_a^{\frac{1}{2}} + y_a^{\frac{1}{2}}$$
$$U_b(x_b, y_b) = (x_b + 1)(y_b + 1)$$

and resources which are given by

$$e(a) = (1, 0)$$
$$e(b) = (2, 0) \; .$$

The preferences are monotonic and strictly convex. For any strictly positive price vector it is easy to calculate that market demand satisfies

$$\varphi(a, p) + \varphi(b, p) \gg 0 \; ,$$

and thus, since there is positive demand for y, it cannot be an equilibrium. Hence, no competitive equilibrium exists, but obviously the core is non–empty and given by $\{e(a),\ e(b)\}$. This example shows also why in the definition of an exchange economy we assumed that total initial endowments were strictly positive.

Example 4.3 "Non–convexities". Consider in Figure 4.8 an Edgeworth box for two individuals, one of whom has non–convex preferences. Suppose that the initial endowments are e. The allocation $\bar{x} = e$ is clearly in the core since it cannot be improved upon by the agents individually or together. Yet it is also evident that we can find no price line which will separate the two preferred sets. Hence, at any price one of the agents will be able to purchase a bundle preferred to $\bar{x}$. Note, in particular, that since we set the initial resources e equal to $\bar{x}$ there is no other point in the core and hence no competitive equilibrium. Yet the solution $\bar{x}$ does not seem unreasonable. In terms of the individuals' preferences it is "self–sustaining", so the fact that this outcome is not encompassed by a competitive solution lends weight to the argument for the core as a more basic concept.

We may also wish to treat economies in which "markets" in the traditional sense do not seem to be very plausible. In such cases, even though formally we may be able to find "competitive prices" it is difficult to envisage the price mechanism as being that which would solve the exchange problem. We repeat that in small economies where negotiations would play an important role, or where there are only a few units of each good, the notion of an accepted or acceptable price system loses much of its credibility.

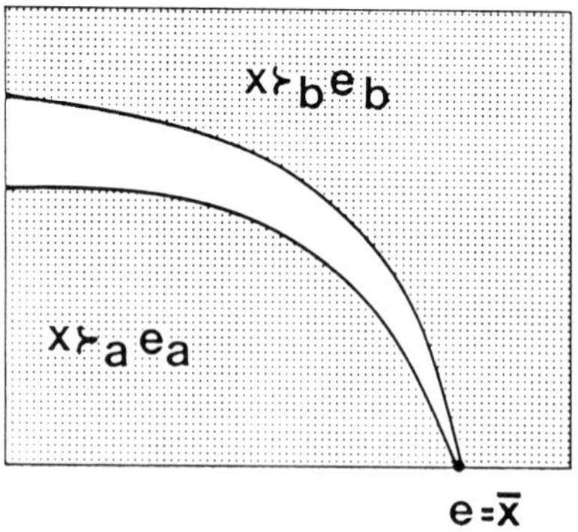

Figure 4.8

If one views, as we do, our second theme as being that the essential purpose of a price system is as a means of permitting decentralized decision–making by individuals, then it is clear that its importance lies in solving large market problems. It is a defect in the standard presentation of an exchange economy that the competitive solution is introduced by some such phrase as "if the price system p obtains ...", with only vague justification as to why it should obtain. The usual motivation given is indeed that no individual is important enough to upset this price system. This brings us back to the "large" economy, where the distinction between core and competitive solution, of course, disappears. (This aspect will be fully developed in Chapter 5.) Yet despite this implicit idea of large numbers, there is much discussion of competitive equilibrium in a two-person economy, for example. While this may be useful from a formal point of view, conceptually it does not merit being regarded as an acceptable solution. We have already seen in Chapter 1 how an individual can in a small economy, by his own actions, change the competitive allocation in his favour. He can do this, for example, by throwing away something. Thus, in such economies, the competitive solution is not very plausible. We will now show examples of some of the many economies which do not seem to be acceptably solved by the competitive mechanism, yet where the core has a certain appeal as a solution.

3.1. Markets with Indivisibilities[2)]

We consider as a first example an economy with goods which are only available in integer quantities. The fundamental commodity space in this case is then a "lattice" of points in $\mathbb{R}^\ell_+$ rather than the whole of $\mathbb{R}^\ell_+$ as before. In particular, we shall first consider an example of a special

---

[2)] The examples of indivisibilities here are based of those on Shapley and Scarf (1974).

economy in which each trader possesses one unit of one good. He does not need more than one unit but has preferences between the different units. Thus for N individuals we have essentially N goods each separate and distinguishable. Assume that individuals have been randomly assigned rooms in college by the college authorities and wish to rearrange these rooms amongst themselves to improve their welfare. Suppose also that the students are too poor to make side payments. This will not be an unfamiliar situation. This would be an example of the sort of game under consideration.

We can simplify matters considerably by reducing all preferences and allocations to $N \times N$ matrices. The *preference matrix* is B where

$$b_{aj} > b_{ak} \text{ means item } j \succ_a \text{ item } k$$

$$\text{and} \quad b_{aj} = b_{ak} \text{ means item } j \sim_a \text{ item } k \,.$$

For convenience we use the first N positive integers for the preference matrix, but since only the order matters any real numbers maintaining this order would also do.

For the reasons we explain below we will only consider those allocations which are redistributions. An allocation is then a matrix D with

$$d_{aj} = 1 \text{ or } 0,$$

$$\sum_{a \in A} d_{aj} = 1 \qquad \text{for all items } j$$

and a *"permutation"* or redistribution D has its additional property

$$\sum_{j=1}^{N} d_{aj} = 1 \quad \text{for all } a \in A \,.$$

That is, individuals will, in these latter allocations, receive only one room each. Such matrices are special doubly stochastic matrices, namely simply permutations of the identity matrix. The game is defined as before with the sets F and $V(S)$ for each coalition as mappings from $\mathcal{A}$, the set of coalitions, into the utility space $\mathbb{R}^N$.

In the games in question we will assign utility level 0 to having no item at all. Since the numbers associated with each item are positive, every allocation that is not a permutation of items among players will be dominated. Recalling that the $V(S)$ consist of allocations which can be improved upon or equalled by the coalition of S, we see directly that any allocation that assigns no item to some individual a will necessarily be in $V(\{a\})$, since he receives positive utility from his own item. Note that a feasible redistribution for S which assigns one item to each member of S will be referred to as an S permutation, written P_S, where $P_S = (p_{aj})$ is an $\#A \times \#A$, i.e., $N \times N$ doubly stochastic matrix with

$$p_{aj} \in \{0,1\} \quad \text{for all} \quad a \in A \qquad \text{and}$$
$$\sum_{a \in S} p_{aj} = 1 \quad \text{for all } j \in S \quad \text{and} \quad \sum_{j \in S} p_{aj} = 1 \quad \text{for all } a \in S\ .$$

In other words the matrix remaining when we delete the columns and rows not corresponding to the members of S is also doubly stochastic. Now we may define our game more carefully:

$$V(S) = \{x \in \mathbb{R}^N |\ \text{there exists } P_S \text{ with } x(P_S) \geq x^S\}\ , \tag{4.4}$$

where

$$x(P_S) \in \mathbb{R}^S \quad \text{such that} \quad x_a = \begin{cases} b_{aj} & \text{if } p_{aj} = 1\ , \\ 0 & \text{if } p_{aj} = 0\ . \end{cases}$$

We take analogously with our previous definition

$$F = \{x \in \mathbb{R}^N |\ \text{there exists } P_A \text{ with } x(P_A) = x\}\ .$$

Now we must show the following:

The game (A, F, V), as defined, is balanced.

We must show that for every balanced collection of sets $\mathcal{B}$,

$$\bigcap_{S \in \mathcal{B}} V(S) \subseteq V(A)\ .$$

Consider $\bar{x}$ in $\bigcap_{S \in \mathcal{B}} V(S)$ for some balanced family of sets $\mathcal{B}$ and the associated weights w_S. This means that there exists for each S a P_S as in (4.4). Now define the following matrix:

$$E(a) = \sum_{S \in \mathcal{B}_a} w_S P_S(a) \ ,$$

where $E(a)$ and $P_S(a)$ denote the a–th rows of the appropriate matrices. E is clearly doubly stochastic but is no longer necessarily a permutation matrix with elements which are only 1 or 0. We must now construct a matrix G which is an N permutation and for which $x(G) \geq \bar{x}$. Note first that if $e_{aj} > 0$ then the j–th item gives at least as great utility to a as $\bar{x}_a$. This follows, since $e_{aj} > 0$ implies there exists a coalition S, such that $a \in S$ and $x(P_S) \geq \bar{x}^S$. So if we can construct G so that G is an N permutation and

$$g_{aj} = 1 \ \text{ implies } \ e_{aj} > 0 \ ,$$

then we will have $\bar{x} \in V(A)$. Take any fractional element in E, say e_{ij}. Now in the same row and column there must also be other fractional elements so we may construct a chain as follows:

$$\begin{array}{llll} e_{ij} & e_{ik} & & \\ & e_{pk} & e_{p\ell} & \\ & & \vdots & \\ & & e_{r\ell} & e_{rq} \end{array}$$

in which all the elements are positive and fractional. Since this chain may be as long as we wish and there are only N^2 elements in the matrix, some element must be repeated so we have, contained in the chain, a loop, say

$$\begin{array}{llll} e_{ij} & e_{ik} & & \\ & e_{pk} & e_{p\ell} & \\ & & \vdots & \\ & & e_{r\ell} & e_{rj} \\ & & & e_{ij} \end{array}$$

Now take the smallest of these elements, say e_{ik}, and alternatively add and subtract this from the elements in turn. This will leave the matrix doubly stochastic and will replace e_{ik} by 0. So now we have at least one more zero in the new matrix E! Repeating this process must eliminate all the fractional elements and leave us with a permutation matrix G with the required properties. Hence, $\bar{x}$ is in $V(A)$ and $\bigcap_{S\in\mathcal{B}} V(S) \subseteq V(A)$. Thus, the game is balanced.

Example 4.4. Consider the preference matrix

$$\begin{bmatrix} 1 & 2 & 3 \\ 2 & 1 & 3 \\ 2 & 3 & 2 \end{bmatrix} = (b_{aj}) \; .$$

Now look at the sets $V(S)$, which are generated by the following points:

$$\begin{aligned}
V(\{1\}) &: (1,-,-), \quad \text{i.e., } x \text{ such that } x_1 \le 1; \\
V(\{2\}) &: (-,1,-); \\
V(\{3\}) &: (-,-,2); \\
V(\{1,2\}) &: (2,2,-), \quad \text{i.e., } x \text{ such that } x_1 \le 2,\ x_2 \le 2; \\
V(\{1,3\}) &: (3,-,2); \\
V(\{2,3\}) &: (-,3,3); \\
V(\{1,2,3\}) &: (3,2,3), \quad \text{i.e., } x \text{ such that } x_1 \le 2,\ x_2 \le 2,\ x_3 \le 3; \\
&\ (1,3,3); \\
&\ (2,3,2).
\end{aligned}$$

Computation of $V(\{1,3\})$ for example is

$$V(\{1,3\}) = \{(x^1,x^2,x^3) |\text{ there exists } P_{(13)} \text{ with } x(P_{(13)}) \ge (x^1,x^3)\} \; .$$

For the two person coalition $\{1,3\}$ there exist exactly two permutation matrices, namely

$$P_{(13)} = \begin{bmatrix} 0 & 0 & 1 \\ 0 & 1 & 0 \\ 1 & 0 & 0 \end{bmatrix} \quad \text{and} \quad \overline{P}_{(1,3)} = \begin{bmatrix} 1 & 0 & 0 \\ 0 & 1 & 0 \\ 0 & 0 & 1 \end{bmatrix}$$

Obviously the second one is dominated by the first one, i.e., $x(P_{(13)}) \geq x(\overline{P}_{(13)})$, hence

$$x(P_{(13)}) \in \mathbb{R}^2 \text{ with } \begin{aligned} x_1 &= b_{13} = 3 \text{ because } p_{13} = 1 \,, \\ x_3 &= b_{31} = 2 \text{ because } p_{31} = 1 \,, \end{aligned}$$

and then

$$V(\{1,3\}) = \{(x^1, x^2, x^3) |\ 3 \geq x^1,\ 2 \geq x^3\} \,.$$

The other $V(S)$ can be obtained analogously.

The points in the core which are permutations are given by the matrices

$$\begin{bmatrix} 0 & 0 & 1 \\ 1 & 0 & 0 \\ 0 & 1 & 0 \end{bmatrix}, \begin{bmatrix} 1 & 0 & 0 \\ 0 & 0 & 1 \\ 0 & 1 & 0 \end{bmatrix}, \begin{bmatrix} 0 & 1 & 0 \\ 0 & 0 & 1 \\ 1 & 0 & 0 \end{bmatrix}.$$

It is important to see that "strict improvement" plays an essential role in determining the core. The requirement that *all* members of a coalition should be able to find something better to improve upon an allocation is now very different from the weaker version. Before with continuous and monotonic preferences, anybody who could obtain something strictly preferred to some allocation, could always give up a little of his bundle, still have something strictly preferred and be able to make the other members of his coalition strictly better off. With indivisibilities there is no way that such small compensations can be made and if we require only "weak improvement" the core may well be empty. To see how the core would change in the current example consider the two core allocations given by the first and third matrices. They give utility vectors of $(3,2,3)$ and $(2,3,2)$. If we required only that a coalition be able to find something better for some member and keep the others in the same position then individuals 2 and 3 would never accept an allocation that gave utility less than $(-,3,3)$. Both the allocations above would be removed from the core. In either case, in the framework of our example, a student could obtain a room which he prefers by exchanging it with another who would be no worse off, but he lacks the means to persuade the other to accept the transaction.

We started this section by observing that certain situations do not correspond to what we normally think of as markets. In the sense in which we have discussed prices, as generally accepted rates of exchange, it is clear that the model which we have just considered would not be decentralized by a price system. We make this point since Shapley and Scarf (1974), using a method suggested by Gale, describe how one may find "competitive prices" for the exchange problem with indivisibilities. The method is very simple and gives an alternative proof of the existence of core allocations. However, the reader should treat the prices with reservation. There is a formal equivalence to the prices which we will discuss later, but not only is the interpretation different, the prices that are obtained are only ordinal. In other words, if for the N goods we have "prices" $p_1, \ldots, p_N$, then any other prices $\bar{p}_1, \ldots, \bar{p}_N$ which have the same order will also work. Individual $\bar{a}$ will choose the most preferred item in the set $\{a|\ p_a \leq p_{\bar{a}}\}$. In other words, if numbers are assigned to each item any individual may choose the best object among those which have a lower number than his own.

3.2. "Prices"

To find the "price system" we proceed as follows. Consider each of the individuals as a point in a graph and construct a directed arc from each individual to the individual whose item he most prefers. Thus we have a graph with incidence matrix H, i.e., $h_{aj} = 1$ if there is an arc directed from a to j and $h_{aj} = 0$ otherwise.

Thus,

$$h_{aj} = \begin{cases} 1 & \text{if } b_{aj} = max_{i=1\ldots N}\{b_{ai}\} \\ 0 & \text{otherwise} \end{cases}$$

Take our earlier "room" example and we see in Figure 4.9 the graph associated with the matrix

$$H = \begin{bmatrix} 0 & 0 & 1 \\ 0 & 0 & 1 \\ 0 & 1 & 0 \end{bmatrix} .$$

Now consider the matrix H and see if there are any "cycles" in the matrix, i.e., closed loops in the graph. A cycle is defined as a chain h_{ij} with elements equal to one such that

$$h_{ij} = h_{jk} = \ldots = h_{ei} = h_{ij} .$$

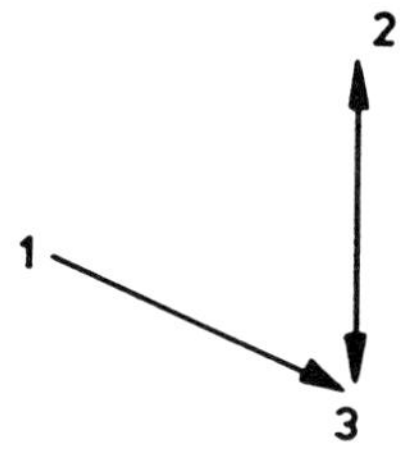

Figure 4.9

Now assign prices p_1 to all items belonging to individuals appearing in the cycle. If there is more than one cycle choose any one and assign p_1 to its elements. In our example individuals 2 and 3 figure in a cycle. Now remove these elements and repeat the procedure with the remaining graph, constructing arcs to the most preferred item in the remaining set. Give prices $p_2 < p_1$ to elements in a cycle or loop in the new graph and repeat the procedure till all elements have a price.

To see that in this way we do actually find a "competitive equilibrium", observe two things. First, there is always a cycle of the sort described (which may of course be degenerate, that is, be a single element) in any subgraph of the original graph. Hence, every item will be assigned a price. Second, performing a cyclical permutation of the items within the cycle will give each individual the most preferred item available to him. In the first, or "top cycle", the individuals obtained their most preferred item. In the second cycle prices were assigned which were lower than those of the top cycle, thus the top cycle items were outside the budget constraint of the second group of inividuals, and they had to be content with the best of the remaining items. In our example then, the top cycle consisted of $(2,3)$ and the remaining individual 1 keeps his own room. Assigning p_1 to the rooms of 2 and 3 allows those individuals to exchange them and giving $p_2 < p_1$ to room 1 means that individual 1 has only his own room in his budget set. Note that the partition of A and the ordering given by the p_i are not unique.

Note that in Figure 4.9 there is only one top cycle and it is easy to see that the only competitive allocation is that which gives the utility pay–off $[1,3,3]$. In fact, an allocation is competitive if and only if it may be arrived at in the above manner. Thus, the other core points are not competitive equilibria. Furthermore, unlike the example of Shapley and Scarf (1974), they are not weakly dominated by the competitive equilibrium.

The same two authors give an example of a plausible exchange game which has an empty core, thus removing any hope that the core might prove to be a panacea for all problems caused by indivisibilities. Thus, one can construct an example where all coalitions other than the individuals and the coalition of the whole can strictly improve upon their initial holdings but where there is no feasible total redistribution which will do this. Thus, the intersection of the *int* $V(S)$ contains elements which are not in F, the feasible outcomes for the whole group. To show how this may happen we consider another exchange problem, due to Shapley and Shubik (1969), and observe that in this case the core is empty.

Example 4.5 (the garbage game). Each individual owns a bag of garbage which he has to deposit in someone's garden. The utility of having b bags of garbage dumped on one's lawn is $-b$. In this special case we may summarize the game in characteristic function form, that is by expressing what a coalition may at least achieve on its own as a number. We then assume that the coalition may redistribute garbage amongst its members. We have then

$$V(S) = -(N - \#S) \text{ for } \#S < N,\ S \subset A \text{ and } F = V(A) = -N .$$

In other words, a coalition can be sure that it can dump its garbage on someone else, but cannot prevent individuals outside the coalition from depositing their refuse in return. Intuitively it is very clear that in a situation with several individuals, say N, the "best" coalition is one with $N - 1$ members. This coalition can deposit everything on the one remaining individual's lawn knowing that in return they will only receive his one bag. The whole coalition, however, must on average receive one bag of garbage per individual and therefore it is not very powerful. Now to see that the core is empty we assume the contrary and arrive at a contradiction.

Suppose that there is an allocation in the core, then it must assign utility α_a to each individual and must satisfy the condition

$$\sum_{a \in S} \alpha_a \geq V(S), \quad \text{for all coalitions } S.$$

There are N coalitions with $N - 1$ members and each individual is a member of $N - 1$, so if we sum these inequalities we have

$$(N-1) \sum_{a \in A} \alpha_a \geq -N .$$

To be feasible, however, we must have

$$\sum \alpha_a = V(A) = -N ,$$

but this gives

$$(N-1)(-N) \geq -N \quad \text{or} \quad 1-N \geq -1 ,$$

i.e., $N \leq 2$. So for the games with more than two players, the core must be empty.

In concluding we make two observations. First, the core is not a satisfactory solution concept for all exchange problems, as we have seen. Second, in the case of small exchange economies it has more appeal than rather artificial "competitive" solutions. Thus, our second theme, if not universally suitable for all orchestras, does sound better when played by small ensembles, than attempted adaptations of the first theme. In Chapter 5 we will discuss what happens when the number of performers increases.

Appendix to Chapter 4

In Chapter 4 we developed the Edgeworth theme at length and, perhaps most important, we showed that for balanced games we do actually have core solutions. Thus, our theme has content. Although the main result of the chapter is quite general it is based on the K-K-M-S theorem which the reader may find lacking in intuitive appeal.

In this appendix we shall give a less general result but one which will include the case that interests us, convex exchange economies. In some ways the approach in these arguments is more elaborate, but each of the steps of the proof has intrinsic interest and the reader's understanding of the problem will be reinforced by working through the proof. Hopefully then, this appendix will clarify the analysis of the core of a game and overcome some of the lack of intuitive content in parts of Chapter 4. We shall not carry out all arguments of the proof; some of the easier steps are left to the reader as an exercise to test his ability and understanding.

Before we start we should mention that our main goal is Proposition 4.2. (the existence of a core allocation for exchange economies with convex preferences). The reader who is primarily interested in the core of the game, will find this appendix less satisfactory, and not sufficiently general. What follows is based on three observations.

Observation A.1. Consider the core $C(\mathcal{E})$ of a convex economy $\mathcal{E} : A \to \mathcal{P}_{co} \times \mathbb{R}^{\ell}_{+}$. Then the core $C(\mathcal{E})$, considered as a subset in $\mathbb{R}^{\ell\#A}$ (every allocation in the core assigns to every individual in A a vector in $\mathbb{R}^{\ell}$) does not suddenly become much larger if the parameters of the economy are slightly altered, that is to say, if the endowments and/or preferences of one or several participating agents are modified slightly.

In more technical language this means that the correspondence $\mathcal{E} \to C(\mathcal{E})$ of the space of all economies with $\#A$ participants into $\mathbb{R}^{\ell\#A}$ is upper hemi-continuous. We shall now explain in more detail what we mean by this. As we have explained in the appendix to Chapter 2 it is clear what is meant by a small change of endowments of an agent, since endowments are described by vectors in the commodity space $\mathbb{R}^\ell$, but the situation is more difficult for preferences. Instead of explaining the meaning of a small change we explained the meaning of a sequence $(\succsim_n)$ of preferences converging to a preference relation $\succsim$. Then repeating our earlier definition, we say that the sequence $(\succsim_n)$ of monotonic preferences on $\mathbb{R}^\ell_+$ converges in $\mathcal{P}_{co}$ to a preference relation $\succsim$ if, whenever $x \succ y$ and $x_n \to x$ and $y_n \to y$, then there is an integer $\bar{n}$ such that $x_n \succ_n y_n$ for all $n \geq \bar{n}$. Let us repeat for those readers familiar with the concept of metric spaces that one can define on the space of preferences $\mathcal{P}_{co}$ a metric which gives rise to the concept of convergence as introduced above. The reader interested in details may consult Hildenbrand (1974).

Equipped with this concept we can define the meaning of "a sequence $(\mathcal{E}_n)$ of economies converging to an economy $\mathcal{E}$".

Definition A.1. Let $\mathcal{E}_n(n = 1, \ldots)$ and $\mathcal{E}$ be economies with the set of agents A with characteristics in $\mathcal{P}_{co} \times \mathbb{R}^\ell_+$. Then the sequence $(\mathcal{E}_n)$ of economies *converges* to the economy $\mathcal{E}$ if $\mathcal{E}_n(a) \to \mathcal{E}(a)$ for every $a \in A$, i.e., ${\succsim_a}^n \to \succsim_a$ and $e^n(a) \to e(a)$, where $({\succsim_a}^n, e^n_a) = \mathcal{E}_a(a)$, $a \in A$.

Observation A.1. can now be stated precisely.

Proposition A.1. Let the sequence $(\mathcal{E}_n)$ of economies be convergent to the economy $\mathcal{E}$. Then for every sequence (f_n) of core allocations, $f_n \in C(\mathcal{E}_a)$, there exists a converging subsequence $(f_{n_q})_{q=1,\ldots}$ such that the limit (i.e., $f(a) = lim_q\ f_{n_q}(a)$, $a \in A$) belongs to the core of $\mathcal{E}$.

We leave the proof of this proposition to the reader observing that the proof is analogous to the proof of the compactness of $C(\mathcal{E})$ in Proposition 4.2.

Observation A.2. We know from the basic approximation theorem of the appendix to Chapter 2 that every convex monotonic preference relation $\succsim$ can be obtained as the limit of a sequence $(\succsim_n)$ of preference relations where every $\succsim_n$ can be represented by a *concave* utility function. Therefore, by Observation A.1. to prove the non–emptiness of the core of an economy $\mathcal{E}$ it suffices to prove this result for economies where every agent has a concave utility function. But these economies give rise to particular games, as explained in the following proposition.

Proposition A.2. Let $\mathcal{E} : A \to \mathcal{P}_{co} \times \mathbb{R}^\ell_+$ be an economy where every preference relation $\succsim_a$ has a concave utility representation. Then the "exchange game" (A, V)[1)] derived from this economy has the following properties:

(i) for every coalition $S \subset A$ the set $V(S)$ is convex;

(ii) the game is "strongly balanced", i.e., for every family $\mathcal{B}$ of coalitions with balancing weights w_S, $S \in \mathcal{B}$, it follows that

$$\sum_{S \in \mathcal{B}} w_S \dot{V}(S) \subset V(A) ,$$

where

$$\dot{V}(S) = \{x \in V(S) |\ x_a = 0 \text{ for } a \notin S\} .$$

Note that every strongly balanced game is balanced.

[1)] In this section we assume $F \subseteq V(A)$ for simplicity, and refer to the game as (A, V).

Proof. The convexity of $V(S)$ follows directly from the concavity of the utility function.
We now prove (ii). For each $S \in \mathcal{B}$ consider $x^S \in \dot{V}(S)$. There exists f^S such that $u_a(f^S(a)) \geq x^S_a$, for all a in S and $\sum_{a \in S} f^S(a) = \sum_{a \in S} e(a)$. Consider further the vector $\sum_{S \in \mathcal{B}} w_S x^S$. For each of its components we have

$$\sum_{S \in \mathcal{B}} w_S x^S_a = \sum_{S \in \mathcal{B}_a} w_S x^S_a \leq \sum_{S \in \mathcal{B}_a} w_S u_a(f^S(a)) \leq u_a(\sum_{S \in \mathcal{B}_A} w_S f^S(a)) \ .$$

The last inequality follows from the concavity of u.
All that remains is to show that the vector $(\sum_{S \in \mathcal{B}_a} w_S f^S(a))_{a \in A}$ is a feasible allocation. But we have

$$\sum_{a \in A} \sum_{S \in \mathcal{B}_a} w_S f^S(a) = \sum_{S \in \mathcal{B}} w_S (\sum_{a \in S} f^S(a)) = \sum_{S \in \mathcal{B}} w_S (\sum_{a \in S} e(a))$$

$$= \sum_{a \in A} e(a) (\sum_{S \in \mathcal{B}_a} w_S) = \sum_{a \in A} e(a) \ .$$

Q.E.D.

Let (A, V) be a game. Choose for every agent $a \in A$ a positive "weight" $\lambda_a > 0$ and define for every coalition $S \subset A$ the number

$$v_\lambda(S) = \max_{x \in V(S)} \sum_{a \in S} \lambda_a x_a \ ,$$

which is well defined because $V(S) \cap \mathbb{R}^N_+$ is compact, and the set

$$V_\lambda(S) = \{x \in \mathbb{R}^N | \sum_{a \in S} \lambda_a x_a \leq v_\lambda(S)\} \ ,$$

as in Figure A.1.

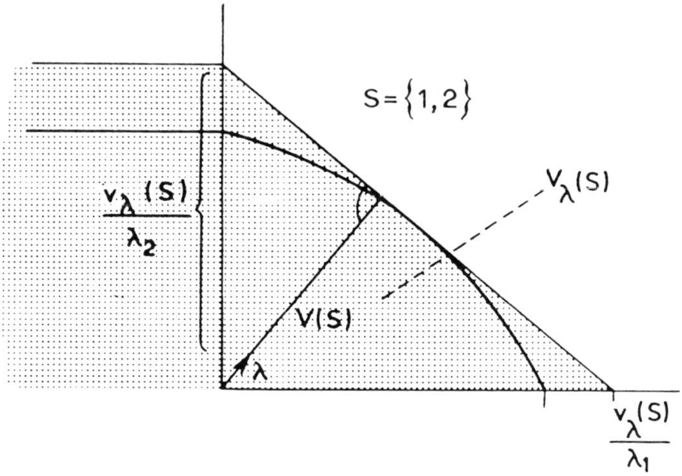

Figure A.1

Observation A.3. We want to show that every convex and strongly balanced game has a non–empty core. For this, we first show that every corresponding λ–weighted transferable utility game (A, V_λ), as defined above, is again strongly balanced (Proposition A.3.) and second, that the core of such a special game is non–empty (Proposition A.4.). Now, if the utility allocation x belongs to the core of (A, V_λ), then the utility allocation x cannot be improved upon in the original game (A, V). Note, however, that x may not belong to $V(A)$. Hence, it remains to show (Proposition A.5.) — using a fixed point theorem — that there is a vector λ^* of weights such that the core of the game (A, V_{λ^*}) has a non–empty intersection with $V(A)$. Here are the details.

Proposition A.3. If the game (A, V) is strongly balanced then the λ–weighted transferable utility game (A, V_λ) is strongly balanced.

Proof. (i) We shall show first that, for every balanced family $\mathcal{B}$ of coalitions

$$\sum_{S\in\mathcal{B}} w_S \dot{V}(S) \subset V(A) \text{ implies } \sum_{S\in\mathcal{B}} w_S v_\lambda(S) \leq v_\lambda(A) .$$

Let x^S be a vector in $\dot{V}(S)$ with

$$\sum_{a\in S} \lambda_a x_a^S = v_\lambda(S) .$$

Now $\sum_{S\in\mathcal{B}} w_S(\sum_{a\in S} \lambda_a x_a^S) = \sum_{a\in A} \lambda_a(\sum_{S\in\mathcal{B}_a} w_S x_a^S) = \sum_{a\in A} \lambda_a(\sum_{S\in\mathcal{B}} w_S x_a^S)$.

The last equality follows since $x^S \in \dot{V}(S)$. But the vector $(\sum_{S\in\mathcal{B}} w_S x_a^S)_{a\in A}$ is in $V(A)$ by assumption; hence

$$\sum_{a\in A} \lambda_a(\sum_{S\in\mathcal{B}} w_S x_a^S) \leq v_\lambda(A) .$$

(ii) We now show that

$$\sum_{S\in\mathcal{B}} w_S \dot{V}_\lambda(S) \subset v_\lambda(A) .$$

Let x^S be a vector in $\dot{V}_\lambda(S)$. Then $\sum_{a\in S} \lambda_a x_a^S \leq v_\lambda(S)$.

But $$\sum_{a\in A} \lambda_a(\sum_{S\in\mathcal{B}} w_S x_a^S) = \sum_{a\in A} \lambda_a(\sum_{S\in\mathcal{B}_a} w_S x_a^S) .$$

It then follows with (i) that

$$\sum_{a\in A} \lambda_a(\sum_{S\in\mathcal{B}} w_S x_a^S) = \sum_{S\in\mathcal{B}} w_S(\sum_{a\in S} \lambda_a x_a^S) \leq \sum_{S\in\mathcal{B}} w_S v_\lambda(S) \leq v_\lambda(A) .$$

Q.E.D.

It should be noted that concavity plays an essential role for the conclusion that (A, V) balanced implies (A, V_λ) balanced. In general this is not true.

Next we show that every strongly balanced and λ–weighted transferable utility game has a non–empty core. We prove a more general result since this generalisation is of independent interest.

We define a special class of games which played an important role in the development of game theory.

Definition A.2. For every coalition $S \subset A$ let $v(S)$ denote a non–negative number, the "pay–off" of coalition S. A *game with transferable utility with characteristic function* v denoted by (A, v) is defined by the sets

$$V(S) = \left\{ x \in \mathbb{R}^N \;\middle|\; \sum_{a \in S} x_a \le v(S) \right\}.$$

Proposition A.4. The core of a game (A, v) with transferable utility and characteristic function v is non–empty if and only if (A, v) is balanced. In particular, every strongly balanced λ–weighted utility game has a non–empty core.

Proof. Let us show that for a balanced game with transferable utility the core is non–empty. The vector $(x_1, \ldots, x_N)$ belongs to the core of (A, v) if

$$\text{(a)} \quad \sum_{i=1}^{N} x_i \le v(A) \qquad \text{and} \qquad \text{(b)} \quad \sum_{i \in S} x_i \ge v(S)$$

for every coalition $S \subset A$. Thus, we consider the linear programming problem of minimizing $x_1 + \ldots + x_N$ subject to the systems of linear inequalities (b). A solution of this linear minimization problem say $\hat{x}_1, \ldots, \hat{x}_N$, will belong to the core of the game (A, v) if the minimum of the objective function is less than or equal to $v(A)$. In order to decide this we consider the dual linear programming problem, i.e., variables w_S. The dual linear programming problem consists of maximizing the linear function $\sum_S v(S) \cdot w_S$, subject to the system of linear equations

$$\sum_{a \in S} w_S = 1, \quad \text{for all } a \in A .$$

Note that the dual constraints are equations which are not inequalities since the primal variables, i.e., x_i, are not restricted in sign. Denote a solution of the dual problem by $(\hat{w}_S)_{S \in A}$. The duality theorem of linear programming says that

$$\sum_{i=1}^{N} \hat{x}_i = \sum_S v(S)\hat{w}_S .$$

Consider now the family $\mathcal{B}$ of those coalitions for whom $\hat{w}_S > 0$. The constraints of the dual just say that this family is balanced with respect to the weights $\hat{w}_S$. Therefore, we obtain $\sum_S v(S)\hat{w}_S \leq v(A)$, since the game (A, v) is strongly balanced. Thus, we have shown that $\sum_{i=1}^{N} \hat{x}_i \leq v(A)$. If we do want to use the fact that for the game (A, v) balanced and strongly balanced are equivalent, one proceeds as follows. It follows from the duality theorem that

$$\sum_{a \in S} \hat{x}_a = v(S) \qquad \text{for every } S \text{ with } \hat{w}_S > 0 .$$

Therefore, $\hat{x} \in V(S)$ and since the family $\mathcal{B}$, as defined above, is balanced we obtain directly $\hat{x} \in V(A)$. The other direction of Proposition A.4. is left for the reader.

Q.E.D.

Proposition A.5. Let (A, V) be a strongly balanced game such that $V(A)$ is convex and compact generated. Then the core of (A, V) is non–empty.

Proof. For every strictly positive vector λ in the unit simplex Δ of $\mathbb{R}^N$ we consider the λ–weighted transferable utility game (A, V_λ).

(i) $C(\lambda)$ is non–empty.

Given the game (A, V_λ) define the game $(A, \hat{V})$ by

$$\hat{V}(S) = \{y \in \mathbb{R}^N \mid y_a = \lambda_a \cdot x_a \quad \text{where } x \in V_\lambda(S)\} \ .$$

It follows that the game $(A, \hat{V})$ is strongly balanced. Indeed, if $\mathcal{B}$ is a balanced family of coalitions with weights w_S then $y^S \in \hat{V}(S)$ (i.e., $\sum_{a \in S} y_a^S \leq v_\lambda(S)$) implies

$$\sum_{a \in A} \sum_{S \in \mathcal{B}_a} w_S y_a^S = \sum_{S \in \mathcal{B}} w_S \Big(\sum_{a \in S} y_a^S\Big) \leq \sum_{S \in \mathcal{B}} w_S v_\lambda(S) \leq v_\lambda(A) \ .$$

Apply Proposition A.4. to the game $(A, \hat{V})$. We can show that

$$\Big(\frac{1}{\lambda_1} y_1, \ldots, \frac{1}{\lambda_N} y_N\Big)$$

belongs to the core of (A, V_λ) if $(y_1, \ldots, y_N)$ belongs to the core of $(A, \hat{V})$.

(ii) The correspondence $\lambda \to C(\lambda)$ is bounded and closed and the set $C(\lambda)$ is convex.

This follows from the fact that the core is defined by inequalities and that the number $v_\lambda(S)$ depends continuously on λ. Now consider the correspondence Ψ defined by

$$\Psi(\lambda) = C(\lambda) - \{x \in \mathbb{R}^N_+ \mid x \in V(A) \text{ and } \sum \lambda_a x_a = \max_{z \in V(A)} \sum \lambda_a z_a\} \ .$$

This correspondence Ψ is bounded and closed. Further, for every λ the set $\Psi(\lambda)$ is convex and has the property $\sum_{a\in A} z_a\lambda_a \leq 0$ for every $z \in \Psi(\lambda)$.

Let

$$\Delta_n = \{\lambda \in \Delta |\ \lambda_a \geq \frac{1}{n},\ a \in A\}\ .$$

By a version of Kakutani's fixed point theorem (Lemma 3.1.) there exists $\lambda^n \in \Delta_n$ and $Z^n \in \Psi(\lambda^n)$ such that $\lambda \cdot z^n \leq 0$ for every $\lambda \in \Delta_N$. Thus, $z^n = x^n - y^n$, where $x^n \in C(\lambda^n)$ and $y^n \in V(A)$. Without loss of generality we can assume that $z^n \to z$, $x^n \to x$, and $y^n \to y$. Clearly, $z \leq 0$, $y \in V(A)$, since $V(A)$ is closed and the utility vector x cannot be improved upon in the game (A, V) since it is the limit of a sequence of vectors with this property. Since $x \leq y$ and since $V(A)$ is comprehensive, we obtain $x \in V(A)$.

Q.E.D.

Conclusion

The core of an economy $\mathcal{E} : A \to \mathcal{P}_{co} \times I\!R^{\ell}_{+}$ *is non–empty.* Indeed, by Observations 1 and 2 it suffices to consider economies where every preference relation has a concave utility representation. By Proposition A.2. these economies lead to convex and strongly balanced games. These games have a non–empty core by Proposition A.5.

Chapter 5

Core and Competitive Equilibria

1. Introduction

We can now come back to our two themes and examine in detail the relationship between them. Up to this point we have established that both competitive equilibria and core solutions exist, and furthermore that the set of one is contained in the set of the other. That is we have for any economy $\mathcal{E}$ (see Proposition 2.4.),

$$W(\mathcal{E}) \subset C(\mathcal{E}).$$

However, we wish to be able to say more. Now, in finite economies the inclusion $W(\mathcal{E}) \subset C(\mathcal{E})$ is typically strict. Indeed if the initial allocation of endowments is not Pareto efficient, which is the usual case, then, if there are any allocations in the core, there are core allocations which are not competitive equilibria.

This leads us to the *basic problem in the theory of the core:* For which kind of economies is the "difference" between the core and the set of competitive equilibria small? Or in other words, under which circumstances does cooperative barter and competition through decentralized markets lead essentially to the same result?

Naturally, the answer depends on the way one measures the "difference" between the two equilibrium concepts. Whatever way we choose to measure this difference the reader will recall from the Introduction that we will need many agents to guarantee that this difference be small.

There are two possible approaches to this problem. Either we look at what happens to the difference between our two themes as we increase the orchestra. Using this approach we must try to show that as economies "become large" the core shrinks to the set of competitive equilibria. That is, as the situation becomes one in which competitive behaviour is more and more plausible, the outcomes of cooperative behaviour are very close to competitive ones. This way of analysing the problem we call the "Limit Theorem" approach. The other approach is to consider straight away the case of an "ideal" orchestra, one in which there are arbitrarily many players none of whom individually makes any noticeable contribution. An economy like this is one which captures exactly the notion of "perfect competition". Although the idea of an infinite number or even of a continuum of agents might appear to be artificial, we may think of this "limit economy" in the same sense that physicists treat a fluid as a continuum of particles even though there are in reality only a finite number of particles in a given volume of a fluid. In this context of "perfect competition" we will be able to show that the two solutions, the Walrasian allocations and the core, are identical, i.e., for such a continuum economy we actually have

$$W(\mathcal{E}) = C(\mathcal{E}).$$

We observe that this second type of result would, although very elegant, be simply an exotic special case if we could not show that the distance between the two solutions diminishes as economies become large.

2. Replica Economies

If we are to adopt the first approach, we have first to define a distance between our two sets, the Walrasian allocations $W(\mathcal{E})$ and the core allocations $C(\mathcal{E})$. If there was only one allocation in the first set, i.e., the competitive equilibria were unique, then the answer would be simple. We would define our distance δ as the smallest number such that all allocations in the core were less than δ away from $W(\mathcal{E})$. However, when we are dealing with sets we have to give a more general definition but its intuitive content is clear. We must now take an allocation in the core and see if there is some Walrasian allocation near to it. Thus we will say that the core is within δ distance from the Walrasian allocations if for every core allocation there is a Walrasian allocation less than δ away from it. More formally then the measure of the difference between the two equilibrium sets, $C(\mathcal{E})$ and $W(\mathcal{E})$, which we shall denote by $\delta(\mathcal{E})$, can be defined as follows.

Let $\delta(\mathcal{E})$ be the smallest number δ with the property: For every allocation $f \in C(\mathcal{E})$ there exists an allocation $f^* \in W(\mathcal{E})$ such that

$$|f(a) - f^*(a)| \leq \delta$$

for every agent a in the economy $\mathcal{E}$.
Thus if $\delta(\mathcal{E})$ is small, then from *every* agent's point of view *any* core allocation is like a competitive equilibrium.

To obtain our result we will need to consider a sequence of economies that become large and show that the distances associated with these economies become small. Thus we define an *increasing sequence of economies* as

$$\mathcal{E}_n : A_n \longrightarrow \mathcal{P} \times \mathbb{R}^\ell_+$$
$$\text{with} \qquad \#A_n \underset{n}{\longrightarrow} \infty \,,$$

where A_n is the set of agents in the economy $\mathcal{E}_n$.

The sort of result that we would like to prove is that for any increasing sequence of economies the distance, as defined, goes to zero

$$\delta(\mathcal{E}_n) \underset{n}{\longrightarrow} 0 .$$

Although very general theorems of this type can be proved this can only be done at the cost of considerable technical complication.

We will therefore first show that such a result holds when we increase economies in a very rigid and symmetric way, i.e., when we "replicate" them and we will come later to discuss more general results.

For now, starting with a given economy $\mathcal{E}$ we will consider its n–fold replica $\mathcal{E}_n$ as simply an economy in which each of the original agents appears n times. Each of the n facsimiles of an agent a has the same preferences and endowments as a had in the economy $\mathcal{E}$ and we will refer to its facsimiles as belonging to "type a". Recall the twins of Ada and Bill in Chapter 1 for example who constitute two types a and b.

More formally then we have

Definition 5.1. With an economy $\mathcal{E} : A \to \mathcal{P} \times \mathbb{R}^\ell_+$, we associate the *n–fold replica* of $\mathcal{E}$

$$\mathcal{E}_n : A \times \{1, \ldots, n\} \to \mathcal{P} \times \mathbb{R}^\ell_+ ,$$

where in the n–th replica the endowments and preferences of agent (a, i) are given by

$$e(a,i) = e(a) \text{ and } \succsim_{(a,i)} = \succsim_a \qquad (i = 1, \ldots, n, \quad a \in A) .$$

Having now defined our special sequences of economies and having defined the notion of distance between the core and the set of competitive equilibria we can give the following basic result.

Theorem 5.1. Let $\mathcal{E} : A \to \mathcal{P}_{\substack{mo \\ sco}} \times \mathbb{R}^{\ell}_{+}$ be an economy and $\mathcal{E}_n$ its n–fold replica. Then the difference between the core and the set of competitive equilibria tends to zero, i.e.,

$$\lim_{n \to \infty} \delta(\mathcal{E}_n) = 0 \ .$$

This is a remarkable result. It says that in large replica economies every core allocation is near to a competitive allocation. In other words, the core is not much larger than the set of competitive allocations. In particular, it implies that every core allocation can be approximately decentralized by a suitable chosen price system.

We will prove this result in two steps. Firstly we will show that in a core allocation in a replica economy, agents of the same type receive the same commodity bundle.

Proposition 5.1 (equal treatment). Let $\mathcal{E} : A \to \mathcal{P}_{\substack{mo \\ sco}} \times \mathbb{R}^{\ell}_{+}$ be an economy with monotonic and strongly convex preferences and $\mathcal{E}_n$ its associated n–fold replica. If f is in the core of $\mathcal{E}_n$ then agents of the same type receive the same commodity bundle, i.e., $f(a,i) = f(a,j)$ for all $a \in A$ and $1 \leq i,\ j \leq n$.

Proof. If Proposition 5.1. did not hold then there would be an allocation $f \in C(\mathcal{E}_n)$, a type $a \in A$, say a^*, and $i \neq j$ such that

$$f(a^*, i) \neq f(a^*, j) \ .$$

For every $a \in A$ there is a least desired commodity bundle among $f(a,1)$, $f(a,2)$, $\ldots, f(a,n)$ according to the common preference $\succsim_a$. Without loss of generality we can assume that $f(a,1) \precsim_a f(a,i)$, $1 \leq i \leq n$. Since preferences are strongly convex we obtain

$$\frac{1}{n}\sum_{i=1}^{n} f(a^*,i) \succ_{a^*} f(a^*,1) \text{ and } \frac{1}{n}\sum_{i=1}^{n} f(a,i) \succsim_a f(a,1), \quad a \in A .$$

Hence, the coalition S consisting of agent $(a,1)$ for every a in A can improve upon the allocation f, by allocating

$$g(a,1) = \frac{1}{n}\sum_{i=1}^{n} f(a,i) \qquad \text{to every } a \text{ in } A.$$

Indeed,

$$\sum_{a\in A} g(a,1) = \sum_{a\in A}\frac{1}{n}\sum_{i=1}^{n} f(a,i) = \frac{1}{n}\sum_{a\in A}\sum_{i=1}^{n} f(a,i)$$
$$= \frac{1}{n}\sum_{a\in A}\sum_{i=1}^{n} e(a,i) = \sum_{a\in A} e(a,1) .$$

Thus, the allocation $g(a,1)$, $a \in A$, is attainable for the coalition S. Now, if agent $(a^*,1)$ gives a sufficiently small amount of his commodities to the other agents of the coalition S then we obtain a feasible allocation g' with $g'(a,1) \succ_a f(a,1)$ for every $a \in A$, since preferences are monotonic.

Q.E.D.

The importance of the "equal treatment" property that we have just proved is that the core is fully described by the core allocations received by one member of each type. Recall again that an allocation in the core of $\mathcal{E}_n$ lies in the Euclidean space of dimension $\ell \cdot \#A \cdot n$. Hence, the core is a subset of this space. Now as n increases, the dimension of this space changes. However, with the "equal treatment" property we need only consider that part of the core denoted by C_n which consists of the allocation to one member of each type, i.e., a subset in Euclidean space of dimension $\ell \cdot \#A$. The fact that the dimension of C_n is independent of

n is essential to our result for replica economies, and indeed has already been used in Chapter 1 where we were able to discuss a two–type replica economy in terms of the Edgeworth box.

The next step is to show that the only allocations that remain in the C_n for all n, are the competitive allocations of the original economy, that is that

$$W(\mathcal{E}) = \bigcap_{n=1}^{\infty} C_n \ .$$

This is the well known result of Debreu–Scarf (1963) which can be stated as follows

Proposition 5.2. If $\mathcal{E} : A \to \mathcal{P}_{mo} \times \mathbb{R}_+^\ell$ is an economy then

$$f \in W(\mathcal{E}) \text{ if and only if } f_n \in C(\mathcal{E}_n),\ n = 1, 2, \ldots$$

where f_n is the n–fold replica of f, i.e., $f_n(a, i) = f(a), i = 1, \ldots, n$.

This gives us a characterisation of Walrasian allocations. An allocation for an economy $\mathcal{E}$ is competitive if and only if its n–fold replica is in the core of the n–fold replica economy $\mathcal{E}_n$ for every n.

Proof. Our argument follows that of Debreu and Scarf (1963). Firstly if $f \in W(\mathcal{E})$ then its n–fold replica f_n is in $W(\mathcal{E}_n)$ and hence by the inclusion $W(\mathcal{E}_n) \subset C(\mathcal{E}_n)$ we have $f_n \in C(\mathcal{E}_n)$.

To prove the other implication consider f, an allocation for $\mathcal{E}$, whose n–fold replica is by assumption in $C(\mathcal{E}_n)$ and this for every n.

We have to show that there exists a price vector p such that p with f forms a competitive equilibrium. That is

(i) $p \cdot f(a) = p \cdot e(a)$

(ii) $x \succ_a f(a)$ implies $p \cdot x > p \cdot e(a)$ for all a in A.

Let us see what this means in geometrical terms. Define for every agent a the set of net trades which give an allocation preferred to $f(a)$, i.e.,

$$\psi_f(a) = \{z \in \mathbb{R}^\ell \mid z + e(a) \succ_a f(a)\} .$$

Thus property (ii) means that, for every agent a the set $\psi_f(a)$ is above the hyperplane $H(p) = \{x \in \mathbb{R}^\ell \mid p \cdot x = 0\}$. That is to say $p \cdot z > 0$ for all z in $\psi_f(a)$ (see Figure 5.1).

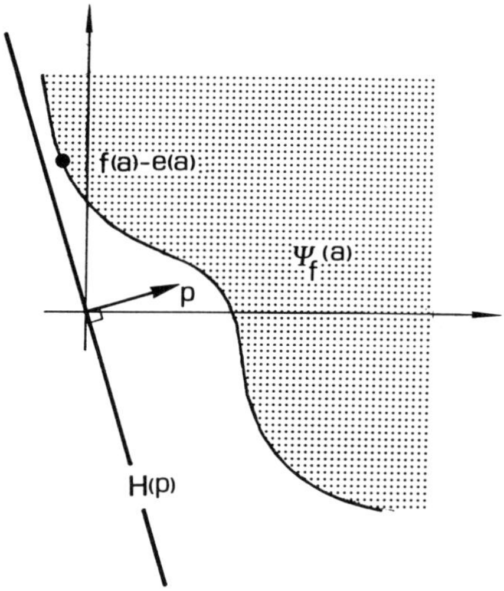

Figure 5.1

Now having seen geometrically what we wish to show we can see how a separation theorem will be used to obtain the required price system.

Firstly we show that the convex hull of the union of the preferred sets $\psi_f(a)$ has an empty intersection with the interior of the negative orthant i.e.,

$$co \bigcup_{a \in A} \psi_f(a) \bigcap int\, \mathbb{R}^\ell_- = \emptyset .$$

Suppose, on the contrary, that there exists a vector $z \ll 0$ contained in $co \bigcup_{a \in A} \psi_f(a)$. Then there exist r numbers $\alpha_i > 0$ with $\sum_{i=1}^{r} \alpha_i = 1$, and $z_i \in \psi_f(a_i)$, where $a_i \in A$ $(i = 1, \ldots, r)$, such that

$$\sum_{i=1}^{r} \alpha_i z_i = z \ll 0 .$$

Note that it may happen that $a_i = a_j$ for $i \neq j$. Since all that we need is that $\sum \alpha_i z_i \ll 0$ we may assume that the numbers α_i are rational. Then there are intergers n and β_i such that

$$\frac{\beta_i}{n} = \alpha_i \qquad (i = 1, 2, \ldots, r) .$$

Now we consider the economy $\mathcal{E}_n$ and form a coalition by choosing β_i agents of type a_i $(i = 1, 2, \ldots, r)$. This coalition can improve upon the n–fold replica of f in $\mathcal{E}_n$. Indeed, to each of the β_i agents of type a_i we allocate the vector $z_i + e(a_i)$, $(i = 1, 2, \ldots, r)$.
Clearly $z_i + e(a_i) \succ_{a_i} f(a_i)$ and

$$\begin{aligned}\sum_{i=1}^{r} \beta_i(z_i + e(a_i)) &= n \sum_{i=1}^{r} \alpha_i(z_i + e(a_i)) \\ &= n \left(\sum_{i=1}^{r} \alpha_i z_i + \sum_{i=1}^{r} \alpha_i e(a_i) \right) \ll \sum_{i=1}^{r} \beta_i e(a_i) .\end{aligned}$$

Clearly since this coalition can improve upon f with less than its initial resources we can give the remainder of the resources to one individual who, by monotonicity, will prefer this even more to the bundle he receives in f, hence the coalition can still improve upon f.

This proves that the two convex sets $co \bigcup_{a \in A} \psi_f(a)$ and $int\, \mathbb{R}^{\ell}_{-}$ are disjoint. Hence by Minkowski's Theorem (see Mathematical Apppendix II.) there exists a hyperplane $H(p)$ with normal p which separates the two sets, the first set lies above, the second one below the hyperplane $H(p)$. Consequently $p \geq 0$ and $p \cdot z \geq 0$ for evey $z \in \psi_f(a)$ for all $a \in A$.

This implies a weakened version of property (ii) that is

(iii) $x \succ_a f(a)$ implies $p \cdot x \geq p \cdot e(a)$.

This gives us essentially what we need and we now only have to show that properties (i) and (ii) follow.

Firstly we show that $f(a)$ is in the budget set, i.e.,

$$p \cdot f(a) = p \cdot e(a) \quad \text{for all } a \in A \; .$$

Indeed, for any $\epsilon > 0$, $f(a) + (\epsilon, \ldots, \epsilon) \succ_a f(a)$ by monotonicity. Thus by property (iii) we have

$$p \cdot f(a) + p \cdot (\epsilon, \ldots, \epsilon) \geq p \cdot e(a) \; .$$

Letting ϵ tend to zero we obtain $p \cdot f(a) \geq p \cdot e(a)$, i.e., $p \cdot (f(a) - e(a)) \geq 0$. Now

$$\sum_{a \in A} p(f(a) - e(a)) = p \cdot \sum_{a \in A} (f(a) - e(a)) = 0 \; ,$$

since f is a redistribution. Therefore we proved property (i), i.e., $p \cdot (f(a) - e(a)) = 0$ for every $a \in A$.

Next we remark that $p > 0$. Otherwise, (i) cannot hold. Simply increase $f^h(a)$ corresponding to $p^h < 0$ improving the bundle and decreasing its value.

Next we show that (iii) implies (ii). Since by the definition of an economy $e(A) \gg 0$ some individual must have positive income, $p \cdot e(a) > 0$. For him $f(a)$ must be a best element in his budget set, otherwise, if there were $x \succ_a f(a)$ with $p \cdot x \leq p \cdot e(a)$, we could find $\overline{x} \succ_a f(a)$ with $p \cdot \overline{x} < p \cdot e(a)$, a contradiction with property (iii). However, if $f(a)$ is a best element in his budget set then p must be strictly positive. If this is so then $f(a)$ is a best element in the budget set for all a in A, even if $p \cdot e(a) = 0$, and we have a competitive equilibrium.

Q.E.D.

We can now proceed to the

Proof of Theorem 5.1. By the definition of $\delta(\mathcal{E})$ and the "equal treatment" property it suffices to show that the distance between C_n and $W(\mathcal{E})$ goes to zero as n becomes large. For this we show that for every sequence (f_n), $f_n \in C_n$, there is a converging subsequence in $\mathbb{R}^{\ell\#A}$ whose limit $\overline{f}$ belongs to $W(\mathcal{E})$. This property clearly implies that $lim\, \delta(\mathcal{E}_n) = 0$.

Let (f_n) be a sequence with $f_n \in C_n$. Recall that the set C_1 is compact and contains the whole sequence. Hence there is a convergent subsequence, which we also call (f_n) and its limit we call $\overline{f}$.

Now choose any integer m, then f_n is in C_m for $n \geq m$, since the sequence C_n is decreasing. Recall that C_m is closed hence $\overline{f}$ belongs to C_m. But this is true for every m. Thus $\overline{f}$ is in $\bigcap_{m=1}^{\infty} C_m$. By Proposition 5.2. we obtain $\overline{f} \in W(\mathcal{E})$.

Q.E.D.

Remark. A natural question that arises is, "how fast" does the sequence (C_n) converge to $W(\mathcal{E})$? Debreu (1975a) has specified with somewhat stronger assumptions than ours on the preferences and endowments of the agents in the economy $\mathcal{E}$, the speed of convergence of C_n to $W(\mathcal{E})$. He shows that the distance $\delta(\mathcal{E}_n)$ goes to zero at least as fast as the inverse of the number of agents in the economy $\mathcal{E}_n$, i.e., $\frac{1}{n\#A}$. In other words, as n tends to infinity $n\delta(\mathcal{E}_n)$ remains bounded.

The whole approach to proving the results of this section depends essentially on the fact that every core allocation in a replica economy has the "equal treatment" property. Thus, every member of a given type receives the same bundle, in a core allocation.

There is a trivial extension of the equal treatment property. If we replace in Proposition 5.1. strong convexity by convexity then one can show analogously that the commodity bundles received by agents of the same type are equivalent in terms of their common preference relation, i.e.,

$$f(a,i) \sim_a f(a,j) \, .$$

Even this property does not hold, however, when we have an economy with different numbers of individuals in each type. To see this we will consider an example of an economy in which two identical individuals receive different treatment in a core allocation.

Example 5.1 (unequal treatment in a core allocation). We consider an economy with three individuals all of whom have the same utiltiy function, but two of whom have identical resources while the third is of a different type. There are two goods and the individuals of the first type, say 1 and 2, have $e(1) = e(2) = (1,14)$ while the individual called 3 of the second type has $e(3) = (27,1)$. All individuals have a utility function $u = u(\xi,\eta) = \xi \cdot \eta$. We consider an allocation which gives the following:

type 1	type 2
$f(1) = (6,6)$	$f(3) = (16,16)$
$f(2) = (7,7)$	

This allocation which gives unequal treatment to the two individuals of type 1 we claim is in the core. To verify this we must check that no coalition can improve upon f. Take the individuals alone and we have

$$\begin{aligned} u(f(1)) &= \ \ 36 > 14 = u(e(1)) \\ u(f(2)) &= \ \ 49 > 14 = u(e(2)) \\ u(f(3)) &= 256 > 27 = u(e(3)) \end{aligned}$$

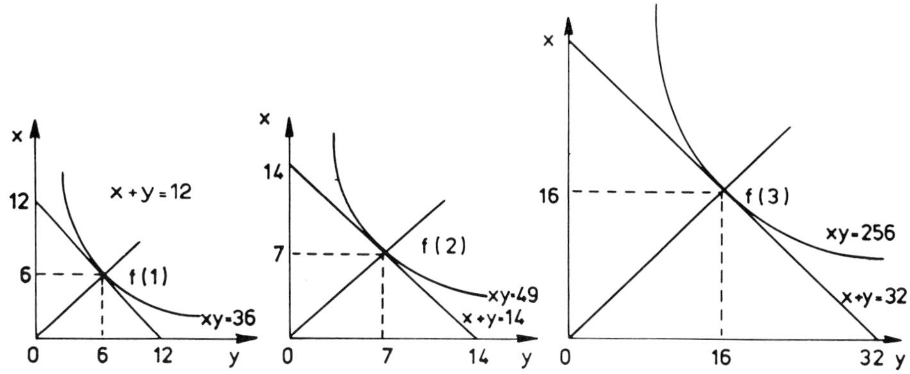

Figure 5.2

Thus, no individual alone can improve upon f. Now consider the coalition of all three agents. It is easily verified that, as can be seen in Figure 5.2 bundles $g(a) = (\hat{x}^a, \hat{y}^a)$ preferred to $f(a)$ must have the following properties:

$$(1) \qquad u(\hat{x}^1, \hat{y}^1) > u(6,6) \quad \text{implies} \quad \hat{x}^1 + \hat{y}^1 > 12,$$

$$(2) \qquad u(\hat{x}^2, \hat{y}^2) > u(7,7) \quad \text{implies} \quad \hat{x}^2 + \hat{y}^2 > 14,$$

$$(3) \qquad u(\hat{x}^3, \hat{y}^3) > u(16,16) \quad \text{implies} \quad \hat{x}^3 + \hat{y}^3 > 32,$$

Hence, for the coalition of all three individuals to improve upon f one must have

$$\sum_{a=1}^{3} (\hat{x}^a + \hat{y}^a) > 58 \, .$$

But since

$$\sum_{a=1}^{3} e(a) = (29, 29)$$

this implies

$$\sum_{a=1}^{3} g(a) \neq \sum_{a=1}^{3} e(a) ,$$

i.e., g is not feasable for the three–man coalition.

Exactly the same argument may be used to show that the two–man coalitions, $\{1,3\}$, $\{2,3\}$ cannot improve upon f as can be seen from inequalities (1), (2), (3).

Now consider the $\{1,2\}$ coalition. If f is not in the core, there exist $g(1) = (x^1, y^1)$ with $g(1) \succ f(1)$ and $g(2) = (x^2, y^2)$ with $g(2) \succ f(2)$, $g(1) + g(2) = (2, 28) = e(1) + e(2)$.

$g(1) \succ f(1)$ is equivalent to $x^1 \cdot y^1 > 36$, $g(2) \succ f(2)$ to $x^2 \cdot y^2 > 49$. But $x^1 \leq 2$, $x^2 \leq 2$, therefore $y^1 > 18$, $y^2 > 24.5$; hence $y^1 + y^2 > 42.5$, but $y^1 + y^2 = 28$, a contradiction.

Before concluding this section we observe an interesting consequence of Proposition 5.2. (Characterization of Walras Allocations). Together with the existence of core allocations (Chapter 4) it implies the following basic existence result which is a corollary to Theorem 3.1. of Chapter 3.

Theorem 5.2 (existence). Let $\mathcal{E} : A \to \mathcal{P}_{\substack{mo \\ co}} \times \mathbb{R}_+^\ell$ be an economy, then there exists a Walrasian equilibrium, i.e., $W(\mathcal{E}) \neq \emptyset$.

Proof. Consider the n–fold replica economy $\mathcal{E}_n$, of the original economy $\mathcal{E}$. We shall construct an allocation for the economy $\mathcal{E}$ whose n–fold replica belongs to the core of $\mathcal{E}_n$. Every economy $\mathcal{E}_n$ is balanced by Proposition 4.1. Hence, by Theorem 4.1. there exists $f_n \in C(\mathcal{E}_n)$. As we remarked above $f_n(a,i) \sim_a f_n(a,j)$ for all $a \in A$ and $i,j \leq n$. Define a new allocation, the average in each type, which we shall call $\overline{f}_n$ as follows:

$$\overline{f}_n(a,i) = \frac{1}{n}\sum_{j=1}^{n} f_n(a,j) \quad \text{for all } a \in A \text{ and } i \leq n \ .$$

Note that since preferences are convex,

$$\overline{f}_n(a,i) \succsim_a f_n(a,i) \ .$$

Hence, $\overline{f}_n \in C(\mathcal{E}_n)$. Thus, we now have a sequence of core allocations $\overline{f}_n$ which give equal bundles to members of the same type. Thus, to describe the allocation $\overline{f}_n$ it suffices to know the values $\overline{f}_n(a,1)$, $a \in A$.

Note furthermore that $\overline{f}_n \in C(\mathcal{E}_n)$ implies that the same allocation restricted to m members of each type is in the core of $\mathcal{E}_m$ for all $m \leq n$. This is clear since any coalition that could improve upon the restricted allocation $\overline{f}_m$ in $\mathcal{E}_m$, i.e., $\overline{f}_n(a,i)$, $a \in A$, $i \leq m$, could also improve upon it in $\mathcal{E}_n$. This means that for any fixed m the restrictions of $\overline{f}_n$ for all $n \geq m$ are in the core of $\mathcal{E}_m$. (This is nothing other than a formulation of Edgeworth's early idea that the core "shrinks".)

Moreover, the $\overline{f}_n$ are bounded since $\overline{f}_n(a,i) \leq \sum_{a\in A} e(a) = e(A)$ for every $n, a \in A$ and $i \leq n$. Hence, the sequence $\overline{f}_n(a,i)$, $n = 1,\ldots$ or a subsequence of it converges to , say, $f(a,i)$. Now it remains to show that the n–fold replica of f, i.e., $f(a,i) = f(a,1)$ for $i \leq n$, is in $C(\mathcal{E}_n)$ for every n.

Choose any integer, say m. By Proposition 4.2. we know that $C(\mathcal{E}_m)$ is closed. We know that for every $n \geq m$ the m restriction of $\overline{f}_n$, i.e., $\overline{f}_n(a,i)$, $i \leq m$ is in $C(\mathcal{E}_m)$. But by the closedness of $C(\mathcal{E}_m)$ the limit of $(\overline{f}_n(a,1))$, i.e., $f(a,1)$, replicated m times is also in the core of $C(\mathcal{E}_m)$. Hence, we have found an allocation $f(a,1)$, $a \in A$ whose replication remains in the core of $\mathcal{E}_n$ and therefore by Proposition 5.2. we conclude that $W(\mathcal{E}) \neq \emptyset$.

Q.E.D.

3. Economies with a Continuum of Agents

Up to this point we have only dealt with finite economies and no matter how large we have never had exact coincidence of our two themes. Suppose that instead of being satisfied with a small difference between these two concepts we now require that they should be identical. This can clearly only be the case if we go to an "ideal" economy which can be viewed as the limit of large economies. What do we require of such an ideal economy? The basic idea is that each of the individuals in such an economy is, by himself, negligible. This has the consequence, that no individual has an influence on the collective outcome of the economy. In particular this means that leaving out one agent or even a finite number of agents leaves us with an equivalent economy. This corresponds, intuitively, to a traditional idea in economics, that of "perfect competition". What we have to find is a mathematical model of an economy which has these properties.

Such a model must, of necessity, be abstract since the properties we require of a perfectly competitive model are themselves abstract. At the risk of being repetitive, we insist that finitely many, and indeed it will become clear that even a countable number of agents, will not be enough. What we need is a continuum of agents.

It should be clear that the sort of economy we are discussing only exists on the conceptual level. No real economic situation that we wish to represent will ever involve a continuum of agents.

There is a mathematical concept, that of a *"measure space"*, which satisfies our requirements exactly. Let us consider a specific example of such a space. Take the closed unit interval $[0,1]$ as a set of agents. Subsets of this interval will play the role of coalitions as before. In particular consider a coalition C which is an interval, the "weight" of this coalition, that is the "fraction" of the total number of individuals contained in it is given by the length of that interval. This number is also called the "measure" $\mu(C)$ of that set. It is clear that by taking unions and intersections of intervals we can give the measure of essentially all the subsets of the unit interval. The measure which we describe informally here is called Lebesgue–measure. However the mathematically trained reader will be aware that there are some subsets to which we cannot associate its measure. The so–called non–measurable subsets present technical problems and hence have to be excluded as possible coalitions. However, this is done for purely mathematical reasons and not as a result of economic considerations.

Clearly, even amongst those sets to which we assign weights (measurable sets) there will be some which will have "measure zero". For example, individual points, finite or even countable subsets will be examples of such sets. We make no distinction between two sets which only differ by a null set (i.e., a set of measure zero) and this implies that any statement we make, can only concern "almost all" agents.

The choice of a continuum to represent the agents in an economy might seem exotic. However this mathematical model of perfect competition has the following fundamental characteristic. Consider a subset C of A and a number ϵ with $0 \leq \epsilon \leq \mu(C)$ then there is a subset B contained in C with measure $\mu(B) = \epsilon$ (Lyapunov's Theorem). Up to this point we have only considered the unit interval with Lebesgue measure. However the property that we have just defined is characteristic of "atomless measure spaces" which are precisely those spaces which have the property that any set C with positive measure $\mu(C)$ contains a set B which has strictly smaller positive measure, i.e., $0 < \mu(B) < \mu(C)$. This implies, in particular, that a point must have measure zero, which corresponds exactly to the idea that we require that individuals are negligible. The reader interested in further details of the use of measure theory in economics should consult Kirman (1982) and the references given there.

In the "ideal" context we have to reformulate some of our definitions. An *economy with a continuum of agents* is now defined by a mapping $\mathcal{E}$ from the unit interval $[0,1]$ into the space of agents' characteristics, i.e.,

$$\mathcal{E} : [0,1] \rightarrow \mathcal{P}_{mo} \times \mathbb{R}^{\ell}_{+} \ .$$

As before, an allocation f is an assignment of commodity bundles to agents, more formally

$$f : [0,1] \to \mathbb{R}^{\ell}_{+} \ .$$

The informed reader knows that both mappings $\mathcal{E}$ and f have to satisfy a technical condition, that of "measurability". In particular we require that the integral denoted symbolically by

$$\int_0^1 f^h(a)d\mu$$

that is the area under the graph of f^h (see Figure 5.3) should be well defined for every commodity h.

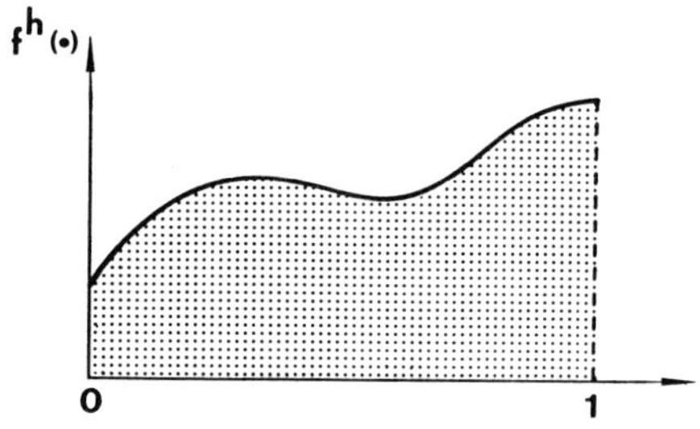

Figure 5.3

This number or integral is interpreted as the *mean* or *per capita* allocation. It should be clear that with an infinite number of agents we have to consider the mean and not the total allocation. In particular an allocation is *feasible*, or a *redistribution* if *mean supply* is equal to *mean demand*, i.e.,

$$\int_0^1 f(a)d\mu = \int_0^1 e(a)d\mu \ .$$

Since, as we explained above, the null sets do not matter in this model we can make no distinction between two allocations which differ only on null sets.

Now we are ready to define in this context our two themes, Walras equilibria and the core. The definitions involved are nothing other than an adaption of 2.11, 2.12 and 2.15.

Definition 5.2. A coalition S can improve upon an allocation f if there exists an allocation g such that

(i) $g(a) \succ_a f(a)$ for almost all $a \in S$

and

(ii) $\int_S g(a) d\mu = \int_S e(a) d\mu$.

Definition 5.3. The core of the economy $\mathcal{E}$, denoted by $C(\mathcal{E})$ is the set of all redistributions for $\mathcal{E}$ that can be improved upon by no coalition.

Definition 5.4. A Walras equilibrium for an economy $\mathcal{E}$ is an allocation f and a price system p in $\mathbb{R}^\ell$ such that

(i) $f(a)$ belongs to $\varphi(\succsim_a, e(a), p)$ for almost all $a \in [0,1]$

and

(ii) $\int_0^1 f(a) d\mu = \int_0^1 e(a) d\mu$.

The set of Walrasian equilibria, we denote as before, $W(\mathcal{E})$. In the present context, by employing the same approach as that used in Chapter 3 it was shown by Aumann (1966) that Walrasian equilibria exist even though preferences are not convex. The technical difficulty involved in this framework is to show that the excess demand correspondence is upper hemi–continuous.

We can now state the following fundamental result due to Aumann (1964).

Theorem 5.3 (Equivalence Theorem). Let $\mathcal{E}$ be an economy with a continuum of agents having their characteristics in $\mathcal{P}_{mo} \times \mathbb{R}^{\ell}_{+}$, then

$$W(\mathcal{E}) = C(\mathcal{E}).$$

Proof. The proof that $W(\mathcal{E}) \subset C(\mathcal{E})$ is analogous to that in Proposition 2.4. To prove that $C(\mathcal{E}) \subset W(\mathcal{E})$ we will use the same strategy as that which we used for the replica case in Proposition 5.3. Choose f in $C(\mathcal{E})$. We have to show that there exists a price vector p such that p with f forms a competitive equilibrium. That is

(i) $p \cdot f(a) = p \cdot e(a)$

and

(ii) $x \succ_a f(a)$ implies $p \cdot x > p \cdot e(a)$ for *almost all* a in A.

Recall that this means in geometrical terms that there is a hyperplane with normal p which supports the set

$$\psi_f(a) = \{z \mid z + e(a) \succ_a f(a)\} .$$

for *almost all* agents in A.

Thus our problem is exactly the same as before except that we now speak of almost all individuals. The difference is essential from a technical point of view for the proof.

Indeed if we were to proceed as before we should show that the convex hull of the union of all agents' preferred net trades has an empty intersection with the interior of the negative orthant that is

$$co \bigcup_{A} \psi_f(a) \bigcap \; int\, \mathbb{R}^{\ell}_{-} = \emptyset \; .$$

Let us try to prove this as before. We then assume that there is a vector $z \ll 0$ contained in $co \bigcup_A \psi_f(a)$. Then there exist r numbers $\alpha_i > 0$ with $\sum \alpha_i = 1$ and $z_i \in \psi_f(a_i)$ where $a_i \in A$ such that

$$\sum_{i=1}^{r} \alpha_i z_i = z \ll 0 \; .$$

Consider for each of these z_i the set

$$A(z_i) = \{a \in A \mid z_i + e(a) \succ_a f(a)\} \; .$$

We will now make use of a basic result (Lyapunov's Theorem for one dimension) which shows the power of the continuum approach. This says that given a set C, then for every ϵ with $0 \le \epsilon \le \mu(C)$ there exists a subset B of C with $\mu(B) = \epsilon$. Let us apply this to find the coalition we need. We choose disjoint subsets B_i of agents from each of the $A(z_i)$ with

$$\mu(B_i) = \lambda \alpha_i$$

where λ is chosen sufficiently small to ensure that the sets B_i can be chosen to be disjoint (see Figure 5.4). For example if the sets $A(z_i)$ are disjoint, then $\lambda = \min_i \mu(A(z_i))$ will do; in general, choose

$$\lambda = \frac{1}{r} \min_i \mu(A(z_i)) \; .$$

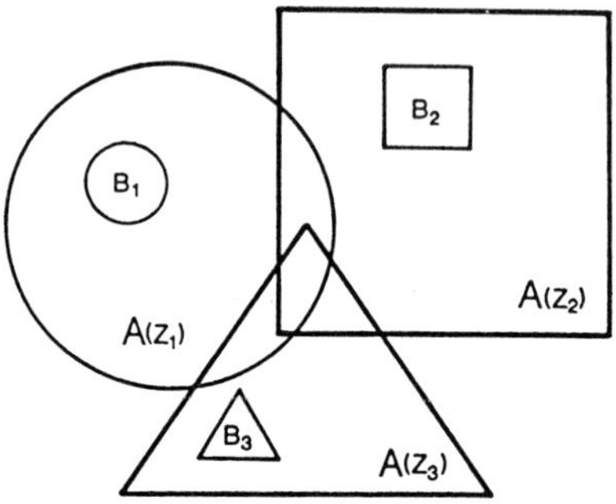

Figure 5.4

We now see clearly where the problem arises. If for one of the i the measure of $A(z_i)$ is zero we cannot form such a coalition.

To be able to guarantee that for each of the z_i, $\mu(A(z_i)) > 0$ we have to modify A slightly to A', keeping the same measure $\mu(A) = \mu(A')$ and then consider

$$co \bigcup_{A'} \psi_f(a)$$

and make the argument. This technical step will not be given here and the interested reader may find details in Hildenbrand (1982).

Assume then that this A' is given and thus that

$$\mu(A(z_i)) > 0$$

for all i.

In this case we form the coalition

$$B = \bigcup_i B_i$$

where B_i is as defined above.

Now this coalition can improve upon the allocation f. Indeed, to every agent in B_i we allocate the vector $z_i + e(a)$, $i = (1, 2, \ldots, r)$. Clearly this is preferred for every agent to f and

$$\begin{aligned}\int_B (z_i + e(a)) &= \sum_i \int_{B_i} (z_i + e(a)) \\ &= \sum_i (\mu(B_i) z_i + \int_{B_i} e(a)) \\ &= \lambda \sum_i \alpha_i z_i + \int_B e(a) \ll \int_B e(a) \,.\end{aligned}$$

This proves that the two convex sets

$$co \bigcup_{A'} \psi_f(a) \quad \text{and} \quad int\, \mathbf{R}^{\ell}_{-}$$

are disjoint.

Now we apply Minkowski's Theorem and proceed exactly as in the proof of Proposition 5.2.

Q.E.D.

4. Finite Economies

What we have just seen is that in an economy with a continuum of agents, every core allocation can be decentralized by a suitably chosen price system. One would like to be able to say that the same is "approximately" true for large but finite economies. What could this posssibly mean? One answer to this question is already discussed in the section on replica economies, where approximate decentralisation means that near to every core allocation there is a Walras allocation. This requirement is, however, too demanding if one wishes to have general results.

We will now define a weaker requirement and for this it is useful to reformulate the definition of a competitive equilibrium f and $p \gg 0$ by the following two properties:

(α) $p \cdot f(a) - p \cdot e(a) = 0$

(β) $inf\ \{p \cdot x \mid x \succ_a f(a)\} - p \cdot e(a) = 0$.

One way to define approximate equilibria is to weaken these two requirements, either on the individual level or to be less exacting, on average. This leads to the following result.

Theorem 5.4. Let $\mathcal{E} : A \to \mathcal{P} \times [0, k]^\ell$ be an economy. Then for every allocation f in the core of $\mathcal{E}$, there is a price vector p with the following properties.

(i) $\frac{1}{\#A} \sum_{a \in A} \mid p \cdot (f(a) - e(a)) \mid \leq \frac{2k\ell}{\#A}$

and

(ii) $\frac{1}{\#A} \sum_{a \in A} \mid inf\{p \cdot x \mid x \succ_a f(a)\} - p \cdot e(a) \mid \leq \frac{2k\ell}{\#A}$.

Proof. The proof follows Anderson (1978). For every agent $a \in A$, let $\psi(a) = \{x - e(a) \in \mathbb{R}^\ell \mid x \succ_a f(a)\} \cup \{0\}$, and define

$$\psi_A = \frac{1}{\#A} \sum_{a \in A} \psi(a) .$$

We now claim that $\psi_A \bigcap \mathbb{R}^\ell_- = \{0\}$. Assume to the contrary that there is a function $h : A \to \mathbb{R}^\ell$ with $h(a) \in \psi(a)$ and $\frac{1}{\#A} \sum_A h(a) < 0$. Then the coalition $S = \{a \in A \mid h(a) \neq 0\}$ can improve upon the allocation f with the allocation

$$g(a) = h(a) + e(a) - \sum_A \frac{h(a)}{\#S}, \qquad a \in S .$$

Indeed, since $h(a) + e(a) \succ_a f(a)$, $a \in S$ it follows by monotonicity of preferences that $g(a) \succ_a f(a)$ for every $a \in S$. Since $\sum_{a \in S} g(a) = \sum_{a \in S} e(a)$ we have shown our claim.

The set ψ_A which contains no strictly negative vector, however, need not to be convex. Hence, its convex hull $co\ \psi_A$ might contain strictly negative vectors. But we shall show that

$$co\ \psi_A \bigcap \{x \in \mathbb{R}^\ell \mid x \ll -b\} = \emptyset, \quad \text{where } b = \frac{\ell \cdot k}{\#A}(1, \ldots, 1)$$

This is illustrated in Figure 5.5.

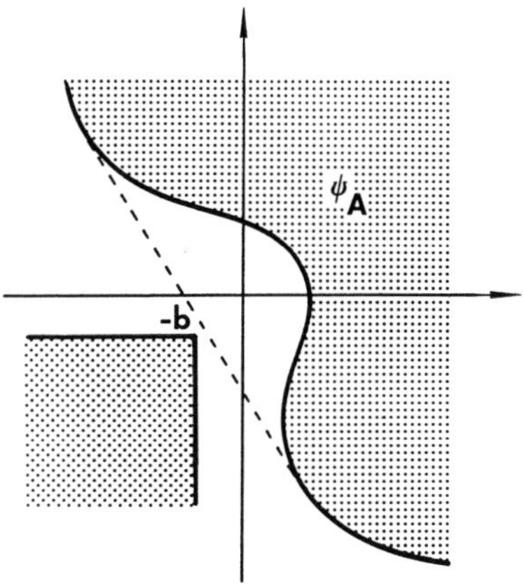

Figure 5.5

Suppose there is a vector $x \in co\ \psi_a$ with $x \ll -b$. Then we shall show that there would be a strictly negative vector y in ψ_A, which is a contradiction. By the Shapley–Folkman Theorem (see Appendix) we can write x in the form $x = \frac{1}{\#A} \sum_{a \in A} g(a)$, where $g(a) \in co\ \psi(a)$ for every $a \in A$ and $\#\{a \in A \mid g(a) \notin \psi(a)\} \leq \ell\}$. Let E denote those agents in A. Define $y = \frac{1}{\#A} \sum_{a \in A \setminus E} g(a)$. Since $0 \in \psi(a)$ we obtain $y \in \psi_A$. Clearly, $\psi(a) \geq -e(a)$, hence $co\ \psi(a) \geq -e(a)$. Now,

$$y = x - \frac{1}{\#A}\sum_{a\in E} g(a) \le x + \frac{1}{\#A}\sum_{a\in E} e(a) \le x + b \ll 0 \ .$$

Thus we have shown that the two sets $co\ \psi_A$ and $\{\in \mathbb{R}^\ell \mid x \ll -b\}$ are disjoint.

By Minkowski's Theorem there exists a hyperplane separating the convex sets $co\ \psi_A$ and $\{x \in \mathbb{R}^\ell \mid x \ll -b\}$. Thus there exists a price vector $p \in \Delta$ such that

$$inf\{p\cdot x \mid x \in \psi_A\} \ge -p\cdot b = -\frac{\ell\cdot k}{\#A}$$

since

$$inf\{p\cdot x \mid x \in \psi_A\} = \frac{1}{\#A}\sum_{a\in A} inf\{p\cdot x \mid x \in \psi(a)\}$$

and by definition $0 \in \psi(a)$ we obtain

$$-\ell\cdot k \le \sum_{a\in A} inf\{p\cdot x \mid x \in \psi(a)\} \le 0 \ .$$

Let $S = \{a \in A \mid p\cdot(f(a) - e(a)) < 0\}$. Since $p\cdot(f(a) - e(a)) \ge inf\ p\cdot\psi(a) \le 0$, it follows that

$$\sum_{a\in S} \mid p\cdot(f(a) - e(a)) \mid \le \sum_{a\in S} -inf\ p\cdot\psi(a) \le \sum_{a\in A} -inf\ p\cdot\psi(a) \le \ell\cdot k \ .$$

Clearly, $\sum_{a\in A} p\cdot(f(a) - e(a)) = 0$, which implies that

$$\sum_{a\in A} \mid p\cdot(f(a) - e(a)) \mid = 2\sum_{a\in S} \mid p\cdot(f(a) - e(a)) \mid \le\ 2\ell\cdot k \ .$$

This proves property (i) of the theorem.

Let $d(a) = inf\{p\cdot x \mid x \succ_a f(a)\} - p\cdot e(a)$. Since $d(a)\ \le p\cdot(f(a) - e(a))$ and $d(a) \ge inf\ \psi(a) \le 0,\ a \in A$, we obtain

$$\sum_{a\in A} | d(a) | = \sum_{a\in A} max(0, d(a)) + \sum_{a\in A} max(0, -d(a))$$
$$\leq \sum_{a\notin S} p\cdot(f(a) - e(a)) + \sum_{a\in A} -inf\ p\cdot\psi(a)$$
$$\leq \ell\cdot k + \ell\cdot k$$

Q.E.D.

Since the bound $B(\mathcal{E}) = 2k\cdot\ell$ in Theorem 5.4. is independent of the number $\#A$ of agents in the economy it follows that the mean deviation (i) and (ii) becomes small as the number of agents becomes large. Therefore if individual characteristics are always chosen in $\mathcal{P}\times[0,k]^\ell$ then every core allocation can be approximately decentralised provided the number of agents is large enough. This formulation does not involve any idea of a sequence of economies, it just requires that there be many agents. Up to this point we have not used any convexity assumptions. If an allocation is "near" in the sense of condition (i) and (ii) of Theorem 5.4. then by adding strong convexity to our assumptions on preferences it is also "near" in terms of commodities. More precisely we have the following result (Hildenbrand (1982)).

Theorem 5.5. Let T be a finite set of agents' characteristics in $\mathcal{P}_{\substack{mo\\sco}}\times\mathbb{R}_+^\ell$ and let b be a strictly positive vector in $\mathbb{R}^\ell$. Then for every $\epsilon > 0$ there exists an integer N such that for every economy

$$\mathcal{E}: A\to T$$

with $\#A\geq N$ and $\frac{1}{\#A}\sum_{a\in A} e(a)\geq b$ and every allocation f in the core $C(\mathcal{E})$ there exists a price system p_f for which

$$\frac{1}{\#A}\sum_{a\in A} | f(a) - \varphi(a,p_f) | \leq \epsilon\ .$$

Thus on average agents receive something close to their demand. However this does not imply that

$$\sum_{a \in A} \varphi(a, p_f) = \sum_{a \in A} e(a)$$

that is, p_f is not necessarily an equilibrium price vector. Therefore we have not shown that the core allocations in such an economy are near to Walras allocations.

5. More General Limit Theorems

Some readers may consider the above results to be a completely satisfactory answer to our basic problem. For such readers the rest of this chapter will be a superfluous intellectual exercise.

However this sort of result is quite different from that for the replica case where we showed that $\delta(\mathcal{E}_n)$ went to zero as n became large. At this point we should mention that there are many results in the literature which fall between the two cases.

Indeed suppose that we do require that for *every individual* the distance of a core allocation from a competitive allocation be small and this is not unreasonable since in finite economies individuals do matter. If we want to sharpen our results in this way then it is not sufficient to restrict the agents' characteristics and require that the number of agents be large. We have to go back to a sequence formulation. How far, in this case, can we extend the replica result? Or, in other words, how robust to modifications of the nature of a sequence of economies is the conclusion $\delta(\mathcal{E}_n) \underset{n\to\infty}{\longrightarrow} 0$ (see Theorem 5.1).

In fact, one can now go very far and obtain very general results in this direction. However, the generality is only obtained at the cost of considerable technical difficulties. We will therefore, in this section, explain where the basic problems in proving such results lie and then give a general theorem for "type economies". This last restriction, to a finite number of types is not bothersome since we can clearly approximate more general economies by appropriately weighting a finite number of characteristics. However even with such sequences of type economies one cannot make a completely general statement. Nevertheless we will show that the replica case is robust to modifications and the particular modification that we make indicates the direction in which we have to go to obtain general results.

Before considering specific results let us just see what we would like to be able to show. Our goal would be to show that in general as economies become large $\delta(\mathcal{E}_n)\underset{n}{\longrightarrow}0$. To make such a statement precise we have to construct a general sequence $(\mathcal{E}_n)$ of economies

$$\mathcal{E}_n : A_n \to \mathcal{P} \times \mathbb{R}^\ell_+$$

where A_n denotes the set of agents in the economy $\mathcal{E}_n$. What conditions must we impose on the sequence $(\mathcal{E}_n)$? The first obvious condition is that

Condition (i): $\#A_n \to \infty$.

Is this condition enough to get the desired result? The answer unfortunately, but not surprisingly, is no, as the following example, due to Gabszewicz (1970), clearly shows.

Example 5.2. Consider an economy with two consumers and two goods. Each consumer has preferences that are represented by the utility function $u(x, y) = (x + 1) \cdot (y + 1)$. These preferences are clearly strictly convex and monotonic. The initial endowments of the two individuals are $e(1) = (3, 0)$ and $e(2) = (0, 3)$. The economy is illustrated in Figure 5.6.

The core consists of the allocations on the line segment a, b and the competitive allocation is given by the point c. Now consider an increasing sequence of economies with, in the nth economy, one consumer of type 1 with resources $(3n,\ 0)$ and n consumers of type 2 each with resources (0,3). *Now as n increases the core shrinks, not to the competitive allocation, which is* $(\frac{3n}{2},\ \frac{3n}{2})$ *and* $(\frac{3}{2}, \frac{3}{2})$, *but to the set of allocations assigning to individual* 1 $(n\alpha,\ n\alpha)$ *and to the individuals of type* 2 $(3-\alpha,\ 3\alpha)$, $\frac{3}{2} \le \alpha \le 2$. To see this we will show that the allocation $(2n,\ 2n)$ for individual 1 and (1,1) for each individual of type 2 is in the core for every n. We leave it to the reader to show that the other allocations mentioned also remain in the core and that any allocation assigning less than $(\frac{3n}{2},\ \frac{3n}{2})$ to individual 1 disappears from the core.

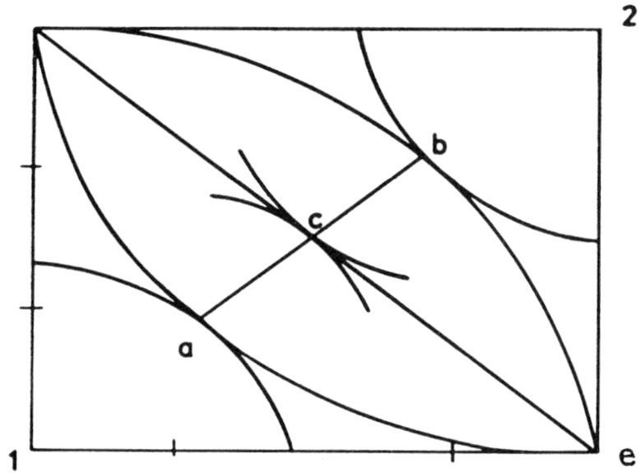

Figure 5.6

Suppose that

$$f(1) = (2n,\ 2n), \qquad f(a) = (1,\ 1), \qquad a = 2, \ldots, n+1\ ,$$

is not in the core for some n, then there exists a coalition S which may improve upon it. Note now that the first individual must participate in such a coalition. Secondly, at the prices $p = (1,1)$, f maximizes u on the sets $\{z \mid p \cdot z \le p \cdot f(a)\}$ for all a, and hence for all a in S. Therefore, the redistribution g with $g(a) \succ_a f(a)$ and

$$\sum_{a \in S} g(a) = \sum_{a \in S} e(a)$$

with which S improves upon f must have the following property:

$$p \cdot \sum_{a \in S} g(a) > p \cdot \sum_{a \in S} f(a) \; .$$

Let $\#S = k + 1$, then

$$p \cdot \sum_{a \in S} f(a) = 2k + 4n \ge p \cdot \sum_{a \in S} e(a) = 3k + 3n$$

since $k \le n$. But then

$$p \cdot \sum_{a \in S} g(a) > p \cdot \sum_{a \in S} e(a)$$

in contradiction to

$$\sum_{a \in S} g(a) = \sum_{a \in S} e(a) \; .$$

Now it is clear that we will have to impose further conditions on our sequence of economies. Before doing this we will introduce some new notation. An economy $\mathcal{E}_n$ in our sequence is depicted in Figure 5.7.

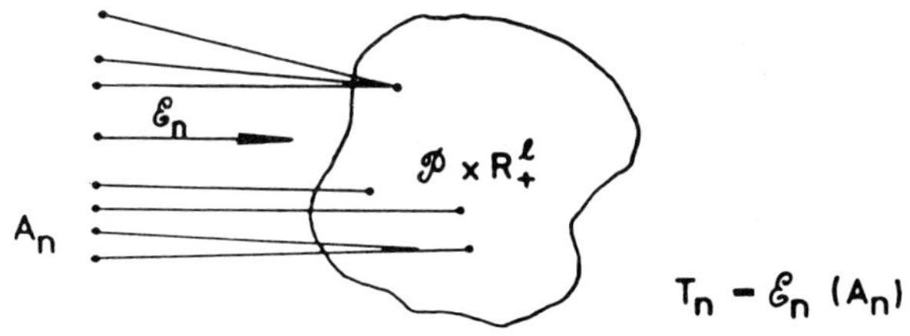

Figure 5.7

Denote the subset of agents' characteristics actually assigned to the individuals A_n by the mapping $\mathcal{E}_n$ as T_n, i.e.,

$$T_n := \mathcal{E}_n(A_n) \subseteq \mathcal{P} \times \mathbb{R}^{\ell}_{+} \ .$$

Every point τ in T_n has a certain weight $\nu_n(\tau)$, the proportion of agents in A_n having that characteristic, i.e.,

$$\nu_n(\tau) := \#\{a \in A_n \mid \mathcal{E}_n(a) = \tau\}/\#A \ .$$

What we will need for our result are two features. Firstly, for large economies, the sets T_n should be very similar, and secondly the "distribution" of weights over the T_n should not change much with large n.

For example, in a sequence of replica economies the situation is trivial. $T_n = T_1$ for all n and the weight distribution is the same for all n. Indeed, $\nu_n(\tau) = \frac{1}{N}$, where $N = \#A_1$. However, in the previous example, consider T_n in commodity space since preferences are constant for all n, and we have $T_n = \{(3n,0)\},\ (0,3)\}$. The weights are

$$\nu_n(0,3) = \frac{n}{n+1} \quad \text{and} \quad \nu_n(3n,0) = \frac{1}{n+1} \ .$$

Now what happens in the limit is that $\nu_n(0,3) \to 1$ and $\nu_n(3n,0) \to 0$. In other words, the n–th man "disappears" and the sets T_n of agents' characteristics do not converge to any set.

With measure theory, we can make the sort of convergence that one needs precise (see Hildenbrand (1974)). However, to keep the analysis on a fairly easy level, we will consider a rather simple case which nevertheless exhibits all the difficulties inherent in the general problem. We will require that T_n shall be independent of n and, moreover, is a finite set. The weights $\nu_n(\tau)$ depend on n but must converge. More formally, we have

Condition (ii): The sequence of economies $\mathcal{E}_n : A_n \to T$, where T is a finite subset of $\mathcal{P} \times \mathbb{R}^\ell_+$ has positive limit frequencies and strictly positive initial endowments, i.e.,

$$\nu_n(\tau) \to \nu^*(\tau) > 0 \text{ for every } \tau \in T \qquad \text{and} \qquad \sum_{\tau \in T} \nu^*(\tau) \cdot e(\tau) \gg 0 \, .$$

Definition 5.5. Let T be a finite subset in $\mathcal{P} \times \mathbb{R}^\ell_+$. A purely competitive sequence $(\mathcal{E}_n)$ of type economies with characteristics in T is a sequence of economies

$$\mathcal{E}_n : A_n \to T, \quad n = 1, 2, \ldots$$

such that conditions (i) and (ii) are satisfied.

With every purely competitive sequence $(\mathcal{E}_n)$ we can associate a limit economy $\mathcal{E}_\infty$ with a continuum of agents (see Section 3 of this chapter for details) in which the set of agents having characteristic τ has measure $\nu^*(\tau)$. We shall then use the shorthand

$$\mathcal{E}_n \to \mathcal{E}_\infty \, .$$

The set of equilibrium prices for this economy we will denote $\Pi(\mathcal{E}_\infty)$.

The idea that a sequence of economies converges in this framework is that the proportion $\nu_n(\tau)$ in each type should converge to some limit frequency $\nu^*(\tau)$. This limit frequency corresponds to the measure of the set associated with that type in the associated limit or continuum economy. In the replica case, $\nu_n(\tau) = \frac{1}{N}$ and hence

$$\nu^*(\tau) = \lim_{n \to \infty} \nu_n(\tau) = \frac{1}{N} \, .$$

Consider now, as we did in Chapter 1, economies increasing in a more general way. For example, suppose that there are two types of individuals. Take a coin and toss it. If it comes down heads, add an individual of type one, if tails, then add one of type two to the previous economy. Repeating this procedure generates a sequence of economies $\mathcal{E}_1 \ldots \mathcal{E}_n$ in each of which the number of agents in the two types may differ, but in the limit the frequences in each type will be $\nu(1) = \nu(2) = \frac{1}{2}$. As another example, think of a sequence of economies with two types generated by the following procedure. Throw a dice and when an odd number occurs add this number of agents to the first type. When an even number happens add this number to the second type. Repeating this will give rise to a sequence of economies and the limit frequencies of the two types will be $\nu(1) = \frac{3}{7}$, $\nu(2) = \frac{4}{7}$. When we consider our sequence of "type economies" we will require for our main limit theorem that

$$\nu(k) = \lim_{n \to \infty} \nu_n(k) > 0.$$

With this in mind we can now examine the one problem that remains before we can state our result. When we increase economies we associate with each of them the set of equilibrium price vectors $\Pi(\mathcal{E}_n)$. Now it may happen that the set of prices for the limit economy $\mathcal{E}_\infty$ is very different from that of $\mathcal{E}_n$. We know, in fact, that the equilibrium price correspondence is upper hemi–continuous (see Hildenbrand (1974)) but what can happen is that $\Pi(\mathcal{E}_\infty)$ contains not only the limits of all the prices from the $\Pi(\mathcal{E}_n)$ but also additional prices that have nothing to do with those in the $\Pi(\mathcal{E}_n)$ even for n large.

To see this consider a sequence of two good economies with excess demand functions $Z_{\mathcal{E}_n}(p)$ of the form illustrated in Figure 5.8.

The sequence $(\mathcal{E}_n)$ converges to $\mathcal{E}_\infty$ but every economy $\mathcal{E}_n$ has just one equilibrium price which converges to $\overline{p}$. However the economy $\mathcal{E}_\infty$ has another equilibrium as well, the price p^* which is far from $\overline{p}$. To give a general result we must exclude this type of "explosion".

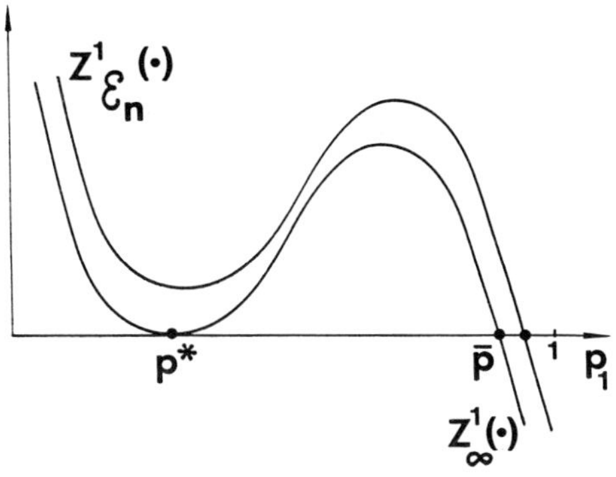

Figure 5.8

Definition 5.6. A purely competitive sequence of type economies is *sleek* if $\Pi(\mathcal{E}_n)$ converges to $\Pi(\mathcal{E}_\infty)$ in the following sense. For every open set $\mathcal{O}$ in $\mathbb{R}^\ell$ with $\mathcal{O} \bigcap \Pi(\mathcal{E}_\infty) \neq \emptyset$ it follows that $\mathcal{O} \bigcap \Pi(\mathcal{E}_n) \neq \emptyset$ for all n sufficiently large.

The reader can easily see that the sequence in the previous example is not sleek.

A simple example of a sleek sequence is one in which the limit economy $\mathcal{E}_\infty$ has a unique competitive price system. Conditions which lead to uniqueness are dealt with in Chapter 6.

Now we give our general result.

Theorem 5.6. For every sleek sequence $(\mathcal{E}_n)$ of economies

$$\lim_{n \to \infty} \delta(\mathcal{E}_n) = 0.$$

The reader will immediately ask how restrictive is the assumption of sleekness? It is not possible to give a general characterisation of sequences of economies which are sleek. However it can be shown that non-sleek sequences are exceptional cases, at least in the differentiable case in the following sense. Represent the weights of the types in every limit economy as a point in the unit simplex in $\mathbb{R}^{\#T}$. Now one can show given the set T of types that there is a negligible (closed and of Lebesgue measure zero) subset C_T such that every purely competitive sequence $\mathcal{E}_n$ of economies whose limit distribution does not belong to the set C_T is sleek.

Here we confined our attention to type economies, that is those in which the characteristics were restricted to a finite set. However the result holds true for any sleek sequence of economies for which the "distribution of characteristics" converges to a "limit distribution". In our particular case this was achieved by the convergence of the weights in each point in T.

Another way of generalising such results is to weaken the notion of the "distance" between the core and the competitive equilibria. We have not entered into details of limit results here but the interested reader should consult Hildenbrand (1974), (1982) and (1987) and the references given there.

Chapter 6

Structure, Uniqueness and Stability[1)]

1. Introduction

What we have seen up to now is that, in our simple model, competitive equilibria exist and have certain properties. In particular, in large economies, they coincide with our second theme or solution, the core. Now if, as we suggest, competitive equilibria have a certain importance, then the economist would clearly like to know more. That equilibrium exists, we might think of as a basic test of the coherence of our model. However, once this test is passed, several questions arise naturally. Firstly, under what conditions will equilibrium be unique? This may seem at first sight a very strong requirement, but the reader should remember that all such statements as the "price of oil is too high", frequently found in the economic literature, implicitly assume a unique equilibrium. If equilibrium is not unique, how conceptually can we do comparative statics since we do not know which equilibria before

---

[1)] In this chapter, we will use some familiar concepts from calculus and linear algebra which are not defined in the mathematical appendix.

and after changes we are to compare? Secondly, if we define some plausible adjustment process, will equilibria be stable? That is, if the economy is disturbed slightly, will it return to an equilibrium, or more, if the economy is not in equilibrium, will it converge to such a state?

Now it is important to recall precisely how we have proceeded. We imposed certain qualitative properties on the characteristics of individuals and then saw whether these properties are enough to yield certain properties of the aggregate excess demand of an economy which in turn guarantee, for example, the existence of equilibria. Now the first question that we might ask is, have we essentially exhausted all the properties of excess demand that our assumptions yield? Or are there still more properties beside the basic four of continuity, homogeneity, satisfying Walras' identity and boundary behaviour. If so, then we could perhaps use these additional properties to start to answer our questions as to uniqueness and stability.

Unfortunately, we will give a clear and unambiguous answer to this question in the first section of this chapter. Our assumptions on individuals yield no more properties than that just described and thus we cannot hope to make progress to answering our other question if we stick to assumptions on individual characteristics alone. Thus, "individualistic microeconomics" will not allow us to progress further.

What should be absolutely clear is that the conditions that we need on excess demand, that is on our system of equations to give us uniqueness and stability, is mathematically very thoroughly understood. Thus, the basic problem is not a technical one but rather one of finding economically interpretable properties that will guarantee the mathematical conditions that we need. Now it is obvious from what we have already said, that "microscopic" or "individualistic" assumptions are not going to help. An alternative approach is to give somewhat "ad hoc" conditions on aggregate excess demand functions themselves which yield the desired results. In doing this, it should be clear to the reader that we are changing our standards.

The sort of assumptions which we will make are of a different nature than those which we have used up to now. This is, of course, unsatisfactory, but within the model we cannot at the current time avoid this.

A hope might be that by some intermediate approach, such as making assumptions about the "distribution of agents' characteristics", we might yield more properties of aggregate excess demand. Although strictly speaking this is not true in finite economies, we do show that we can obtain a well–known economic property, the so–called "Law of Demand" by making assumptions on the distribution of characteristics in a continuum economy.

That the distribution of characteristics plays a role is clearly illustrated in the section on stability, where the stability of equilibrium in an example is shown to depend on the distribution of initial endowments. Thus a prevailing notion that it is the nature of preferences or utility functions that essentially determines stability or uniqueness is unfounded.

In our discussion of uniqueness and stability we will often work with differentiable excess demand. This is not incompatible with our initial approach since it can be derived from a property of individual preferences, that is "smoothness". We will not, however, go into a proof of how this is done.

To sum up then, if equilibrium is of real interest, we will want to know if there are likely to be several of them, in which case analysis of change, i.e., comparative statics, has no theoretical foundation. We also want to know if they are stable, since if not, they would be unlikely to be attained and hence would lose their intrinsic interest. The mathematical conditions required for these properties are well–known and we will show some of the rather unsatisfactory conditions on aggregate excess demand that do guarantee us these properties. The thoughtful student will realize that there is a gap between the "economic" and the mathematical conditions given and may be motivated to find other "economic" conditions which approach the generality of the mathematical ones.

2. Structure: Properties of Excess Demand

Our task now is to see whether there are any additional properties of aggregate excess demand to be obtained within our model of an exchange economy. We recall from Chapter 3.3. that the aggregate, or total, excess demand function $Z_{\mathcal{E}}$ of an exchange economy,

$$\mathcal{E} : A \to \mathcal{P}_{\substack{mo \\ sco}} \times \mathbb{R}^{\ell}_{+}$$

is defined on P, i.e., for all strictly positive prices. By definition $Z_{\mathcal{E}}$ enjoys three properties:

(i)	*Continuity*	$Z_{\mathcal{E}}(\cdot)$ is continuous on P
(ii)	*Homogeneity*	$Z_{\mathcal{E}}(p) = Z_{\mathcal{E}}(\lambda p)$ for all $\lambda > 0$ and $p \in P$
(iii)	*Walras' Law*	$p \cdot Z_{\mathcal{E}}(p) = 0$ for all $p \in P$.

In addition we also know that excess demand satisfies a boundary condition, property (4) in Proposition 3.2., which says that if any price goes to zero then excess demand becomes arbitrarily large. We will not take this directly into consideration in what follows since we will confine our attention to the behaviour of $Z_{\mathcal{E}}(p)$ on prices which are bounded away from zero.

These three properties impose very few restrictions on excess demand and we might well pose the following question first asked by Sonnenschein: Do the rather strong assumptions that we have made on individual preferences not imply any further properties of aggregate excess demand? It would be comforting if the reply were in the affirmative since this might encourage the hope that, in a more general setting, assumptions on individual characteristics might restrict aggregate behaviour to some specific class of functions. This in turn might give some hope of testable implications of our assumptions.

Unfortunately, the reply is negative and unequivocally so. If we exclude prices close to zero to avoid problems with boundary behaviour then we have the following result due to Debreu (1974).

Theorem 6.1. Given any function g from P into $\mathbb{R}^\ell$ with properties (i), (ii) and (iii) then for every compact subset K of P there exists an exchange economy $\mathcal{E} : A \rightarrow \mathcal{P}_{\substack{mo\\sco}} \times \mathbb{R}^\ell_+$ with ℓ agents, i.e., $\#A = \ell$, such that the aggregate excess demand of $\mathcal{E}$ is equal to $g(p)$ on K, i.e.,

$$Z_{\mathcal{E}}(p) = g(p) \text{ for all } p \in K.$$

This result shows clearly that no further restriction other than Continuity, Homogeneity and Walras' Law can be imposed on the aggregate excess demand function of an exchange economy if we neglect prices close to zero.

We now give a guide to how the above Theorem is proved. First we show how the given function $g(p)$ is decomposed into ℓ functions $z_i(p)$ which satisfy conditions (i), (ii) and (iii). It then has to be shown that these are in fact individual excess demand functions on K.

For any $p \in K$ consider the vector $g(p)$ which, by Walras' Law, lies on the hyperplane $H(p) = \{z \in \mathbb{R}^\ell \mid p \cdot z = 0\}$. Since p is strictly positive we can choose a constant $k > 0$ to make the vector $g(p) + \frac{k}{|p|}p$ strictly positive. Since K is compact, we can in fact find a constant k such that $g(p) + \frac{k}{|p|}p$ is strictly positive for all $p \in K$.

To understand the basic idea involved in decomposing the function g into ℓ functions z_i consider Figure 6.1. The reader can easily see that $g(p) = z_1(p) + z_2(p)$, and that the functions $z_i(\cdot)$, constructed in this way, have properties (i) – (iii) on K.

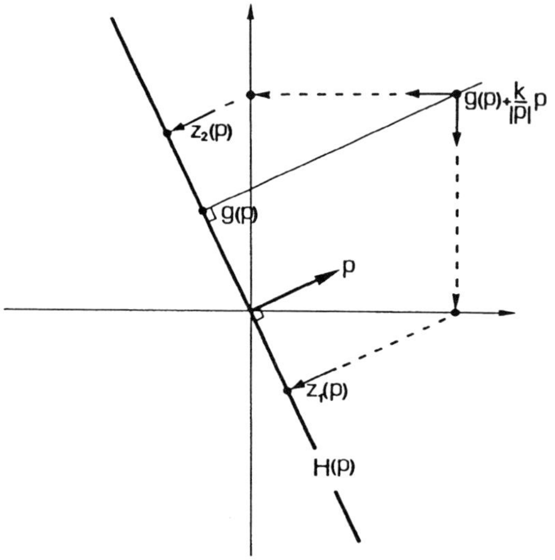

Figure 6.1

We shall now give the expressions corresponding to the geometrical construction in Figure 6.1 for the ℓ good case.

We can write

$$g(p) + \frac{k}{|p|}p = \sum \gamma_i(p)\mathbf{1}_i \ ,$$

where $\gamma_i(p) > 0$. That is to say, $\gamma_i(p)$ is the i–th coordinate of the vector $g(p) + \frac{k}{|p|}p$. If $proj_{H(p)}$ denotes the orthogonal projection of $\mathbb{R}^\ell$ onto the hyperplane $H(p)$, we obtain from the above expression

$$\begin{aligned} g(p) &= proj_{H(p)}\left(g(p) + \frac{k}{|p|}p\right) \\ &= proj_{H(p)}\left(\sum_{i=1}^{\ell} \gamma_i(p)\mathbf{1}_i\right) = \sum_{i=1}^{\ell} \gamma_i(p) proj_{H(p)}\mathbf{1}_i \ . \end{aligned}$$

Let us denote by $b_i(p)$ the orthogonal projection on $H(p)$ of the i–th unit vector $\mathbf{1}_i$, i.e., $b_i(p) = proj_{H(p)}\mathbf{1}_i$. Hence, the expression for $b_i(p)$ is given by

$$b_i(p) = \mathbf{1}_i - \frac{p_i}{p \cdot p} p.$$

The functions $z_i(\cdot)$, illustrated in the figure, are given by

$$z_i(p) = \gamma_i(p) b_i(p), \qquad p \in K.$$

Thus, the given function $g(p)$ is nothing other than the weighted sum of the functions $b_i(\cdot)$, which themselves are independent of g. Only the weights $\gamma_i(p)$ depend on the given function g. We are thus tempted to call the functions $b_i(\cdot)$ "base excess demand functions". Since the functions $z_i(p)$ sum up to $g(p)$ and satisfy conditions (i), (ii) and (iii) on K we have completed the first step.

The second step, unfortunately, is more complicated. For this we have to show that there exist preference relations $\succsim_i$ in $\mathcal{P}_{\substack{mo\\sco}}$ which, together with appropriately chosen initial endowments e_i, yield $z_i(p)$ as an excess demand function on K, i.e.,

$$z_i(p) = \varphi(\succsim_i, e_i, p) \; - \; e_i \qquad \text{for every} \quad p \in K.$$

Observe that the only restriction on the choice of the initial endowment vector e_i is that it must be large enough for $z_i(p) + e_i$ to be positive on K. Note that the i–th agent, defined by $(\succsim_i, e_i)$, has a positive net demand only for the i–th good.

We now show how the second step is achieved for the "base" functions $b_i(p)$, but will not complete the argument for the functions $z_i(p) = \gamma_i(p) b_i(p)$, which is the difficult part of the proof. The procedure for the functions b_i is illustrated in Figure 6.2.

Consider the point $b_2(p)$ on $H(p)$. Since by definition $b_2(p)$ is the orthogonal projection of the unit vector $\mathbf{1}_2$ on $H(p)$, it is the nearest point on $H(p)$ to the vector $\mathbf{1}_2$. Thus, the circle through $b_2(p)$ with centre $\mathbf{1}_2$ is

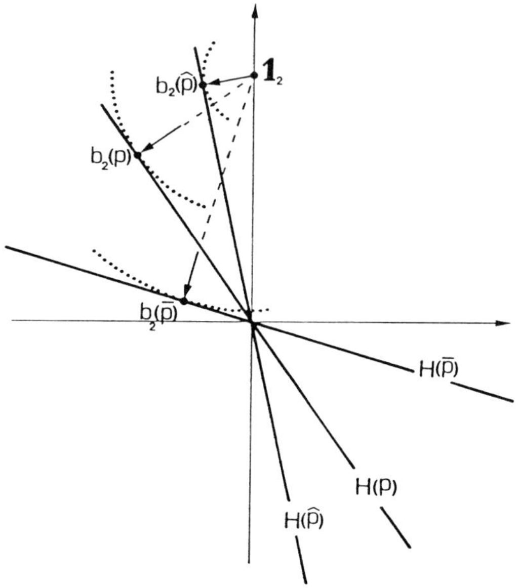

Figure 6.2

tangent to $H(p)$ at $b_2(p)$. A segment of this circle, when lifted up by the amount of the initial endowment vector (for example, choose the vector (1,0)) will form the essential part of the desired indifference curve. The initial endowment can be any vector provided that the lifted excess demand, that is to say, the demand, is positive for all p in K. The same argument will work in ℓ dimensions. The circles become spheres with centre $\mathbf{1}_i$ and the i–th initial endowment vector must be sufficiently large. For example, the vector with zero of the i–th good and one unit of all other goods will do.

What we have seen so far is that the functions $b_i(p)$ are indeed individual excess demand functions, derived from the characteristics in $\mathcal{P}_{\substack{mo\\sco}} \times \mathbf{R}^{\ell}_{+}$. As we mentioned before, to show the same for the functions $z_i(p) = \gamma_i(p)b_i(p)$ is difficult and delicate. We shall not give the argument here but, by looking at Figure 6.3, where we have drawn the functions $b_i(p)$ and $z_i(p)$ for p in K, the reader should be able to persuade himself that he could draw indifference curves corresponding to $z_i(p)$. A reader who is not satisfied with this geometrical reasoning is referred to Debreu (1974) for the complete proof.

A striking strengthening of Theorem 6.1. with differentiability assumptions on the function g was obtained by Mantel (1976). He showed that the preferences generating the individual excess demand function $z_i(p)$ can be made not only strictly convex and monotonic but even *homothetic*, that is to say, they have the following property: $x \succsim y$ if and only if $\lambda x \succsim \lambda y$ for every $\lambda > 0$. These are very special preference relations since they imply that an individual always spends a fixed proportion of his income on each good, independent of the level of his income. We have never used these preferences but they play an important role in applied work.

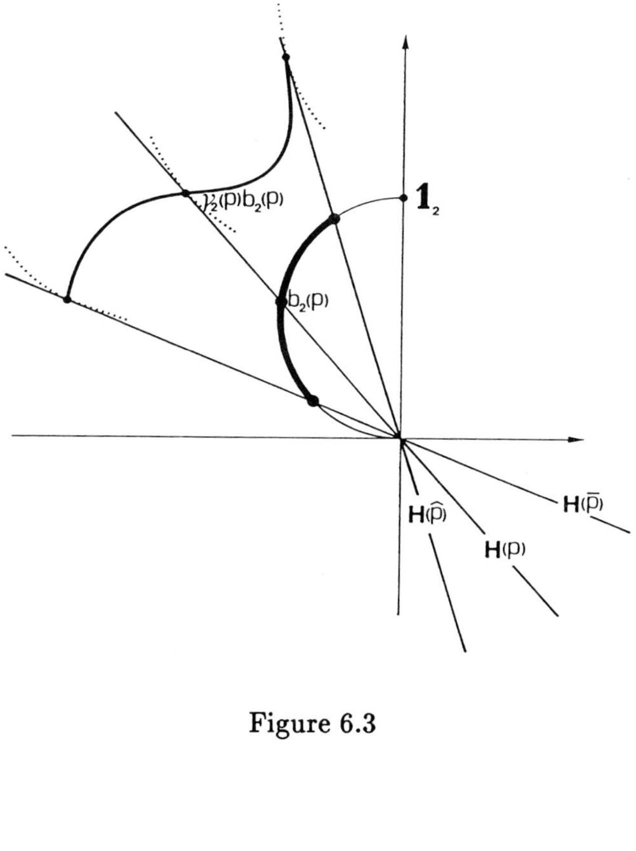

Figure 6.3

A strong objection has been raised to these results, or rather to their significance for economics, by those concerned with the practical problem of estimating demand functions. Basically, it is argued, in constructing the appropriate economy, no restriction whatsoever is placed on the *distribution of characteristics* of the individuals chosen. Thus the economic theorist allows himself the liberty of choosing as widely dispersed preferences and endowments as he pleases, whilst the practitioner may feel that he does not deal with economies in which individuals have arbitrarily different preferences and that he knows something about the distribution of endowments or income. Hence it is argued, as soon as we restrict the "dispersion" of preferences and the income distribution, then perhaps we may impose meaningful restrictions on aggregate excess demand functions.

Thus although all the players in the orchestra may satisfy our basic criteria we can choose them in such peculiar combinations that they can perform virtually any musical work. However, if we were to restrict the combinations allowed, then we might also limit the resulting music!

Unfortunately, this is not the case. In finite economies even if we require that all preferences are identical and furthermore if we restrict ourselves to *price independent relative income distributions*, chosen a priori, there is still no further restriction on possible aggregate excess demand functions. We now give an extension of our previous result which makes this precise.

Theorem 6.2. Given any function $g : P \to \mathbb{R}^\ell$ which satisfies conditions (i) – (iii) and arbitrarily chosen positive numbers $\alpha_1, \ldots, \alpha_n$ with $\sum \alpha_i = 1$, $\alpha_i \neq \alpha_j$ for $i \neq j$, where $n \geq \ell$ then the following holds: For every compact subset K of P there is an economy $\mathcal{E} : A \to \mathcal{P}_{\substack{mo\\sco}} \times \mathbb{R}^\ell_+$ with $\#A = n$, in which every agent has the same preferences, (i.e., $\succsim_i = \succsim$ for all i in A) and endowments are collinear, (i.e., $e(i) = \alpha_i \sum_{j \in A} e(j)$ for all i in A) such that

$$Z_{\mathcal{E}}(p) = g(p) \quad \text{for all} \quad p \in K.$$

In other words economies with a fixed, price independent relative income distribution and in which all individuals have identical preferences, can generate, as their excess demand functions on K, any function satisfying conditions (i) – (iii).

We will not formally prove this extension but we will give an indication of how it is obtained.

First a simple observation. It is not hard to see that in Theorem 6.1. we can choose $\#A$ to be any number $n \geq \ell$. Secondly, as mentioned above, we can increase the individual endowments beyond the required minimum as much as we wish. In particular we can do this in such a way that all endowments are collinear, that is, of the form

$$e_i = \beta_i e$$

for some fixed strictly positive vector e and positive real numbers β_i. We can further multiply these endowments by factors greater than one so that we have as required

$$e_i = \alpha_i \sum_{j \in A} e_j \ .$$

So far, then, we have obtained an economy with the required relative income distribution with the given $g(p)$ as excess demand for all prices p in K.

The only remaining step is to show that we can, in fact, give all consumers the same preferences. Consider the case of two agents, say a and b, and two commodities. The price consumption curves of each individual of our economy, that is, the demand at each price $p \in K$ are given by the heavy black lines in Figure 6.4. In this figure, the income shares are $\alpha_a = \frac{1}{3}$ and $\alpha_b = \frac{2}{3}$ and total resources are (9,6). The compact set K of prices is given by

$$K = \{p \in P \mid \overline{p}_1 \leq p_1 \leq \hat{p}_1 \ , \ \hat{p}_2 \leq p_2 \leq \overline{p}_2\} \ .$$

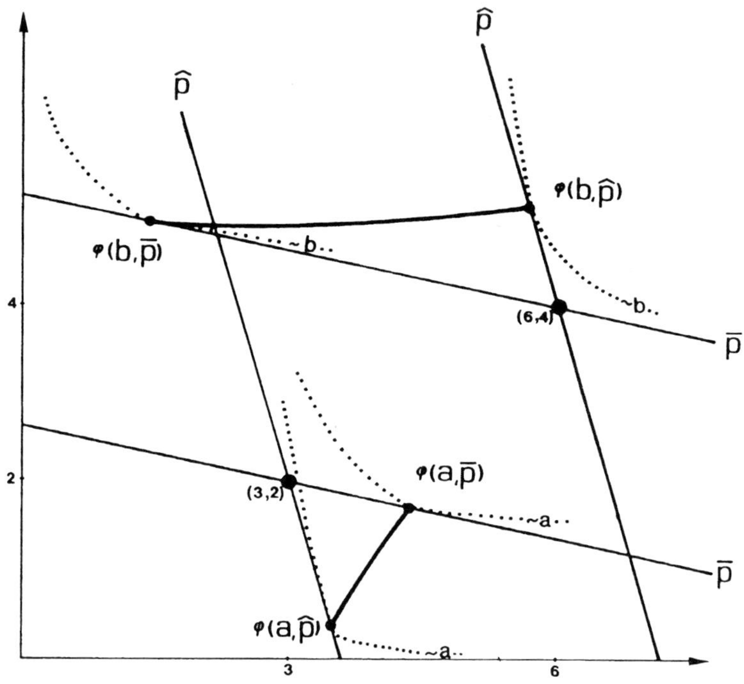

Figure 6.4

It is clear that *a* and *b* *cannot have* the same preferences since their indifference curves *must* cut each other due to the location of their price consumption curves.

However, now suppose that we multiply total resources by 3, keeping income shares the same. Since we still want to generate the same excess demand as before we will merely shift the "relevant" parts of the indifference curves upwards for each individual. Thus although their demands will change, their excess demands will remain the same as before (see Figure 6.5).

Consumer *a*'s endowment $\hat{e}(a)$, is now (9,6) and consumer *b*'s endowment $\hat{e}(b)$, is now (18,12). It is clear that every indifference curve

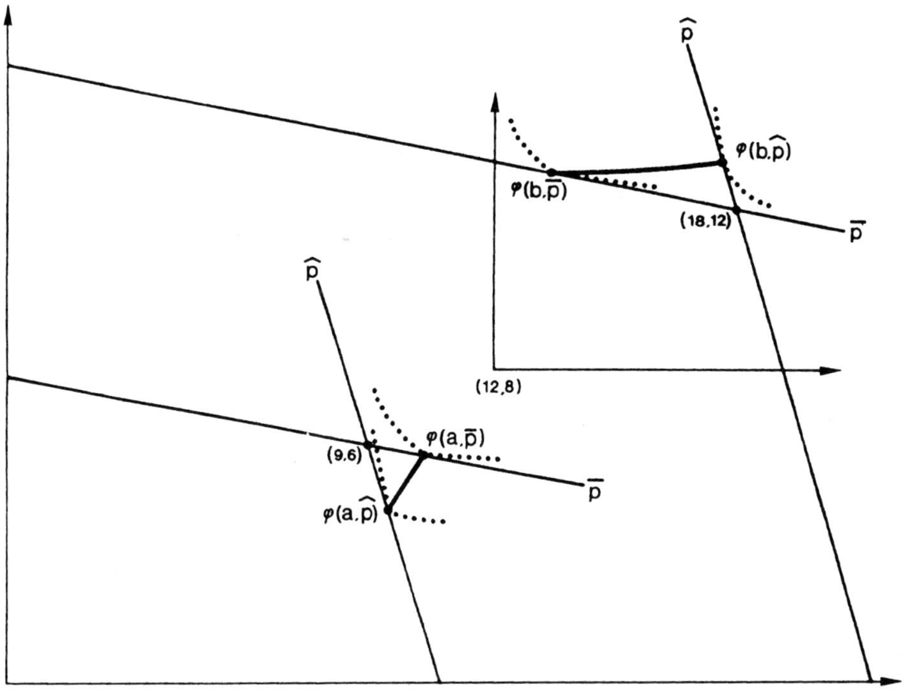

Figure 6.5

of agent b corresponding to a level of satisfaction achieved over the demand at prices in K lies above the point $\hat{e}(b) - (6,4) = (12,8)$. Since $\varphi(a,\overline{p}) < (12,8)$, no indifference curve of agent a that corresponds to a level of satisfaction achieved over the demand at prices in K has an intersection with $\{x \in \mathbb{R}^2_+ \mid x \geq (12,8)\}$. Hence the relevant part of a's indifference curves are now separated from the relevant part of b's curves (see Figure 6.5). Hence by filling in indifference curves appropriately we can construct a family which represents both a's and b's preferences, that is a and b have the same preferences and the economy still has the same excess demand as before. This argument can be extended to the ℓ good case. For a formal proof see Kirman and Koch (1986).

3. Income Distribution and Properties of Excess Demand

What we have just shown is that exchange economies, where the agents have *identical preferences* and *collinear endowments*, can generate essentially any function satisfying properties (i) – (iii) as an aggregate excess demand function. Thus, even this very restricted class of economies yields no useful additional properties which might, for example, lead to uniqueness or stability. However, the picture changes drastically if we consider *this* restricted class of economies with a *continuum of agents*, and if we make an assumption on the *shape of the income distribution.* This is worth noting, not because this class of economies is of any particular intrinsic interest, but because it is a clear example of a case where the *distribution of characteristics*, to which we have often referred, plays a decisive role.

As defined in Chapter 5.3., let

$$\mathcal{E} : [0,1] \to \mathcal{P}_{\substack{mo \\ sco}} \times \mathbb{R}^{\ell}_{+}$$

be an economy with a continuum of agents each of whom has the same preferences, say $\succsim$, and collinear endowments $e(a)$, i.e., $e(a) = \alpha(a)\bar{e}$, $\alpha(a) > 0$, where $\bar{e}$ denotes the mean endowment vector $\int_0^1 e(a)da \gg 0$.

For a given price vector $p \in P$, the income $w(a)$ of agent a is given by $w(a) = p \cdot e(a) = \alpha(a)p \cdot \bar{e}$. The income distribution in this economy can be described by the distribution function $V_p : \mathbb{R}_+ \to [0,1]$. That is to say, $V_p(w)$ gives the proportion of agents in the economy $\mathcal{E}$ whose income is less than or equal to w, i.e.,

$$V_p(w) = \text{ measure } \{a \in [0,1] \mid p \cdot e(a) \leq w\}\,.$$

The derivative of $V_p(w)$, denoted by $\rho_p(w)$, is called the *density of the income distribution.*

The essential assumption now is that this density $\rho_p(\cdot)$ is a *decreasing function on* $\mathbb{R}_+$, as in Figure 6.6.

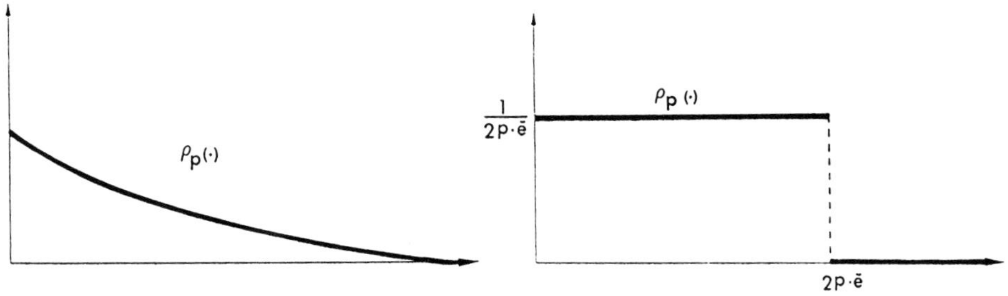

Figure 6.6

Note that this assumption on the shape of the density ρ_p is independent of the price vector p used to define income, even though the density ρ_p itself depends, of course, on the price vector p. Indeed, one easily verifies $V_p(w) = V_q\left(\frac{q\cdot\bar{e}}{p\cdot\bar{e}}w\right)$, hence $\rho_p(w) = \frac{q\cdot\bar{e}}{p\cdot\bar{e}}\,\rho_q\left(\frac{q\cdot\bar{e}}{p\cdot\bar{e}}w\right)$; consequently, if $\rho_p(\cdot)$ is decreasing on $\mathbb{R}_+$, then $\rho_q(\cdot)$ has the same property.

The reader might object that this assumption is not realistic since fortunately there is always some income level below which there are only relatively few individuals. Something can still be said in this case but we will stick to our simple assumption since we only want here to give an illustration of the important role of an assumption on the income distribution. This is the first time we use a "non individualistic" assumption.

Theorem 6.3. Let $\mathcal{E}$ be an exchange economy with a continuum of agents in which each agent has the same preference relation $\succsim$ in $\mathcal{P}_{\substack{mo\\sco}}$ and where the vectors $e(a), a \in A$, of initial endowments are collinear. Assume that the density ρ of the income distribution is decreasing on $\mathbb{R}_+$. Then the excess demand function $Z_{\mathcal{E}}(p)$ has the following property

$$(p-q)\cdot(Z_{\mathcal{E}}(p)-Z_{\mathcal{E}}(q))\leq 0$$

for all price vectors $p, q \in P$ with $p\cdot\bar{e} = q\cdot\bar{e}$, where $\bar{e}$ denotes the mean endowment vector.

Remark . The conclusion of Theorem 6.3. can be strengthened to a strict inequality, i.e.,

$$(p-q)\cdot(Z_{\mathcal{E}}(p)-Z_{\mathcal{E}}(q))< 0$$

for every $p, q \in P$ with $p \neq q$ and $p\cdot\bar{e} = q\cdot\bar{e}$, if we assume that the common preference relation $\succsim$ admits a continuously differentiable utility function with $\partial u(x) \neq 0$ and that the demand function $f(p,b)$ is continuously differentiable in p and b.

Finally we have succeeded in obtaining an additional property of the excess demand function of a class of economies. Let us now look carefully at what this hard–won condition means.

Firstly, it is clear that the property is in fact a property of the mean demand function

$$\Phi_{\mathcal{E}}(p) = \int_{[0,1]} \varphi(\succsim, e(a), p)da$$

of the economy $\mathcal{E}$. The inequality

$$(p-q)\cdot(\Phi_{\mathcal{E}}(p)-\Phi_{\mathcal{E}}(q))\leq 0$$

means that the vector $(p-q)$ of price changes and the vector $(\Phi_{\mathcal{E}}(p) - \Phi_{\mathcal{E}}(q))$ of demand changes point in "opposite" directions, see Figure 6.7.

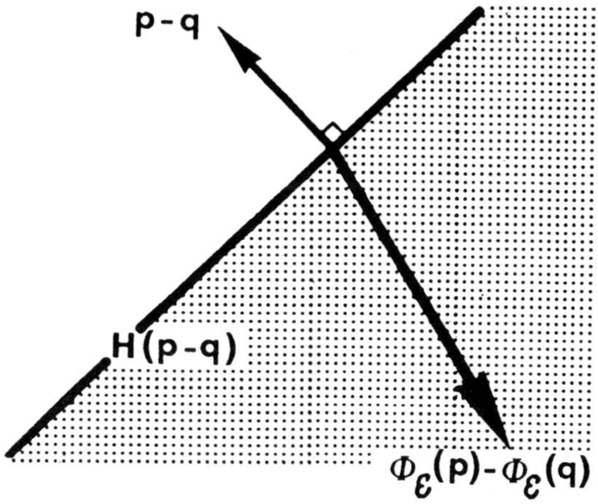

Figure 6.7

Thus our property would correspond to the familiar "law of demand", if it were not for the annoying restriction

$$p \cdot \bar{e} = q \cdot \bar{e}.$$

Unfortunately, this normalization of prices cannot be avoided since the "monotonicity" property of mean demand cannot hold for all prices. Indeed, if there is a price vector $p \in P$ with $Z_{\mathcal{E}}(p) \neq 0$, then there is a price vector $q \in P$ such that $q \cdot Z_{\mathcal{E}}(p) < 0$. Hence we obtain by Walras' Law $q \cdot (\Phi_{\mathcal{E}}(q) - \Phi_{\mathcal{E}}(p)) > 0$. Now, for any $\lambda > 0$ we obtain by homogeneity, $(\lambda p - q) \cdot (\Phi_{\mathcal{E}}(\lambda p) - \Phi_{\mathcal{E}}(q)) = \lambda (p \cdot (\Phi_{\mathcal{E}}(p) - \Phi_{\mathcal{E}}(q)) + q \cdot (\Phi_{\mathcal{E}}(q) - \Phi_{\mathcal{E}}(p))$. The last term is positive, and hence, for λ sufficiently small, the whole expression is positive.

Observe that this "restricted" monotonicity condition is very strong. It does not even hold, in general, for an individual demand function $\varphi(\succsim, e, p)$. In what went before we have lost properties possessed by individual demand functions when we aggregated over agents. Here we gain a property. This shows clearly that in this setting, market demand functions are of a *different nature* than individual demand functions.

Proof of Theorem 6.3. We shall give the proof here under the additional assumption that the common demand function $f(p, w)$ is continuously differentiable in p and w. Furthermore we shall assume that the density is constant on the interval $[0, \overline{w}]$, $\overline{w} = 2p \cdot \overline{e}$, i.e., income is uniformly distributed over $[0, \overline{w}]$. For a proof of the general result we refer to Hildenbrand (1983).

Let $\partial\Phi(p)$ denote the Jacobian matrix of the mean demand function Φ of the economy $\mathcal{E}$, i.e., $\partial\Phi(p)$ is the matrix of partial derivatives

$$\partial\Phi(p) = \begin{pmatrix} \partial_{p_1}\Phi_1(p) & \cdots & \partial_{p_\ell}\Phi_1(p) \\ \vdots & & \vdots \\ \partial_{p_1}\Phi_\ell(p) & \cdots & \partial_{p_\ell}\Phi_\ell(p) \end{pmatrix}$$

Now there is a mathematical result which says that the claimed "restricted" monotonicity property in Theorem 6.3. holds if (and only if) the Jacobian matrix $\partial\Phi(p)$ is *negative semi definite on the hyperplane* $H(\overline{e})$, i.e.,

> for every $p \in P$, and every vector $v \in \mathbb{R}^\ell$, $v \neq 0$, and $v \cdot \overline{e} = 0$ it follows that
> $$v \cdot \partial\Phi(p)v = \sum_i \sum_j v_i v_j \partial_{p_i}\Phi_j(p) \leq 0.$$

We shall prove this result later and show first that the Jacobian matrix $\partial\Phi(p)$ is negative semi definite on $H(\overline{e})$ for every $p \in P$.

We denote the demand function which is derived from the common preference relation $\succsim$ by $f(p, w)$, where w denotes income. To link this definition to our usual notation, observe that $f(p, p \cdot e) = \varphi(\succsim, e, p)$.

If we consider the demand for the i–th good and differentiate it with respect to the price p_j we obtain

$$\partial_{p_j} f_i(p, w(a)) + \partial_w f_i(p, w(a))e_j(a),$$

where $w(a) = p \cdot e(a)$. We denote the Jacobian matrix of the function $p \mapsto f(p, p \cdot e)$ by $\partial f(p, p \cdot e)$. Then we obtain the matrix equation

$$\partial f(p, p \cdot e(a)) = \partial_p f(p, w(a)) + D(p, e(a)),$$

where the element (i, j) of the $(\ell \times \ell)$–matrix D is given by

$$\partial_w f_i(p, w(a))e_j(a).$$

The reader will recall from standard microeconomic theory that the price derivative $\partial_{p_j} f_i(p, w)$ can be decomposed into the Slutsky–substitution term s_{ij} and the income effect term,i.e.,

$$\partial_{p_j} f_i(p, w) = s_{ij}(p, w) - f_j(p, w)\partial_w f_i(p, w).$$

The Slutsky–decomposition reads in matrix notation as

$$\partial_p f(p, w) = S(p, w) - A(p, w),$$

where S is the Slutsky–substitution matrix and A the matrix of income effects.

Hence we obtain for the Jacobian matrix of the demand function $f(p, p \cdot e(a))$,

$$\partial f(p, p \cdot e(a)) = S(p, w(a)) - A(p, w(a)) + D(p, e(a)).$$

From now on we drop the price vector in the notation of the matrices S, A and D since this vector is fixed.

Consequently, the Jacobian matrix $\partial\Phi(p)$ of the mean demand function Φ is given by

$$\begin{aligned}\partial\Phi(p) &= \int_0^1 \partial f(p, p\cdot e(a))da \\ &= \int_0^1 S(w(a))da - \int_0^1 A(w(a))da + \int_0^1 D(e(a))da\ ,\end{aligned}$$

where the integral of a matrix is to be understood as the matrix of the integrals of its elements.

It is well–known that the Slutsky–substitution matrix S is negative semi definite. Consequently, the matrix $\overline{S} = \int S(w(a))da$ is also negative semi definite.

Since initial endowments $e(a)$ are collinear, one easily verifies that the matrix $\overline{D} = \int D(e(a))da$ is of the special form

$$\overline{D} = (d_i \cdot \overline{e}_j)$$

with $d_i = \int \partial_w f_i(p, w(a))\alpha(a)da$, where $e(a) = \alpha(a)\overline{e}$. Hence we obtain

$$\overline{D}v = 0 \text{ for every vector } v \in \mathbb{R}^\ell \text{ with } v\cdot\overline{e} = 0.$$

Thus, it remains to analyze the matrix $\overline{A} = \int A(w(a))da$, the matrix of the mean income effects. Here we shall make use of our assumption on the shape of the density ρ. Since we made the simplifying assumption that income is distributed uniformly, the density ρ is constant on the interval $[0, \overline{w}]$, where $\overline{w} = 2p\cdot\overline{e}$. Thus we obtain

$$\overline{A} = \int_0^1 A(w(a))da = \int_0^\infty A(w)\rho(w)dw = \frac{1}{\overline{w}}\int_0^{\overline{w}} A(w)dw.$$

For the following argument we can assume that $\overline{w} = 1$. Let $v \in \mathbb{R}^\ell$, $v \neq 0$. Then we obtain by definition of $\overline{A}$

$$v\cdot\overline{A}v = \sum_{i=1}^{\ell}\sum_{j=1}^{\ell} v_i v_j \int_0^1 f_j(p,w)\partial_w f_i(p,w)dw$$

$$
\begin{aligned}
&= \int_0^1 \left(\sum_{j=1}^{\ell} v_j f_j(p,w) \right) \left(\sum_{i=1}^{\ell} v_i \partial_w f_i(p,w) \right) dw \\
&= \int_0^1 (v \cdot f(p,w)) \partial_w (v \cdot f(p,w)) dw \\
&= \frac{1}{2} \int_0^1 \partial_w (v \cdot f(p,w))^2 dw \\
&= \frac{1}{2} \left[(v \cdot f(p,1))^2 - (v \cdot f(p,0))^2 \right] \\
&= \frac{1}{2} (v \cdot f(p,1))^2 \geq 0
\end{aligned}
$$

since $f(p,0) = 0$.

To sum up, we have

$$v \cdot \partial\Phi(p) v = v \cdot \overline{S} v - v \cdot \overline{A} v + v \cdot \overline{D} v \ .$$

If $v \cdot \overline{e} = 0$, then we have shown that $\overline{D} v = 0$. Since $v \cdot \overline{S} v \leq 0$ and $v \cdot \overline{A} v \geq 0$, we obtain $v \cdot \partial\Phi v \leq 0$ for every v with $v \cdot \overline{e} = 0$.

This completes the proof that the Jacobian matrix $\partial\Phi$ is negative semi definite on the hyperplane $H(\overline{e})$ which, in turn by the lemma below, implies that the mean demand function has the claimed "restricted" monotonicity property.

Lemma 6.1. Let $F : P \to \mathbb{R}^{\ell}$ be a continuously differentiable function and e any vector in $\mathbb{R}^{\ell}$. Then the following two properties are equivalent:

(i) for every $p \in P$, the Jacobian matrix $\partial F(p)$ is negative semi definite on $H(e)$

(ii) $(p - q) \cdot (F(p) - F(q)) \leq 0$

for every $p, q \in P$ with $p \cdot e = q \cdot e$.

Proof. Given $p, q \in P$, let $v = p - q$ and

$$p(\alpha) = \alpha p + (1-\alpha)q, \qquad 0 \leq \alpha \leq 1 .$$

Define the function $g : [0,1] \to \mathbb{R}$ by

$$g(\alpha) = v \cdot (F(p(\alpha)) - F(q)) .$$

Then we obtain, $g(0) = 0$, $g(1) = (p-q)\cdot(F(p)-F(q))$ and the derivative

$$g'(\alpha) = v \cdot \partial F(p(\alpha))v.$$

Now assume that property (i) holds. If $p \cdot e = q \cdot e$, i.e., $v \cdot e = 0$, then we obtain

$$g'(\alpha) = v \cdot \partial F(p(\alpha))v \leq 0 .$$

Since $g(0) = 0$ and $g'(\alpha) \leq 0$ for all α, it follows that $g(1) \leq 0$, which implies property (ii), since $g(1) = (p-q)\cdot(F(p) - F(q))$.

Conversely, assume property (ii). If $v \cdot e = 0$, then $(p(\alpha) - q) \cdot e = 0$, since $p(\alpha) - q = \alpha(p-q)$. Since $g(\alpha) = \frac{1}{\alpha}(p(\alpha) - q) \cdot (F(p(\alpha)) - F(q))$ it follows by property (ii) that $g(\alpha) \leq 0$ for $\alpha > 0$. Since $g(0) = 0$, this implies that $g'(0) \leq 0$, which proves property (i).

Q.E.D.

Remark. The proof of the lemma shows that the function F is strictly monotonic, i.e.,

$$(p-q) \cdot (F(p) - F(q)) < 0$$

for every $p, q \in P$ with $p \neq q$ and $p \cdot e = q \cdot e$ if for every $p \in P$, the Jacobian matrix $\partial F(p)$ is negative definite on $H(e)$, i.e., $v \cdot \partial F(p)v < 0$ for every $v \neq 0$ and $v \cdot e = 0$. The converse is not true.

The monotonicity property of the excess demand function $Z_{\mathcal{E}}(\cdot)$ has an important consequence on the structure of the set of equilibrium price vectors of the economy $\mathcal{E}$. Indeed, we shall show in the next section that "typically", that is to say for "regular" economies, the set $\Pi_{\mathcal{E}}$ of normalized equilibrium price vectors is a finite set. Thus, if we can show that the set $\Pi_{\mathcal{E}} = \{p \in \Delta \mid Z_{\mathcal{E}}(p) = 0\}$ is convex, then it consists of one vector only, that is to say, for such an economy, the equilibrium price vector is unique (up to normalization).

Proposition 6.2. Let $\mathcal{E}$ be an exchange economy such that the excess demand function $Z_{\mathcal{E}}(\cdot)$ has the restricted monotonicity property:

$$(p - q) \cdot (Z_{\mathcal{E}}(p) - Z_{\mathcal{E}}(q)) \leq 0 \quad \text{for all } p, q \in P \quad \text{with } p \cdot \overline{e} = q \cdot \overline{e}.$$

Then the set $\{p \in P \mid Z_{\mathcal{E}}(p) = 0\}$ of equilibrium price vectors is convex.

Proof. We shall show that

$$\{p \in P \mid Z_{\mathcal{E}}(p) = 0\} = \bigcap_{q \in P} \{p \in P \mid p \cdot Z_{\mathcal{E}}(q) \geq 0\} .$$

This identity then clearly implies the claimed convexity, since the intersection of the convex sets $\{p \in P \mid p \cdot Z_{\mathcal{E}}(q) \geq 0\}, q \in P$, is again convex.

Let $p^* \in P$ with $Z_{\mathcal{E}}(p^*) = 0$. For every $q \in P$, there exists $\lambda > 0$ such that $q \cdot \overline{e} = \lambda p^* \cdot \overline{e}$, since the mean endowment vector $\overline{e}$ belongs to P. Since $Z_{\mathcal{E}}(\lambda p^*) = Z_{\mathcal{E}}(p^*) = 0$ and $q \cdot Z_{\mathcal{E}}(q) = 0$ we obtain

$$-\lambda p^* \cdot Z_{\mathcal{E}}(q) = (\lambda p^* - q) \cdot (Z_{\mathcal{E}}(\lambda p^*) - Z_{\mathcal{E}}(q)) \leq 0$$

by the restricted monotonicity of $Z_{\mathcal{E}}(\cdot)$. Hence we showed that $p^* \cdot Z_{\mathcal{E}}(q) \geq 0$ for all $q \in P$.

Conversely, let $\overline{p} \in P$ be such that $\overline{p} \cdot Z_{\mathcal{E}}(q) \geq 0$ for all $q \in P$. Let $p_\lambda = \lambda q + (1 - \lambda)\overline{p}$. Since $p_\lambda \in P$ we obtain $\overline{p} \cdot Z_{\mathcal{E}}(p_\lambda) \geq 0$. Thus $0 \leq (\overline{p} - p_\lambda) \cdot Z_{\mathcal{E}}(p_\lambda) = \lambda(\overline{p} - q) \cdot Z_{\mathcal{E}}(p_\lambda)$, hence $(\overline{p} - q) \cdot Z_{\mathcal{E}}(p_\lambda) \geq 0$. For λ converging to zero we obtain $(\overline{p} - q) \cdot Z_{\mathcal{E}}(\overline{p}) \geq 0$, hence $q \cdot Z_{\mathcal{E}}(\overline{p}) \leq 0$ for all $q \in P$. This implies $Z_{\mathcal{E}}(\overline{p}) \leq 0$, and consequently, by Walras' Law, we obtain $Z_{\mathcal{E}}(\overline{p}) = 0$.

Q.E.D.

The reader who compares Theorems 6.2. and 6.3. may be a little puzzled. He may believe that there is a contradiction of Theorem 6.3. with the conclusion of Theorem 6.2. where one could choose the relative income distribution at will. Why can one not use the method employed in the proof of Theorem 6.2. to construct a sequence of economies converging to an economy with a continuum of agents as in Theorem 6.3.? Recall the definition of an economy with a continuum of agents, the mean endowment vector must be finite for these economies!

4. Uniqueness

Having seen that the excess demand function of an economy can take essentially any form provided that it satisfies the three basic conditions (i) – (iii) of Section 6.1., we cannot hope that assumptions on individual characteristics alone will help us to establish uniqueness, where uniqueness here, of course, means unique up to normalization of prices. However, it should be emphasized that the *mathematical conditions* needed to guarantee a unique solution to our system of equations are well known and we shall now explain them. The problem is then to find some economically interpretable conditions which will ensure that the mathematical conditions will be satisfied:

Consider a continuously differentiable excess demand function $Z(p)$ of an economy $\mathcal{E}$ and denote by $\Pi_{\mathcal{E}}$ the set of equilibrium prices in Δ.

Recall that the Jacobian matrix, the matrix of partial derivatives,

$$\partial Z(p) = \begin{pmatrix} \partial_{p_1} Z^1(p) & \cdots & \partial_{p_\ell} Z^1(p) \\ \vdots & & \vdots \\ \partial_{p_1} Z^\ell(p) & \cdots & \partial_{p_\ell} Z^\ell(p) \end{pmatrix}$$

is always singular since

$$\partial Z(p) p = 0 \ .$$

Indeed, this follows from homogeneity $Z(\lambda p) = Z(p)$. Differentiating with respect to λ we obtain $\partial Z(\lambda p)p = 0$. Obviously $\lambda = 1$ gives the required property.

In what follows the rank of the Jacobian matrix $\partial Z(p)$ will play an essential role. From the above observation, the rank can at most be $\ell - 1$.

The class of economies $\mathcal{E}$ for which the rank of the Jacobian matrix is maximal, will play an important part in what follows. In view of this we give the following

Definition 6.1. The economy $\mathcal{E}$ is called *regular* if the excess demand $Z(p)$ is continuously differentiable and the Jacobian matrix $\partial Z(p)$ has rank $\ell - 1$ at every p in $\Pi_{\mathcal{E}}$.

The following figures illustrate this concept in the case of two goods:

Figure 6.8

The reader should note, and indeed this is clear from the above diagrams, that the assumption of a regular economy is not restrictive in the differentiable framework. Indeed, if an economy is not regular then by an arbitrarily small change in the initial endowments, keeping preferences fixed, we obtain a regular economy.

The following remark will be useful to establish the regularity of an economy. If p is in $\Pi_{\mathcal{E}}$, then the rank of $\partial Z(p) = \ell - 1$ if and only if the determinant

$$det\ \partial\widehat{Z(p)} \neq 0,$$

where $\partial\widehat{Z(p)}$ is a matrix obtained by deleting the j–th row and the j–th column of $\partial Z(p)$, where j can be chosen arbitrarily. Furthermore, if $p \in \Pi_{\mathcal{E}}$ then the sign of $det\ \partial\widehat{Z(p)}$ does not depend on the index j which is used to delete the row and column.

Theorem 6.4. For every regular economy $\mathcal{E}$ the set $\Pi_{\mathcal{E}}$ of equilibrium price vectors is finite and

$$\sum_{p \in \Pi_{\mathcal{E}}} sign\ det\ - (\partial\widehat{Z(p)}) = 1\ .$$

The first part of this fundamental result is due to Debreu (1970) and the second to Dierker (1982). For more details see Mas–Colell (1985).

The importance of the above result is that it gives a simple mathematical condition for uniqueness. Indeed, if *det* $(-\partial\widehat{Z(p)})$ has *the same sign for all* p in $\Pi_{\mathcal{E}}$ then equilibrium is unique.

The reader should observe that this theorem in no way gives a useful procedure for checking for uniqueness for a particular economy since one has to know all equilibria, and in particular how many there are, in order to verify that *sign det* $(-\partial\widehat{Z(p)}$ is the same for every equilibrium.

Thus, if we can find conditions which guarantee that at any equilibrium price p, *det* $(-\partial\widehat{Z(p)})$ is positive, this theorem gives us uniqueness directly. On the other hand, if there is at least one equilibrium price p^* for which *det* $(-\partial\widehat{Z(p)}) < 0$, then there must be more than one equilibrium.

We now give examples of economically interpretable conditions on the excess demand function of an economy which allow us to apply the theorem, i.e., conditions that guarantee that $det\ (-\partial \widehat{Z(p)}) > 0$. We repeat that these conditions are *ad hoc* and are not derived from underlying individualistic assumptions. It is important to note that all the following conditions are in fact *conditions on the total demand function* of an economy since

$$\partial Z(p) = \partial \Phi(p) \ .$$

I. Gross Substitutability

> **Definition 6.2.** An excess demand function $Z(p)$ has the gross substitutability property at p if the Jacobian matrix $\partial Z(p)$ has positive off diagonal elements.

Since $\partial Z(p)p = 0$, it is clear that then the diagonal elements must be negative.

The economic interpretation of gross substitutability is clear: Demand curves in own prices are decreasing and all complementarities at the aggregate level are excluded. This is clearly a quite restrictive condition. We shall not show that gross substitutability leads to $det\ (-\partial \widehat{Z(p)}) > 0$ since this is implied by the following property, which is itself implied by gross substitutability.

II. Dominant Diagonal

A matrix $A = (a_{ij})$ has dominant diagonal if there exist positive weights w_i such that

$$w_i |a_{ii}| > \sum_{\substack{j=1 \\ j \neq i}}^{n} w_j |a_{ij}| \qquad \text{for all } i \ .$$

It is a standard result that an $n \times n$ matrix with the dominant diagonal property is non singular and furthermore, if it has a *positive* dominant diagonal, i.e., $a_{ii} > 0$ for all i, then $det\ A > 0$.

Clearly the Jacobian of Z(p) cannot have a dominant diagonal since the rank of the matrix $\partial Z(p)$ is at most $\ell - 1$. Therefore, we formulate our definition in terms of $\widehat{\partial Z(p)}$. However, it might happen that the matrix $\widehat{\partial Z(p)}$ has a dominant diagonal if we delete the j–th row and column but not if we delete the row and column for another index.

Definition 6.3. An excess demand function $Z(p)$ has the dominant diagonal property at p if there exists an index j such that the matrix $\widehat{\partial Z(p)}$, where the j–th row and column is deleted, has a negative dominant diagonal.

Loosely speaking, this means that own price effects are more important than all cross price effects together, given a suitable choice of weights. The difference with gross substitutability is that some complementarity is allowed.

If $\widehat{\partial Z(p)}$ has a negative dominant diagonal then $-\widehat{\partial Z(p)}$ has a positive dominant diagonal which implies as we have said that

$$det\ (-\widehat{\partial Z(p)}) > 0\ .$$

III. Negative Definiteness

Recall that a matrix $A = (a_{ij})$ is called negative (resp. positive) definite

$$\text{if} \quad v \cdot Av = \sum_{i,j=1}^{n} v_i v_j a_{ij} < 0 \qquad (\text{resp. } > 0) \qquad \text{for all } v \neq 0 \text{ in } \mathbb{R}^n\ .$$

To see the link between properties II. and III. we remark that a symmetric matrix A is negative definite if and only if it has a negative dominant diagonal. Without symmetry, however, neither property implies the other.

Obviously, a negative definite matrix is non singular. Therefore, for the same reasons as before, we again use $\widehat{\partial Z(p)}$ in the following

Definition 6.4. An excess demand function $Z(p)$ has the negative definite property at p if there exists an index j such that the matrix $\widehat{\partial Z(p)}$, where the j–th row and column is deleted, is negative definite.

Since the determinant of a positive definite matrix is positive then clearly to require that $\widehat{\partial Z(p)}$ be negative definite gives us the condition we need.

To interpret this condition assume that we drop the last row and column of $\partial Z(p)$ and that we set the price $p_\ell = 1$. In effect, we are choosing the ℓ–th good as numéraire. Then our condition implies (see the remark after Lemma 6.1. in the previous section) the following restricted monotonicity property (which now really corresponds to the so–called "Law of Demand") for the total demand system

$$(p - q) \cdot (\Phi(p) - \Phi(q)) < 0 \qquad p \neq q \qquad p_\ell = q_\ell = 1 \ .$$

This condition means that the vector of price changes $p-q$ and the vector of demand changes $\Phi(p) - \Phi(q)$ go in opposite directions. In particular, this implies that for all goods (other than the numéraire) the partial demand curves are downward sloping.

Each of the above conditions leads very directly to the required sign of the determinant. In fact, they are so strong that each of them admits a direct and simple proof of uniqueness. This is particularly obvious for the last condition. There are other conditions available in the literature but they are of the same ad hoc nature, and those that we have given here are enough to illustrate the problem.

To understand why the above conditions can only be derived from individual characteristics in very special examples, it is helpful to examine the Jacobian matrix of the total demand $\Phi(p)$.

Recall that the total demand function $\Phi(p)$ of an exchange economy is defined by

$$\Phi(p) = \sum_{a \in A} \varphi(\succsim_a, e_a, p).$$

It is important to remember that prices intervene in two ways, directly and through income, where the income $w(a)$ of agent a is defined by $w(a) = p \cdot e(a)$. To make this more explicit we denote by $f(\succsim, p, w)$ the demand of an agent with preferences $\succsim$ and income w. Obviously the link between the functions φ and f is

$$f(\succsim, p, p \cdot e) = \varphi(\succsim, e, p).$$

Therefore, we obtain for the Jacobian matrix the following expression (which we used in the proof of Theorem 6.3.)

$$\partial\Phi(p) = \sum_{a \in A} \Big(\partial p_j f_i(\succsim_a, p, w(a))\Big)_{i,j} + \sum_{a \in A} \Big(\partial_w f_i(\succsim_a, p, w(a)) \cdot e_j(a)\Big)_{i,j}$$

We refer to the first matrix as $J(p)$ and the second as $D(p)$.

Recall that our basic question was, can we find individualistic assumptions which will give us the required mathematical property of the total demand function which we discussed above. Now we make the following important observation.

The first matrix, J, depends only on preferences since, once preferences are given, the individual demand function f is completely specified. However, the second matrix although depending, to some extent, on preferences through "the marginal propensity to consume" is crucially influenced by the distribution of initial endowments. Thus, properties of the first matrix can only be obtained by appropriate assumptions on preferences whilst properties of the second depend in an essential way on the distribution of initial resources.

Up to this point we have never imposed any restriction on the distribution of endowments when defining an economy. This is because, a priori, no one distribution is any more acceptable than another. The only distinction that we have made was between the case where the initial endowments were distributed arbitrarily and the extreme case where the endowments were collinear.

In the light of this let us now look at properties of each of the two matrices J and D.

The traditional but somewhat simplistic approach to obtain properties of J is to find conditions on individual preferences which give in turn conditions on individual demand which are preserved if we sum over individuals. If all players are playing the same tune then it is not surprising if the orchestra is playing that tune. An obvious condition on individual demand which has this property is that the Jacobian matrix $\partial_p f(\succsim_a, p, w(a))$ be negative definite. Since the sum of negative definite matrices is negative definite, this gives us the same property on the matrix J. For example, it is well–known that the class of *homothetic* preferences, widely used in the traditional economic literature, yields a negative definite Jacobian.

Another case, but in an economy with a continuum of agents, in which the matrix J can be shown to be negative definite (without assuming that the individual demand functions have this property) was given in the proof of Theorem 6.3.

Now, if we could, by making suitable assumptions, obtain the same property for the matrix D, then we would have completed our task. However, the nature of the matrix D is quite different. For example, if all goods are normal, i.e., if the "marginal propensities to consume " $\partial_w f_i(\succsim_a, p, w(a))$ are positive, then the matrix D has all positive elements. Thus the matrix D is certainly not negative definite. Furthermore, when D is added to J, even if J is negative definite for example, it may destroy this property. Indeed, it can destroy any of the conditions mentioned except for gross substitutability in the following sense that if J has nonnegative off diagonal elements, then $\partial\Phi(p)$ will have the property of gross substitutability, again if all goods are normal. This is independent of the distribution of initial resources. This is the case if utility functions are of the beloved Cobb–Douglas type where all off diagonal elements of J are zero.

Thus, even if, as may be possible, J is manageable, D may create problems. This is true in our simple economies since we impose no restrictions on the distribution of initial endowments. Now one way to avoid this problem would be to impose requirements on this distribution which would make D highly degenerate. Thus if the matrix J is negative definite and if initial endowments are collinear, for example, then the rank of D is one. In this case this implies that the Jacobian $\partial\Phi(p)$ would be negative definite on a hyperplane, which is enough to guarantee that $det\ (-\partial\widehat{Z(p)}) > 0$. Recall that this is precisely the property which we obtained in the proof of Theorem 6.3.

After our classical themes the reader may find this music somewhat difficult to appreciate but we will now give a simple example in which the role of D will become very clear.

Example . We will consider the example which we have already used in Chapter 3.4 since it will be useful for our discussion of stability.

The economy has three individuals and three commodities. We will give directly the individual demand functions although the preferences from which they are derived can be specified.

This example shows very neatly that even with fixed preferences and total endowments, changing the distribution of individual endowments changes radically the properties of the Jacobian matrix $\partial\Phi(p)$. It can have all the desirable properties or none of them.

individual a: $\quad f_a(p,w_a) = \left(\frac{w_a}{p_1+p_2}\,,\ \frac{w_a}{p_1+p_2}\,,\ 0\right)$

individual b: $\quad f_b(p,w_b) = \left(0\,,\ \frac{w_b}{p_2+p_3}\,,\ \frac{w_b}{p_2+p_3}\right)$

individual c: $\quad f_c(p,w_c) = \left(\frac{w_c}{p_1+p_3}\,,\ 0\,,\ \frac{w_c}{p_1+p_3}\right)$

To complete the specification of the economy we have to give the individual endowment vectors $e(a)$, $e(b)$ and $e(c)$. We will fix the total endowment vector at (1,1,1) and consider three possible distributions.

Case 1: $\quad e(a) = (1,0,0),\ e(b) = (0,1,0),\ e(c) = (0,0,1)$

Case 2: $\quad e(a) = (\frac{2}{3},\frac{1}{6},\frac{1}{6}),\ e(b) = (\frac{1}{6},\frac{2}{3},\frac{1}{6}),\ e(c) = (\frac{1}{6},\frac{1}{6},\frac{2}{3})$

Case 3: $\quad e(a) = e(b) = e(c) = (\frac{1}{3},\frac{1}{3},\frac{1}{3})$.

In all three cases, the reader can easily check that there is a unique equilibrium price vector $p^* = (1,1,1)$.

The reader who is still with us at this point will have no difficulty in calculating the matrices J and D at the equilibrium price p^* in each of the three cases. Observe that the matrix J is, of course, the same in each case.

Case 1:

$$\partial\Phi(p^*) = \qquad J \qquad + \qquad D$$

$$= \frac{1}{4}\begin{pmatrix} -2 & -1 & -1 \\ -1 & -2 & -1 \\ -1 & -1 & -2 \end{pmatrix} + \frac{1}{2}\begin{pmatrix} 1 & 0 & 1 \\ 1 & 1 & 0 \\ 0 & 1 & 1 \end{pmatrix} = \frac{1}{4}\begin{pmatrix} 0 & -1 & 1 \\ 1 & 0 & -1 \\ -1 & 1 & 0 \end{pmatrix}$$

One can verify that the matrix $\widehat{\partial\Phi(p^*)}$ has none of the desirable properties; $\widehat{\partial\Phi(p^*)}$ is not negative definite and does not have a dominant diagonal, although the matrix J is negative definite. Observe that the nonnegative matrix D is positive definite.

Case 2:

$$\partial\Phi(p^*) = J + \frac{1}{12}\begin{pmatrix} 5 & 2 & 5 \\ 5 & 5 & 2 \\ 2 & 5 & 5 \end{pmatrix} = \frac{1}{12}\begin{pmatrix} -1 & -1 & 2 \\ 2 & -1 & -1 \\ -1 & 2 & -1 \end{pmatrix}$$

Observe that $\partial\Phi(p^*)$ does not have the gross substitutability property and $\widehat{\partial\Phi(p^*)}$ does not have a dominant diagonal but it is negative definite.

Case 3:

$$\partial\Phi(p^*) = J + \frac{1}{3}\begin{pmatrix} 1 & 1 & 1 \\ 1 & 1 & 1 \\ 1 & 1 & 1 \end{pmatrix} = \frac{1}{12}\begin{pmatrix} -2 & 1 & 1 \\ 1 & -2 & 1 \\ 1 & 1 & -2 \end{pmatrix}$$

In this case $\partial\Phi(p^*)$ has the gross substitutability property and hence $\widehat{\partial\Phi(p^*)}$ has a negative dominant diagonal. Furthermore $\widehat{\partial\Phi(p^*)}$ is negative definite.

5. Stability

Let us now return to our discussion of the adjustment process in Chapter 3.4. As we argued, an equilibrium concept is unsatisfactory, even if it can be shown to be unique, if one cannot specify some adjustment process which will attain it. Any price adjustment process which one might consider is likely to contain an ad hoc element. Yet the idea that economies have a tendency to adjust towards equilibrium is so prevalent in economics that we cannot overlook this question. To illustrate the difficulties, both conceptual and technical, we shall now look at Scarf's example which we discussed both in Chapter 3.4. and in the last section.

Recall the classical tâtonnement adjustment process

$$p(t+1) = p(t) + \lambda Z(p(t))$$

In what follows, when we illustrate the process we will normalize the prices at each step in order to show it in the simplex. In our examples we must, of course, given the initial prices, choose the adjustment speed λ sufficiently small to ensure that we are never led to negative prices.

The evolution of the prices in the three cases of the example we studied in the last section are shown in Figures 6.9, 6.10 and 6.11. In

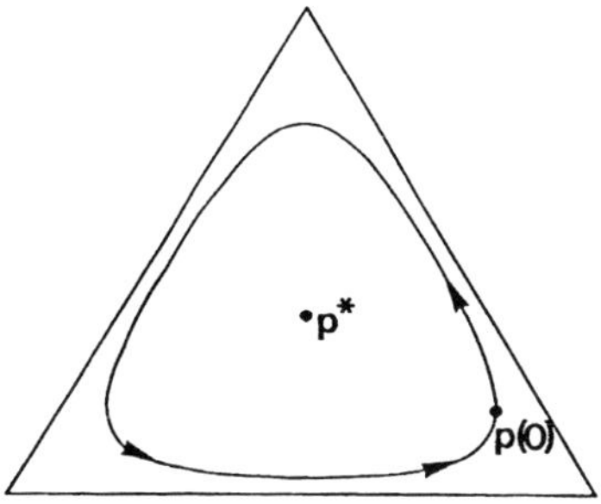

Figure 6.9

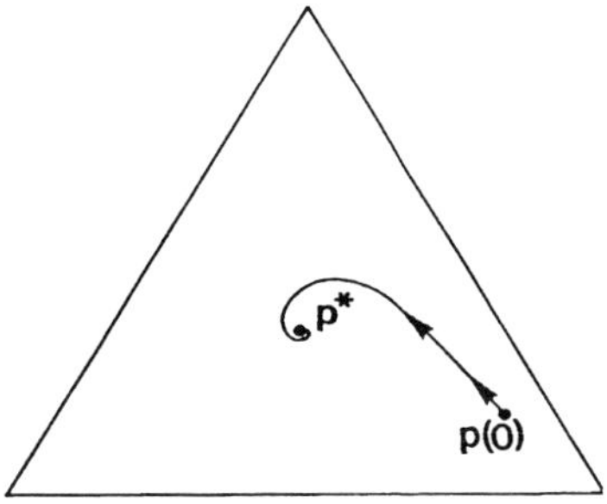

Figure 6.10

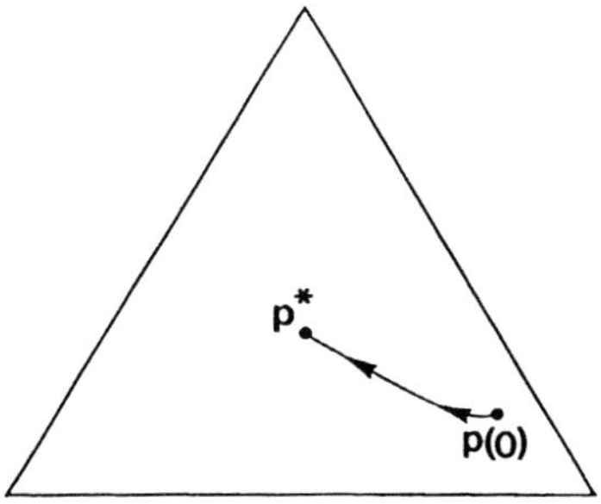

Figure 6.11

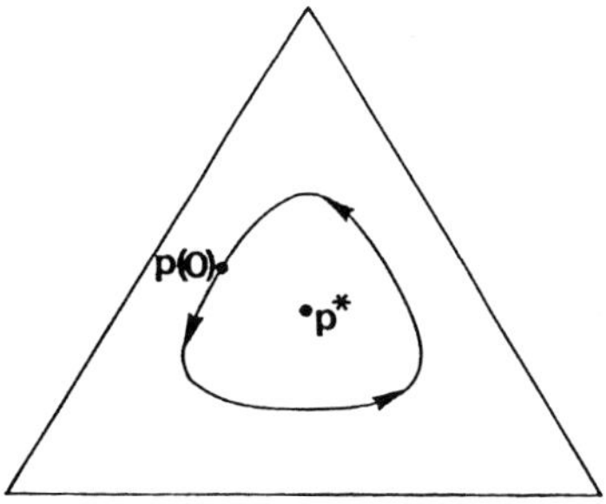

Figure 6.12

each case we started from the initial prices $p(0) = (0.08,\ 0.75,\ 0.17)$ and used $\lambda = 0.0004$. Starting from a different initial price vector we get similar pictures in each case. To illustrate this in case 1 we also initiated the process at $p = (0.43,\ 0.14,\ 0.43)$ (see Figure 6.12).

Recall that in all three cases there is a unique equilibrium vector $p = (\frac{1}{3}, \frac{1}{3}, \frac{1}{3})$ but the Jacobian matrix at these prices has quite different properties. This clearly shows that the problems of uniqueness and stability must not be confounded.

Next we want to point out that although the equilibrium prices do not depend on the adjustment process that we choose, the evolution of prices, however, does. In case 1 of our example consider the alternative adjustment process that we specified in Chapter 3.4.

$$p(t+1) = p(t) + \lambda\, max\ (0, Z(p)).$$

As before we normalize at each step. We illustrate the evolution of prices from two starting vectors $p(0) = (0.08,\ 0.75,\ 0.17)$ and p(0)=(0.333, 0.333, 0.334) (see Figures 6.13, 6.14).

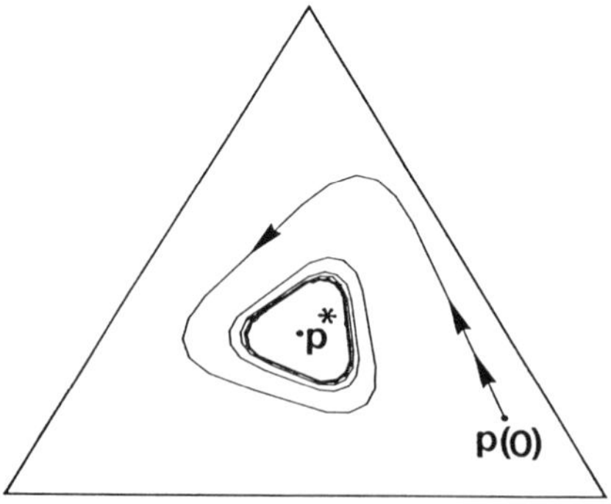

Figure 6.13

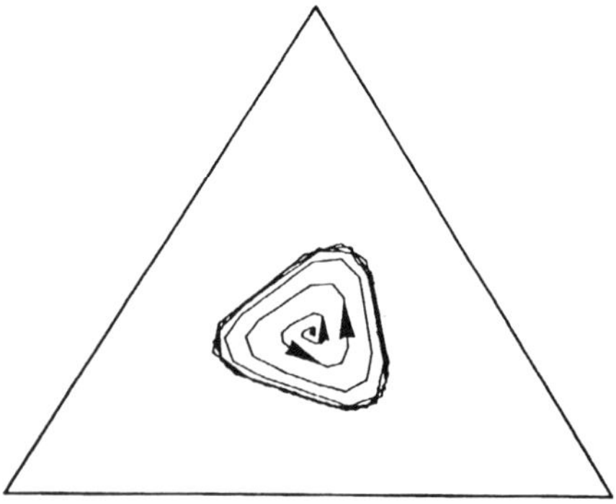

Figure 6.14

The main difference between the two adjustment processes is that in the first case starting near equilibrium we remain near equilibrium but in a closed orbit. In the second case even starting very close to equilibrium we move out to a closed orbit which may be far from equilibrium.

Finally we want to illustrate the importance of the choice of the speed of adjustment λ even in the case where the prices always converge to the unique equilibrium. In this case we do not specify the excess demand function which is derived from so–called "constant elasticity of substitution" utility functions. In Figure 6.15 we chose λ to be fifty times larger than in Figure 6.16.

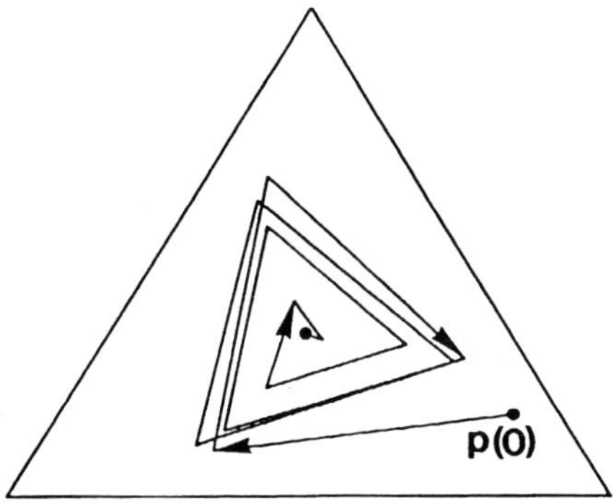

Figure 6.15

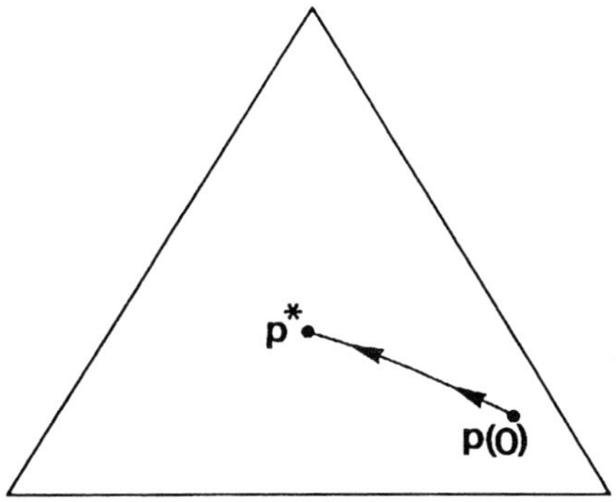

Figure 6.16

The figures clearly show how by diminishing the adjustment speed we smooth the price path. This suggests pushing this idea to the limit and formulating an adjustment process in continuous time. This instantaneous adjustment process might seem far–fetched to the reader but it simplifies the mathematical treatment considerably.

6. Tâtonnement in Continuous Time

In this context the evolution of prices $p(t)$ is considered to be a differentiable function where t goes from 0 to infinity and the price adjustment rule is given by

$$\frac{d}{dt}p(t) = Z(p(t)) .$$

It can be shown that, under suitable conditions, this differential equation always has a solution. That is to say, for every starting point p_0 there exists a differentiable function $p(t)$ with $p(0) = p_0$ which satisfies the equation

$$\frac{d}{dt}p(t) = Z(p(t)) .$$

There are various stability concepts in the mathematical literature. Three are of particular interest. The first requires that if the process starts sufficiently near equilibrium it should stay near equilibrium. This, of course, would not rule out the sort of behaviour illustrated in Figure 6.9 and 6.12. For an economist a concept more in keeping with the idea of the "invisible hand" is that if the process starts sufficiently near an equilibrium it converges to this equilibrium. Both of these concepts are "local" concepts. If in the second case the process converges to an equilibrium from any price vector then we speak of "global stability".

We will not give a thorough treatment of this problem on which there is an extensive literature. We shall confine ourselves to studying a particular case. We shall examine the case in which we consider exchange economies with one commodity, say the last, chosen as "numéraire". That is, we fix the price of that commodity once and for all to be equal to one. This implies of course that we have to slightly modify the adjustment process we specified and adjust only the remaining $\ell - 1$ prices.

Theorem 6.5. Let $\mathcal{E}$ be an exchange economy with a continuously differentiable excess demand function $Z(p)$. Assume that $Z(p)$ is monotonic in prices in terms of the numéraire, i.e., for every pair of price vectors p and q with $p \neq q$ and $p_\ell = q_\ell = 1$ we have

$$(p - q) \cdot (Z(p) - Z(q)) < 0 .$$

Then the equilibrium price p^* is unique and globally stable.

Proof. Let $p(t)$ denote the solution of the system of differential equations

$$\begin{aligned}\frac{d}{dt}p_1(t) &= Z_1(p_1(t), \ldots, p_{\ell-1}(t), 1)\\ \frac{d}{dt}p_{\ell-1}(t) &= Z_{\ell-1}(p_1(t), \ldots, p_{\ell-1}(t), 1)\\ \frac{d}{dt}p_\ell(t) &= 0\end{aligned}$$

with the arbitrary positive starting price vector $p(0) = (p_1(0), \ldots, p_{\ell-1}(0), 1)$. We have already shown that the equilibrium price vector $p^* = (p_1^*, \ldots, p_{\ell-1}^*, 1)$ is unique. We shall now show that the distance between $p(t)$ and p^* goes to zero as t goes to infinity. For this we show that the function

$$L(p(t)) = \frac{1}{2}\sum_{i=1}^{\ell}(p_i(t) - p_i^*)^2$$

tends to zero as t goes to infinity. First we show that $\frac{d}{dt}\, L(p(t)) < 0$ for all t. Indeed,

$$\frac{d}{dt}L(p(t)) = \sum_{i=1}^{\ell}(p_i(t) - p_i^*)\frac{d}{dt}p_i(t).$$

Since $p(t)$ is a solution of the system of differential equations, $p_\ell(t) = p_\ell^* = 1$, and $Z(p^*) = 0$ we obtain

$$\frac{d}{dt}L(p(t)) = \sum_{i=1}^{\ell}(p_i(t) - p_i^*)(Z_i(p(t)) - Z_i(p^*)) < 0,$$

by monotonicity.

Thus we have shown that the function $t \mapsto L(p(t))$ – and hence the distance of $p(t)$ to p^* – is strictly decreasing as t becomes large. Therefore to show that $lim_{t\to\infty} L(p(t)) = 0$, it suffices to show that there is at least one sequence (t_n) converging to infinity such that $lim_{n\to\infty} L(p(t_n)) = 0$. Since $\frac{d}{dt}L(p(t)) < 0$ and $L(p(t)) \geq 0$ for all t, there exists a sequence (t_n) converging to infinity such that

$$\frac{d}{dt}L(p(t_n)) \longrightarrow 0 .$$

The sequence $(p(t_n))_{n=1,\ldots}$ of price vectors is bounded since the function $L(p(t))$ is decreasing. Hence, there exists a converging subsequence $(p(t_{n_k}))_{k=1,\ldots}$, say $p(t_{n_k}) \to \overline{p}$. Since

$$\frac{d}{dt}L(p(t_{n_k})) = (p(t_{n_k}) - p^*) \cdot (Z(p(t_{n_k})) - Z(p^*)) ,$$

we obtain as k goes to infinity,

$$0 = (\overline{p} - p^*) \cdot (Z(\overline{p}) - Z(p^*)) .$$

Hence, by monotonicity of $Z(\cdot)$, we obtain $\overline{p} = p^*$.

Q.E.D.

The reader may well feel disappointed that we have only shown stability in a special case and, of course, one can find other assumptions in the literature which also give stability. However, as he will be well aware from the previous discussion, there is no hope that we can avoid restricting ourselves to more or less ad hoc assumptions and we have just chosen one which allows a very simple proof.

7. Conclusions

Let us recall in concluding this chapter and our book how far we have come and, more importantly, how far we have to go. We have shown that under standard assumptions on individual characteristics we can prove the existence of competitive equilibrium. Furthermore these assumptions can be weakened in large economies. Large orchestras can cover up erratic individual performances! We have shown the relationship between our two themes — those of competition and cooperation — and in large economies found them to be in harmony, and in very large economies, identical.

However, when we attempted to give the competitive solution more content by examining the questions of its uniqueness and its stability in terms of the classical "tâtonnement" adjustment process, we ran into a fundamental problem. There are no assumptions on the isolated individuals which will give us the properties of aggregate behaviour which we need to obtain uniqueness and stability. Thus we are reduced to making assumptions at the aggregate level which we cannot justify by the usual individualistic assumptions. This problem is usually avoided in the macroeconomic literature by assuming that the economy behaves as an individual. Such an assumption cannot be justified in the context of the standard economic model and the way to solve this problem may involve rethinking the very basis on which this model is founded. The reader who has successfully accompanied us to this point should therefore now understand both the essential content and the fundamental limitations of modern economic analysis. As we said at the outset, maybe one of our readers will compose the new theme which will enable us to find our way out of this impasse!

Mathematical Appendix I

Topological Concepts in $\mathbb{R}^\ell$

The topological structure of $\mathbb{R}^\ell$ is built on the topological properties of the real numbers $\mathbb{R}$. We can safely assume that the reader is familiar with $\mathbb{R}$. Let us just recall the fundamental properties of $\mathbb{R}$.

Proposition AI.1. Every non–empty subset S of $\mathbb{R}$ which is bounded from below (above) has an infimum (supremum). The infimum of S, written $inf(S)$, is defined by the properties:

(i) $inf(S) \leq x$ for every $x \in S$,

(ii) for every $\epsilon > 0$ there exists $x \in S$ with $x < inf(S) + \epsilon$.

The supremum of S, written $sup(S)$, is defined by the properties:

(i) $x \leq sup(S)$ for every $x \in S$,

(ii) for every $\epsilon > 0$ there exists $x \in S$ with $sup(S) - \epsilon < x$.

If the number $inf(S)$ ($sup(S)$) belongs to the set S then we express this by writing $min(S)$ instead of $inf(S)$ ($max(S)$ instead of $sup(S)$).

Definition AI.1. A sequence $(\lambda_n)_{n=1,\ldots}$ in $\mathbb{R}$ is said to be convergent to $\lambda \in \mathbb{R}$ if for every $\epsilon > 0$ there exists an integer $\bar{n}$ such that

$$\lambda - \epsilon < \lambda_n < \lambda + \epsilon \qquad \text{for all } n > \bar{n} .$$

This can be written as

$$|\lambda_n - \lambda| < \epsilon \qquad \text{for all} \quad n > \bar{n} .$$

It follows immediately from the fundamental property (i) that every increasing (decreasing) sequence $(\lambda_n)_{n=1\ldots}$ which is bounded from above (below) in $\mathbb{R}$ converges to $sup\{\lambda_1, \lambda_2, \ldots\}$ ($inf\{\lambda_1, \lambda_2, \ldots\}$).

1. Convergence in $\mathbb{R}^\ell$

Definition AI.2. A sequence $(x_n)_{n=1,2,\ldots}$ of points in $\mathbb{R}^\ell$ is said to converge to the point $x \in \mathbb{R}^\ell$ (written $x_n \to x$) if the sequence (x_n) converges coordinate–wise, that is to say, if for every $h = 1, \ldots, \ell$ the sequence $(x_n^h)_{n=1,\ldots}$ of real numbers converges to the real number x^h.

The point x is called the *limit* of the sequence (x_n); this is also written $x = lim_{n \to \infty} x_n$. Alternatively, we could have defined convergence of a sequence (x_n) in $\mathbb{R}^\ell$ by using the concept of distance between two points x, y in $\mathbb{R}^\ell$, e.g.,

the *Euclidean distance* $\quad \|x - y\| = \sqrt{(x^1 - y^1)^2 + \ldots + (x^\ell - y^\ell)^2}$,

the *sum distance* $\quad |x - y| = |x^1 - y^1| + \ldots + |x^\ell - y^\ell|$,

the *sup distance* $\quad |||x - y||| = sup_{h=1,\ldots,\ell} |x^h - y^h|$.

One can easily verify that $x_n \to x$ according to our original definition if and only if $\|x_n - x\| \to 0$, $|x_n - x| \to 0$, or $|||x_n - x||| \to 0$. This fact is expressed by saying that convergence of a sequence in $\mathbb{R}^\ell$ is a topological concept. It does not depend on the particular choice of one of the three distances (indeed there are more than three!).

2. Closed and Open Sets

Definition AI.3. A subset F of $\mathbb{R}^\ell$ is said to be closed if the limit of every convergent sequence in F belongs to F, i.e., if $x_n \to x$ and $x_n \in F$ for $n = 1, 2, \ldots$ then $x \in F$.

Examples. Given a point $z \in \mathbb{R}^\ell$ and a real number $r > 0$, the sets

$$F_1 = \{x \in \mathbb{R}^\ell \mid |x - z| \leq r\},$$
$$F_2 = \{x \in \mathbb{R}^\ell \mid \|x - z\| \leq r\}$$
and
$$F_3 = \{x \in \mathbb{R}^\ell \mid |||x - z||| \leq r\}$$

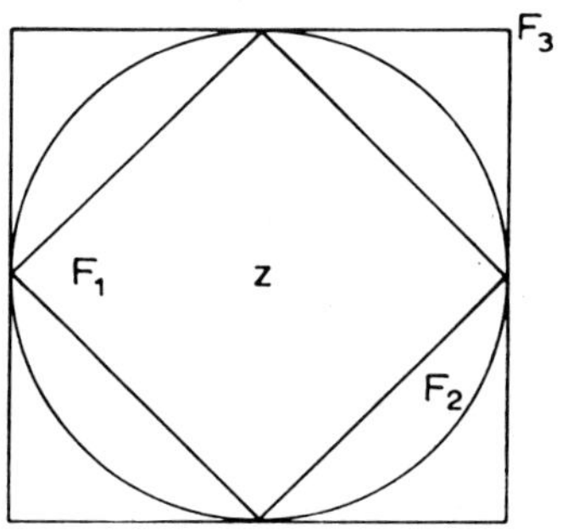

Figure AI.1

are closed. These sets are called "balls" with centre z and radius r. Of course, as is clear from Figure AI.1., only the set F_2, which is defined with respect to the Euclidean distance, coincides with the intuitive meaning of the word "ball".

Proposition AI.2. The intersection of any collection of closed sets is closed. The union of finitely many closed sets is closed.

Proof. Denote the collection of closed sets by $\{F_i\}_{i\in I}$. Let $x_n \in \bigcap_{i\in I} F_i$ $(n = 1,\ldots)$ and $x_n \to x$. Since F_i is closed it follows that $x \in F_i$, $i \in I$. Hence $x \in \bigcap_{i\in I} F_i$.

Let $x_n \in F_1 \cup \ldots \cup F_n$ and $x_n \to x$. Since there are only finitely many sets F_i there must be at least one such set, say F_i, which contains infinitely many points x_n, say $x_{n_1}, x_{n_2}, \ldots$. The subsequence (x_{n_q}) also converges to x and since F_i is closed it follows that $x \in F_i$. Hence $x \in F_1 \cup \ldots \cup F_n$.

Q.E.D.

Definition AI.4. The closure of a set $S \subset \mathbb{R}^\ell$ is the smallest closed set which contains the set S; it is denoted by $\bar{S}$.

More precisely, $\bar{S}$ is the intersection of all the closed sets in $\mathbb{R}^\ell$ which contain the set S. By Proposition AI.2., $\overline{S}$ itself is closed.

$$\bar{S} = \bigcap \{G \mid G \text{ is closed and } S \subset G\} .$$

Definition AI.5. A subset G of $\mathbb{R}^\ell$ is said to be open if its complement $\mathbb{R}^\ell \setminus G$ is closed.

Examples. Given a point $z \in \mathbb{R}^\ell$ and a real number $r > 0$ the sets

$$G_1 = \{x \in \mathbb{R}^\ell \mid |x - z| < r\},$$
$$G_2 = \{x \in \mathbb{R}^\ell \mid \|x - z\| < r\}$$
$$\text{and} \qquad G_3 = \{x \in \mathbb{R}^\ell \mid |||x - z||| < r\}$$

are open; they are called *open* balls with centre z and radius r.

Proposition AI.3. A subset G of $\mathbb{R}^\ell$ is open if and only if for every $z \in G$ there exists a ball with centre z and radius $r > 0$ which is contained in G.

Proof. Let G be open. Assume to the contrary that there is a point $z \in G$ such that every ball $B_r(z)$ with centre z and radius $r > 0$ contains a point, say x_r, which does not belong to G. By setting $r = \frac{1}{n}$ $(n = 1, \ldots)$ we obtain a sequence of balls becoming smaller and smaller. But $\mathbb{R}^\ell \setminus G$ is closed, therefore we obtain $z \in \mathbb{R}^\ell \setminus G$ which is a contradiction.

Assume now that for every point z in G there is also a ball $B_r(z)$ in G with $r > 0$. We have to show that $\mathbb{R}^\ell \setminus G$ is closed. Thus, let (x_n) be a sequence in $\mathbb{R}^\ell \setminus G$ and assume $x_n \to x$. If x belonged to G then there would exist a ball $B_r(x) \subset G$ with centre x and radius $r > 0$. But then it follows that $x_n \in B_r(x)$ for n large enough since the sequence (x_n) converges to x. Hence, $x \in \mathbb{R}^\ell \setminus G$ which proves that $\mathbb{R}^\ell \setminus G$ is closed, and hence that G is open.

Q.E.D.

Considering the complements of the appropriate sets, it follows immediately from Proposition AI.2. that:

Proposition AI.4. The union of any collection of open sets is open. The intersection of finitely many open sets is open.

Definition AI.6. A neighbourhood U of a point x in $\mathbb{R}^\ell$ is a subset which contains an open set G such that the point x belongs to G. Thus,

$$x \in G \subset U, \qquad \text{where } G \text{ is open.}$$

A ball with centre x and radius $r > 0$ is a special neighbourhood of the point x. Conversely, every neighbourhood U of a point x contains a ball $B_r(x)$ with centre x and radius $r > 0$.

Definition AI.7. A neighbourhood U of a subset S of $\mathbb{R}^\ell$ is a subset containing an open set G which contains S, i.e.,

$$S \subset G \subset U, \qquad \text{where } G \text{ is open.}$$

A particular neighbourhood of a set S is given by

$$\{x \in \mathbb{R}^\ell |\ \|x - z\| < r \ \text{ for some } z \in S\}\ ,\ r > 0\ .$$

By abuse of language we call this set a ball around the set S with radius r as in Figure AI.2.

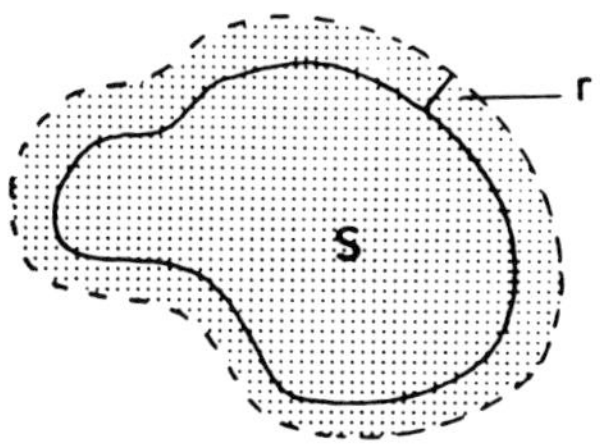

Figure AI.2

Definition AI.8. A point x is called a boundary point of the set $S \subset \mathbb{R}^\ell$ if every neighbourhood U of x has a non–empty intersection with S and $\mathbb{R}^\ell \setminus S$. The set of all boundary points of S is called the boundary of S and is denoted by ∂S.

Thus $x \in \partial S$ if and only if for every neighbourhood U of x it follows that

$$U \cap S \neq \emptyset \quad \text{and} \quad U \cap (\mathbb{R}^\ell \setminus S) \neq \emptyset \, .$$

Clearly, $\partial S \subset \bar{S}$, hence a closed set contains its boundary.

In many applications one only considers sets which belong to a certain given subset X of $\mathbb{R}^\ell$. In this case one must be careful to make the distinction between the terms "open" or "closed" referring to the whole space $\mathbb{R}^\ell$ and "open" or "closed" relative to the subset X.

Definition AI.9. A subset F of $X \subset \mathbb{R}^\ell$ is said to be closed relative to X if $x_n \to x$, $x_n \in F$ and $x \in X$ implies $x \in F$.

Clearly, if $F \subset \mathbb{R}^\ell$ is closed in $\mathbb{R}^\ell$ then $F \cap X$ is closed relative to X. If the set X is closed in $\mathbb{R}^\ell$ then every subset of X which is closed relative to X is also closed in $\mathbb{R}^\ell$. However, if X is not closed, then there are subsets of X which are closed relative to X but not closed in $\mathbb{R}^\ell$ (e.g. X itself)!

Definition AI.10. A subset G of $X \subset \mathbb{R}^\ell$ is said to be open relative to X if $X \setminus G$ is closed relative to X.

Clearly, if $G \subset \mathbb{R}^\ell$ is open in $\mathbb{R}^\ell$ then $G \cap X$ is open relative to X. If the set X is open, then every subset of X which is open relative to X is also open in $\mathbb{R}^\ell$. However, if X is not open, then there are subsets of X which are open relative to X but not open in $\mathbb{R}^\ell$ (e.g. X itself)! For example, the "preferred sets" $\{x \in \mathbb{R}^\ell_+ \mid x \succ z\}$ of a continuous preference relation are open relative to $\mathbb{R}^\ell_+$.

Definition AI.11. A subset B of $\mathbb{R}^\ell$ is called bounded if there are two points $\underline{x}$ and $\overline{x}$ of $\mathbb{R}^\ell$ such that

$$\underline{x} \leq x \leq \overline{x} \qquad \text{for every } x \in B\ .$$

Alternatively, we can define $B \subset \mathbb{R}^\ell$ to be bounded if there is a ball $B_r(0)$ with centre 0 and radius $r < \infty$ which contains the set B.

The following result is fundamental and was basic to arguments in the earlier chapters.

Proposition AI.5. Let K be a subset of $\mathbb{R}^\ell$. Then the following assertions are equivalent:

(i) K is closed and bounded.

(ii) For every sequence $(x_n)_{n=1,2,\ldots}$ in K there exists a convergent subsequence $(x_{n_q})_{q=1,2,\ldots}$ whose limit belongs to K.

(iii) For every open covering $\{G_i\}_{i\in I}$ of K (i.e., the sets G_i are open and $K \subset \bigcup_{i\in I} G_i$) there exists a finite sub–covering of K (i.e., there exists a finite subset $E \subset I$ such that $K \subset \bigcup_{i\in E} G_i$).

(iv) Every collection $\{F_i\}_{i\in I}$ of closed sets with the finite intersection property (i.e., for every finite subset $E \subset I$ follows $\bigcap_{i\in E} F_i \neq \emptyset$) has a non–empty intersection, i.e., $\bigcap_{i\in I} F_i \neq \emptyset$.

A subset $K \subset \mathbb{R}^\ell$ having these properties is called *compact*. It is worth noting that the above result only holds since K is a subset of $\mathbb{R}^\ell$, and these statements are not equivalent for subsets of more general spaces.

Definition AI.12. Let $S \subset \mathbb{R}^\ell$ and $T \subset \mathbb{R}^m$. A mapping f of S into T is said to be continuous at $x \in S$ if for every sequence $(x_n)_{n=1,\ldots}$ converging to x it follows that the sequence $(f(x_n))_{n=1,\ldots}$ converges to $f(x)$. The mapping $f : S \to T$ is said to be continuous if it is continuous at every point of S.

Alternatively, instead of using converging sequences we can define continuity of $f : S \to T$ at x in terms of neighbourhoods: f is continuous at x if for every neighbourhood U of $f(x)$ there exists a neighbourhood V of x such that $f(z) \in U$ for every $z \in V$.

Proposition AI.6. The mapping $f : S \to T$ is continuous if and only if the inverse image $f^{-1}(G) = \{x \in S |\ f(x) \in G\}$ of open (closed) subsets in T is open (closed) in S.

Proposition AI.7. If $f : S \to T$ is continuous then the image $f(K)$ of a compact subset K in S is compact.

Proposition AI.8. Every closed subset K of a compact set X is compact.

Since we know that every bounded and closed subset of $\mathbb{R}$ has a greatest and smallest number it follows from Proposition AI.7. that

Proposition AI.9. Every continuous function of a compact set S into $\mathbb{R}$ admits a maximum and minimum, i.e., there exist points x_* and x^* in S such that

$$f(x_*) \leq f(x) \leq f(x^*) \qquad \text{for every } x \in S \ .$$

Mathematical Appendix II

Separation of Convex Sets

Definition AII.1. A subset C of $\mathbb{R}^\ell$ is said to be *convex* if for $x, y \in C$ the segment

$$[x, y] = \{z \in \mathbb{R}^\ell |\ z = \lambda x + (1 - \lambda)y,\ 0 \leq \lambda \leq 1\}$$

belongs to C, i.e., $\lambda x + (1 - \lambda)y \in C$ for every λ with $0 \leq \lambda \leq 1$. In Figure AII.1 the set C is convex but D is not.

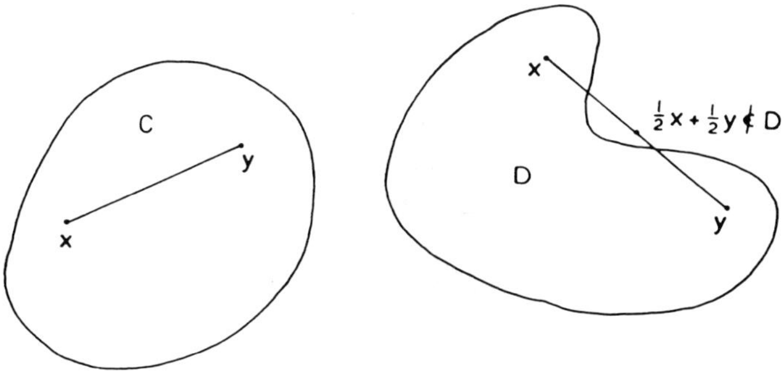

Figure AII.1

Examples.

(1) The ball $B_r(z)$ with centre z and radius $r > 0$ is convex.

(2) The positive (negative) orthant $\mathbb{R}^\ell_+$ ($\mathbb{R}^\ell_-$) is convex.

(3) The cube $Q = \{x \in \mathbb{R}^\ell | \; 0 \leq x \leq \bar{x}\}$, $\bar{x} \in \mathbb{R}^\ell$ is convex.

(4) The solution set of a system of linear equations (inequalities) in ℓ variables forms a convex set.

The following results are easy to prove:

(1) The closure $\bar{C}$ of a convex set C in $\mathbb{R}^\ell$ is convex.

(2) If C is a convex set in $\mathbb{R}^\ell$ and λ any number, then the set

$$\lambda C := \{z \in \mathbb{R}^\ell | \; z = \lambda x, \; x \in C\}$$

is convex.

(3) The sum

$$A + B := \{z \in \mathbb{R}^\ell | \; z = x + y, \; x \in A, \; y \in B\}$$

of convex sets is convex.

(4) Let $\{C_i\}_{i \in I}$ be a collection of convex sets in $\mathbb{R}^\ell$ then the set

$$\bigcap\nolimits_{i \in I} C_i$$

is convex.

(5) Let X be a subset of $\mathbb{R}^\ell$ then

$$co \; X = \bigcap \{C \subset \mathbb{R}^\ell | C \text{ is convex and } \; X \subset C\} \; ,$$

called convex hull of X, is the smallest convex subset of $\mathbb{R}^\ell$ containing X.

Definition AII.2. The set of solutions of one linear equation in ℓ variables is called a *hyperplane* in $\mathbb{R}^\ell$, that is to say, for every vector $p \in \mathbb{R}^\ell$, $p \neq 0$, and every $\alpha \in \mathbb{R}^\ell$ the set

$$H(p,\alpha) := \{x \in \mathbb{R}^\ell |\ p^1x^1 + p^2x^2 + \ \ldots\ + p^\ell x^\ell = \alpha\}$$

is a hyperplane. The vector p is called a normal to the hyperplane $H(p,\alpha)$.

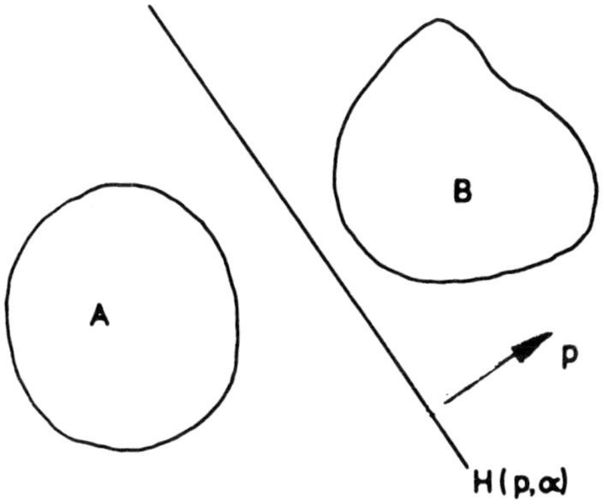

Figure AII.2

We say that the hyperplane $H(p,\alpha) \subset \mathbb{R}^\ell$ *separates* the two sets A and B in $\mathbb{R}^\ell$ if

$$p \cdot x \leq \alpha \leq p \cdot y \quad \text{for every } x \in A \text{ and every } y \in B.$$

This is also expressed by saying that the sets A and B lie in different half–spaces generated by the hyperplane $H(p,\alpha)$, as in Figure AII.2.

Proposition AII.1. Let C be a non–empty closed and convex subset in $\mathbb{R}^\ell$ and $z \notin C$. Then there exist a point $y \in C$ and a hyperplane $H(p, \alpha)$ through y (i.e., $\alpha = y \cdot p$) such that

$$p \cdot z < p \cdot y = inf_{x \in C}\, p \cdot x \ ,$$

that is to say, the point z lies below the hyperplane and the set C lies on or above the hyperplane.

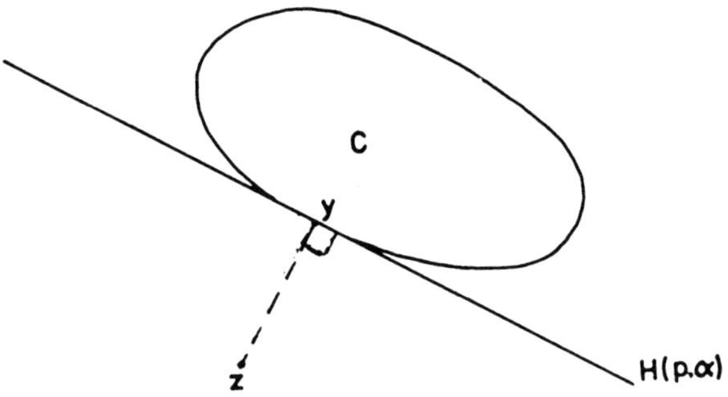

Figure AII.3

Proof. First we show that there is a point $y \in C$ which is nearest to the point z (see Figure AII.3), where the nearness is measured by the Euclidean distance $\|z - y\|$. In order to show this let x_0 be any point in C. The set

$$B = \{x \in C |\ \|z - x\| \leq \|z - x_0\|\}$$

is compact (and non–empty). The distance function $x \to \|z - x\|$ is continuous on B. Therefore (Mathematical Appendix I, Proposition AI.9.), there exists a minimum, i.e., a point $y \in C$ such that

$$0 < \|z - y\| \leq \|z - x\| \quad \text{for every } x \in C \ .$$

Now we define $p = y - z$ and $\alpha = p \cdot y$ and claim that $H(p, \alpha)$ is the desired hyperplane. Indeed, z lies below the hyperplane $H(p, \alpha)$ since

$$p \cdot z = p \cdot z - p \cdot y + p \cdot y = -p \cdot p + p \cdot y < p \cdot y = \alpha \, .$$

Assume the set C does not lie on or above the hyperplane, i.e., assume there is a point $x \in C$ with $p \cdot x < \alpha$. Let $x_\lambda = \lambda x + (1 - \lambda)y$. By a simple calculation we obtain

$$\|z - y\|^2 - \|z - x_\lambda\|^2 = \lambda[2p \cdot (y - x) - \lambda(y - x) \cdot (y - x)] \, .$$

Since by assumption $p \cdot (y - x) > 0$ we obtain, for λ sufficiently small,

$$\|z - y\| > \|z - x_\lambda\|.$$

Since $x_\lambda \in C$ for $0 < \lambda < 1$ we have a contradiction as the point y was chosen as the nearest point in C to z.

Q.E.D.

The following separation theorem was used in Chapter 5.

Theorem AII.1. Let C be a convex set of $\mathbb{R}^\ell$ and $z \notin C$. Then there exists a hyperplane $H(p, \alpha)$ through z which separates z and C, i.e.,

$$p \cdot z = \alpha \leq p \cdot x \quad \text{for every } x \in C \, .$$

Proof. If $z \notin \bar{C}$, the closure of C, then there exists by Proposition AII.1., a vector $p \in \mathbb{R}^\ell$, $p \neq 0$, such that $p \cdot z < p \cdot x$ for every $x \in C$. Hence, the desired hyperplane is $H(p, p \cdot z)$. If $z \in \bar{C}$ there exists a sequence $(z_n)^*$ converging to z with $z_n \notin \bar{C}$ $(n = 1, \ldots)$. Hence there exist normals $p_n \in \mathbb{R}^\ell$, $p_n \neq 0$, such that

$$p_n \cdot z_n < p \cdot x \quad \text{for every } x \in \bar{C} \ .$$

Let $q_n = p_n/|p_n|$ $(n = 1, \ldots)$. The sequence of vectors q_n is bounded (it belongs to the unit simplex) and therefore (Mathematical Appendix I, Proposition AI.5) there exists a converging subsequence, say $q_{n_t} \underset{t}{\rightarrow} p$. Clearly, $p \neq 0$. Since the scalar product is continuous it follows that

$$p \cdot z \leq p \cdot x \quad \text{for every } x \in \bar{C} \ .$$

Hence, $H(p, p \cdot z)$ is the desired hyperplane.

Q.E.D.

Corollary (Minkowski's theorem). Let A and B be non–empty convex subsets in $\mathbb{R}^\ell$ with $A \cap B = \emptyset$. Then there exists a hyperplane separating the sets A and B.

Proof. The set $C = A - B$ is convex and $0 \notin C$. Hence, there exists $p \in \mathbb{R}^\ell$, $p \neq 0$, such that $0 \leq p \cdot x$ for every $x \in C$. Thus, if $y \in A$ and $z \in B$, then $x = z - y \in C$ and we have $0 \leq p \cdot x$, i.e., $p \cdot y \leq p \cdot z$ for every $y \in A$ and every $z \in B$.

Q.E.D.

We close this section by stating the following result.

Proposition AII.2 (Caratheodory). Let A be a subset of $\mathbb{R}^\ell$. Then every point $x \in co\ A$ is the convex combination of $\ell + 1$ points in A.

Mathematical Appendix III

Continuous Correspondences

1. Introduction

We have observed at several points in the book, for example in considering demand relations, that the actions taken by an individual are determined by the values of those variables which constitute his economic "environment". If these values uniquely determined the action to be taken then we could have worked with "point–to–point" relations, known as functions. However, when the action to be taken is not uniquely determined there will be a set of possible actions and in our analysis we must use "point–to–set" relations or *correspondences*. More formally, we have

Definition AIII.1. A *correspondence* φ of a set S into a set T is a "rule" which associates to every element $x \in S$ a non–empty subset $\varphi(x) \subset T$.

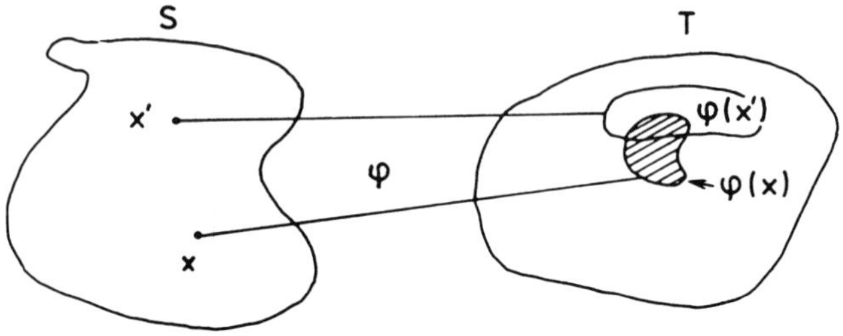

Figure AIII.1

We write for this $x \mapsto \varphi(x)$. The set S is called the *domain* and the set T the *range* of the correspondence φ, see Figure AIII.1.

Obviously, a *function* (mapping) of S into T is a special correspondence which associates with every element $x \in S$ an element $y \in T$. In saying this we are not making the distinction between the element y in T and the subset $\{y\}$ of T which consists of one point only. Given a correspondence φ of S into T we consider the subset G_φ in $S \times T$ defined by

$$G_\varphi := \{(x, y) \in S \times T | \ y \in \varphi(x)\} .$$

The set G_φ is called the *graph* of φ. Conversely, if G is a subset in $S \times T$ such that for *every* $x \in S$ the set of points $y \in T$ with $(x, y) \in G$ is *non–empty,* then G is the graph of a correspondence (see Figure AIII.2), i.e.,

$$\varphi(x) := \{y \in T | \ (x, y) \in G\} .$$

In what follows we will examine how the set $\varphi(x)$ depends on the argument x when x is changed slightly. To make the idea of "changing slightly" precise, we have to endow the sets S and T with a *topological structure*. In all the applications that we have encountered in this book the domain S and range T were subsets in some Euclidean space $\mathbb{R}^m$. In this case the topological concepts *neighbourhood* of a point (set) or

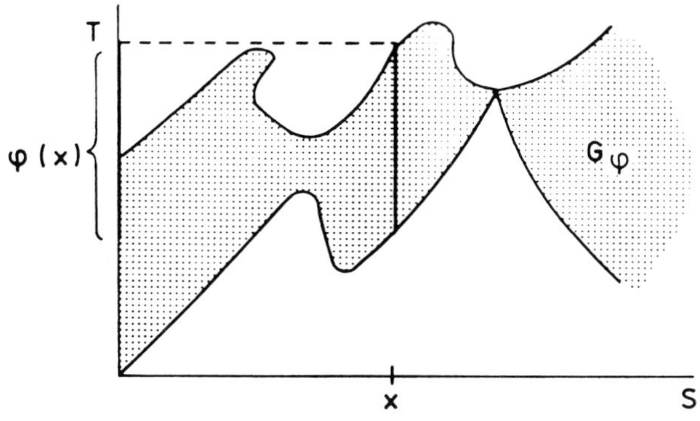

Figure AIII.2

open (closed) subset are well defined (see Mathematical Appendix I). We emphasize, however, that all the results (though not the simple proofs given in this section) hold true for general metric spaces S and T. (For details, see Hildenbrand (1974).)

From now on, unless specifically stated otherwise, the sets S and T are subsets of some Euclidean space, say $S \subset \mathbb{R}^s$ and $T \subset \mathbb{R}^t$.

2. Upper Hemi–Continuous Correspondences

A correspondence φ of S into T is said to be *u.h.c.* (upper hemi–continuous) *at the point* $x \in S$ if the set $\varphi(x)$ does not "suddenly become much larger with a small change in the point x". In other words, the set $\varphi(x)$ does not "explode" if one changes the argument x slightly. Note, however, that we do allow the set $\varphi(x)$ to suddenly become much smaller, thus the set $\varphi(x)$ may "implode" (see, for example, the point x_2 in Figure AIII.4). More formally, we have the following definition.

Definition AIII.2. The correspondence φ of S into T is said to be *u.h.c. at x* if for every open set $\mathcal{O}$ containing $\varphi(x)$ there exists a neighbourhood V of x such that

$$\varphi(x') \subset \mathcal{O} \quad \text{for every } x' \in V$$

(see Figure AIII.3). The correspondence φ is called *u.h.c.* if it is u.h.c. at every point $x \in S$.

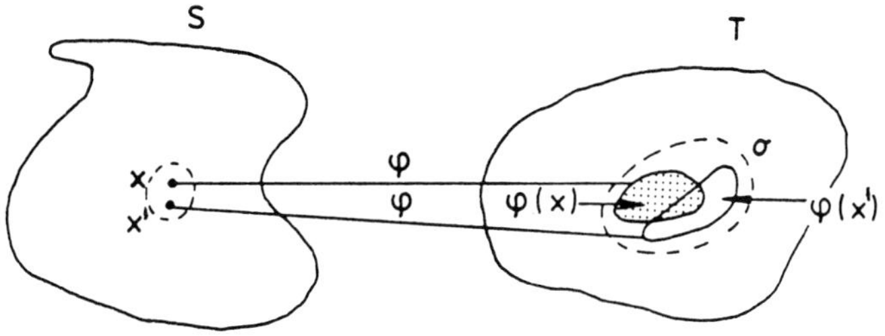

Figure AIII.3

In Figure AIII.4, φ is u.h.c. at x_1, x_2 and x_4, and at x_2 there is an "implosion". However, φ is not u.h.c. at x_3 where φ has an "explosion". Indeed, if $x' < x_3$ there is a small enough neighbourhood $\mathcal{O}$ of $\varphi(x_3)$ such that $\varphi(x')$ is not contained in this neighbourhood.

Obviously, a function f of S into T (considered as a correspondence) is u.h.c. if and only if it is continuous. This fact explains why we have chosen the somewhat esoteric term *"hemi"* and have refrained from using upper *semi*–continuous, even though this is widely employed in the literature. Indeed, a function of S into the real line $\mathbb{R}$ may be upper (or lower) semi–continuous without being continuous. Recall that a function f is called upper semi–continuous at $x \in S$ if for every $\lambda > f(x)$ there

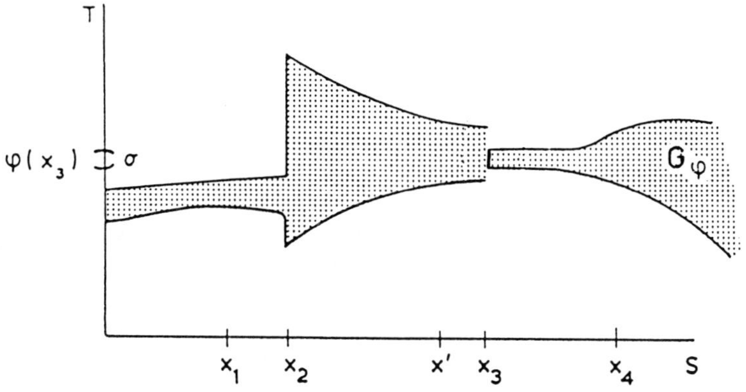

Figure AIII.4

exists a neighbourhood V of x such that $f(z) < \lambda$ for every $z \in V$. If the reader makes a quick drawing he will see immediately that u.s.c. functions need not be continuous.

To familiarize himself with the definition of u.h.c. the reader should verify the following simple assertions:

(i) If the correspondence φ of S into T is u.h.c. at x then the *closure* of φ, i.e., the correspondence

$$x \mapsto \overline{\varphi(x)} \quad \text{(closure of the subset } \varphi(x))$$

is also u.h.c. at x. However, the converse is false.

(ii) If the correspondences φ_i of S into T $(i = 1, \ldots, n)$ are u.h.c. at x then their *union*, i.e., the correspondence

$$x \mapsto \bigcup_{i=1}^{n} \varphi_i(x)$$

is also u.h.c. at x.

(iii) Let the correspondences φ of S into T and ψ of T into U be u.h.c. Then the *composition* $\psi \circ \varphi$, i.e.,

$$x \mapsto \psi(\varphi(x)) = \bigcup_{y \in \varphi(x)} \psi(y)$$

is u.h.c.

In most applications the correspondences are *compact-valued,* i.e., $\varphi(x)$ is a compact subset of T for every $x \in S$. In this case the general definition of u.h.c. in terms of neighbourhoods has an easy equivalent formulation in terms of sequences. In many proofs it is easier to work with this alternative definition of u.h.c.

Theorem AIII.1 (characterization of u.h.c. by sequences) . The compact–valued correspondence φ of S into T is u.h.c. at x if and only if for every sequence (x_n) congerging to x in S and every sequence (y_n) with $y_n \in \varphi(x_n)$ there exists a converging subsequence of (y_n) whose limit belongs to $\varphi(x)$.

Proof. (a) Let φ be u.h.c. at x. The proof consists of two steps: Firstly we show that the sequence (y_n) is bounded and consequently possesses a convergent subsequence. Then we show that the limit of the subsequence belongs to $\varphi(x)$.

Since $\varphi(x)$ is bounded there exists a bounded and open set B containing $\varphi(x)$. By definition of u.h.c. there exists a neighbourhood V of x such that $\varphi(z) \subset B$ for every $z \in V$. Since the sequence (x_n) converges to x there exists an integer $\bar{n}$ such that $x_n \in V$ for $n \geq \bar{n}$. Consequently, we have $\varphi(x_n) \subset B$ and therefore $y_n \in B$ for $n \geq \bar{n}$. Thus, the sequence (y_n) is bounded. Hence, there exists a converging subsequence, say $(y_{n_q}) \underset{q}{\rightarrow} y$.

Assume now that $y \notin \varphi(x)$. Clearly, there exists a *closed* neighbourhood of $\varphi(x)$ not containing the point y, for example the closed ball B_ϵ

around the set $\varphi(x)$ with radius $\epsilon > 0$, where the number ϵ is smaller than the distance of y to any point z in $\varphi(x)$ (see Figure AIII.5) i.e.,

$$B_\epsilon = \{v \in T | \; inf_{z \in \varphi(x)} \; d(z, v) \leq \epsilon\} \; .$$

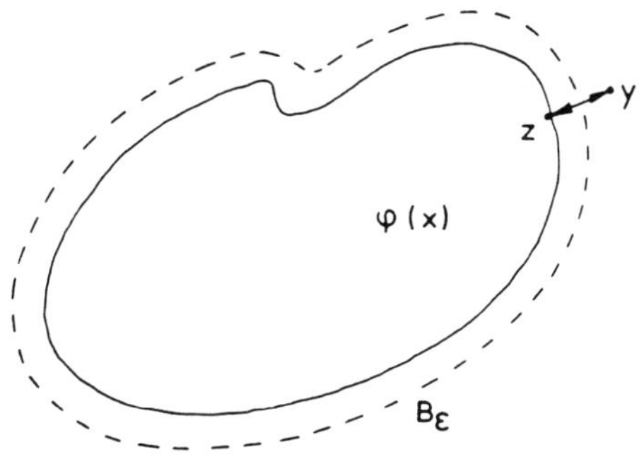

Figure AIII.5

Since φ is u.h.c. it follows that for n large enough we have $\varphi(x_n) \subset B_\epsilon$ and consequently $y_n \in B_\epsilon$. Since the subsequence (y_{n_q}) converges to y and since B_ϵ is, by assumption, closed it follows that the limit point $y \in B_\epsilon$. But this is a contradiction since by construction $y \notin B_\epsilon$.

(b) To prove the converse we assume that φ is not u.h.c. at x, i.e., there *exsits* an open set $\mathcal{O}$ containing $\varphi(x)$ such that *every* neighbourhood V of x contains a point z_V with $\varphi(z_V) \not\subset \mathcal{O}$. By choosing the sequence of neighbourhoods $B_{1/n}(x)$ $(n = 1, \ldots)$, i.e., the ball with centre x and radius $\frac{1}{n}$, we therefore obtain a sequence (x_n) converging to x and a sequence (y_n), with $y_n \in \varphi(x_n)$ and $y_n \notin \mathcal{O}$. By assumption we know that there exists a converging subsequence of (y_n) whose limit belongs to $\varphi(x)$. But this is impossible since the set $T \backslash \mathcal{O}$ is closed. Thus $y_n \in T \backslash \mathcal{O}$ for every n implies that the limit point of no converging subsequence of (y_n) will belong to $\mathcal{O}$ and *a forteriori* to $\varphi(x)$ which is contained in $\mathcal{O}$.

Q.E.D.

Remark . The reader familiar with elementary topology will have observed that in the first part of the proof we made use of our special situation, $T \subset \mathbb{R}^m$, when we concluded that there is a *compact* neighbourhood of the compact set $\varphi(x)$. However, as mentioned before, the theorem is true for all metric spaces S and T. Then one has to show first that for a u.h.c. correspondence φ the image $\varphi(K)$ of a compact set K (in our case the converging sequence $x_1, x_2, \ldots, x$) is again compact.

The following results, which have been used frequently in the book, are immediate consequences of the definition of u.h.c. in terms of sequences. Roughly speaking, they show that set–theoretic operations like *union, product, sum* and *convex hull* applied "point–wise", preserve u.h.c.

Proposition AIII.1. Let the correspondence φ of S into T be compact–valued and u.h.c. Then, the image

$$\varphi(K) = \bigcup_{x \in K} \varphi(x)$$

of a compact set K is compact.

Proof. We have to show that every sequence (y_n) in the image $\varphi(K)$ has a converging subsequence whose limit belongs to $\varphi(K)$. Let the sequence (y_n) belong to $\varphi(K)$. For every y_n there is an $x_n \in K$ such that $y_n \in \varphi(x_n)$. Since K is compact there exists a converging subsequence (x_{n_q}) whose limit $x = lim_q \, x_{n_q} \in K$. Thus, we can apply Theorem AIII.1. to the subsequences (x_{n_q}) and (y_{n_q}) and this gives us the desired converging subsequence of (y_{n_q}).

Q.E.D.

Proposition AIII.2 (u.h.c. of the product correspondence). Let the correspondences φ_i of S into T $(i = 1, 2, \ldots, k)$ be compact–valued and u.h.c. Then the product correspondence

$$x \mapsto \varphi_1(x) \times \varphi_2(x) \times \ldots \times \varphi_k(x)$$

of S into the product space $T \times \ldots \times T$ is compact–valued and u.h.c. at x.

Proof. We have to show that for every sequence (x_n) converging to x and for every sequence $y_n = (y_n^1, y_n^2, \ldots, y_n^k)_{n=1,\ldots}$ with $y_n^i \in \varphi_i(x_n)$ $(i = 1, \ldots, k)$, there exists a converging subsequence whose limit belongs to the product $\varphi_1(x) \times \ldots \times \varphi_k(x)$. Recall that a sequence $(y_n^1, y_n^2, \ldots, y_n^k)$ in the product space converges to $(y^1, y^2, \ldots, y^k)$ if and only if every sequence $(y_n^i)_{n=1,\ldots}$ of its coordinates converges to y^i. Thus, by applying Theorem AIII.1. in succession to the first, second, ... coordinates we obtain the desired convergent sequence in the product space.

Q.E.D.

Proposition AIII.3 (u.h.c. of the sum correspondence). Let the correspondences φ_i of S into $\mathbb{R}^m$ $(i = 1, \ldots, k)$ be compact–valued and u.h.c. at x. Then the sum correspondence

$$x \mapsto \varphi_1(x) + \varphi_2(x) + \ldots + \varphi_k(x)$$

of S into $\mathbb{R}^m$ is compact–valued and u.h.c. at x.

Proof. Let the sequence (x_n) be convergent to x and let

$$y_n \in \varphi_1(x_n) + \varphi_2(x_n) + \ldots + \varphi_k(x_n) , \qquad n = 1, 2, \ldots .$$

Thus, the vector y_n is of the form $y_n = y_n^1 + y_n^2 + \ldots + y_n^k$, where $y_n^i \in \varphi_i(x_n)$ $(i = 1, \ldots, k)$. By Theorem AIII.1. there exists for every sequence $(y_n^i)_{n=1,\ldots}$ $(i = 1, \ldots, k)$ a converging subsequence whose limit y^i belongs to $\varphi_i(x)$. Consequently, there exists a converging subsequence $(y_{n_q})_{q=1,\ldots}$ of (y_n) such that the coordinate sequence $y_{n_q}^i$ converges to y^i. Hence,

$$\lim_q y_{n_q} = y^1 + y^2 + \ldots + y^k \in \varphi_1(x) + \varphi_2(x) + \ldots + \varphi_k(x) .$$

Q.E.D.

Proposition AIII.4 (u.h.c. of the convex hull correspondence). Let the correspondence φ of S into $\mathbb{R}^m$ be compact–valued and u.h.c. at x. Then the convex hull correspondence

$$x \mapsto co\ \varphi(x) \quad \text{(convex hull of } \varphi(x))$$

of S into $\mathbb{R}^m$ is compact–valued and u.h.c at x.

Proof. Let the sequence (x_n) be convergent to x and let $y_n \in co\ \varphi(x_n)$. By the well–known *result of Caratheodory* every vector $y_n \in co\ \varphi(x_n)$ can be written as a convex sum of $m+1$ vectors in $\varphi(x_n)$, i.e.,

$$y_n = \lambda_n^0 \cdot z_n^0 + \lambda_n^1 \cdot z_n^1 + \ldots + \lambda_n^m \cdot z_n^m .$$

where

$$z_n^i \in \varphi(x_n), \quad \lambda_n^0 + \lambda_n^1 + \ldots + \lambda_n^m = 1 \text{ and } \lambda_n^i \geq 0 .$$

By Theorem AIII.1. there exists for every $i = 0, \ldots, m$ a converging subsequence of $(z_n^i)_{n=1,\ldots}$ whose limit belongs to $\varphi(x)$. Furthermore, the sequence $(\lambda_n^i)_{n=1,\ldots}$ is bounded and therefore possesses a converging subsequence. Consequently, there exists a converging subsequence (y_{n_q}) of (y_n) such that the corresponding subsequences $(z_{n_q}^i)_{q=1,\ldots}$ and $(\lambda_{n_q}^i)_{q=1,\ldots}$ are convergent, say $(z_{n_q}^i) \mapsto z^i$ and $(\lambda_{n_q}^i) \mapsto \lambda^i$. Clearly, we have $\lambda^0 + \lambda^1 + \ldots + \lambda^m = 1$ and $\lambda^i \geq 0$. Hence

$$\lim_q y_{n_q} = \lambda^0 z^0 + \ldots + \lambda^m z^m \in co\, \varphi(x) \; .$$

Q.E.D.

We now mention another continuity concept which is closely related to u.h.c. We should add that, to avoid a common error, the reader would be well advised to make a careful note of the difference between the two concepts.

Definition AIII.3. A correspondence φ of S into T is said to be *closed* if the graph $G_\varphi = \{(x, y) |\; y \in \varphi(x)\}$ of φ is a closed subset in $S \times T$.

Clearly, a closed correspondence is closed–valued (i.e., $\varphi(x)$ is a closed subset in T for every $x \in S$), and it follows immediately from Theorem AIII.1. that a closed–valued and u.h.c. correspondence has a closed graph. The example illustrated in Figure AIII.6. shows that a correspondence may be closed — even compact–valued — but not u.h.c. The graph of φ is closed but φ is not u.h.c. at $x = 0$.

Note, however, that if the range T is a compact space — which indeed is the case in many applications — then, of course, every closed correspondence is u.h.c. This follows immediately from Theorem AIII.1.

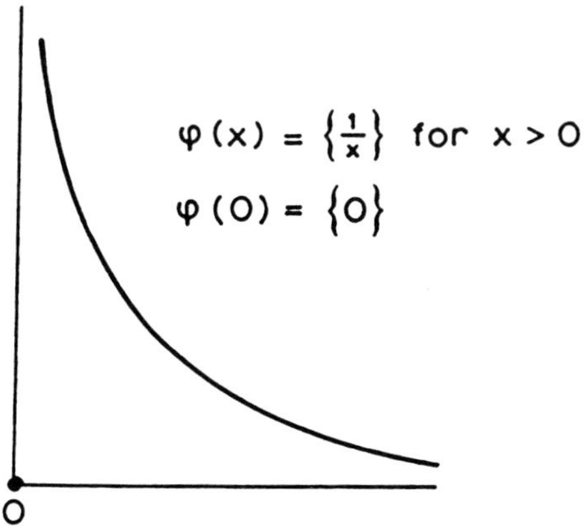

Figure AIII.6

For this reason a closed correspondence is sometimes called u.h.c. in the literature. However, since there are applications where the range space T is not compact it seems more appropriate to distinguish the two concepts.

One can show that the intersection (provided it is non–empty) of two close–valued and u.h.c. correspondences is again u.h.c. In the following particularly useful result we strengthen the assumptions about one correspondence and make it compact–valued, while the other we only require to be closed rather than u.h.c.

Proposition AIII.5. Let the correspondence φ of S into T be compact–valued and u.h.c., the correspondence ψ of S into T be closed and assume $\varphi(x) \cap \psi(x) \neq \emptyset$. Then the intersection correspondence

$$x \mapsto \varphi(x) \cap \psi(x)$$

is compact–valued and u.h.c.

Proof. We have to show that for every sequence (x_n) converging to x and every sequence (y_n) with $y_n \in \varphi(x_n) \cap \psi(x_n)$ there is a converging subsequence of (y_n) whose limit belongs to $\varphi(x) \cap \psi(x)$. Applying Theorem AIII.1. to the correspondence φ it follows that there is a converging subsequence (y_{n_q}) of (y_n) such that its limit y belongs to $\varphi(x)$. In order to show that y belongs to $\psi(x)$ we observe that $(x_{n_q}, y_{n_q}) \in G_\psi$ and $(x_{n_q}, y_{n_q}) \to (x, y)$. Since, by assumption, the graph G_ψ of ψ is closed, it follows that $(x, y) \in G_\psi$, i.e., $y \in \psi(x)$.

Q.E.D.

3. Lower Hemi–Continuous Correspondences

A correspondence φ of S into T is said to be *l.h.c.* (lower hemi–continuous) at the point $x \in S$ if the set $\varphi(x)$ does not "suddenly become much smaller with a small change in point x". In other words, the set $\varphi(x)$ does not "implode" if one moves the argument x slightly. Note, however, that we now allow the set $\varphi(x)$ to become much larger suddenly. Thus, the set $\varphi(x)$ may "explode". More formally, we have the following definition.

Definition AIII.4. The correspondence φ of S into T is said to be *l.h.c.* at x if for every open set $\mathcal{O}$ in T with $\varphi(x) \cap \mathcal{O} \neq \emptyset$ there exists a neighbourhood V of x such that

$$\varphi(x') \cap \mathcal{O} \neq \emptyset \qquad \text{for every } x' \in V$$

(see Figure AIII.7.). The correspondence is called l.h.c. if it is l.h.c. at every point $x \in S$.

The correspondence drawn in Figure AIII.8. is l.h.c at x_1 and x_3 but not l.h.c. at x_2 where φ is u.h.c. As in the case of u.h.c. a function of S into T (considered as a correspondence) is l.h.c. if and only if it is continuous. Thus, the two concepts of continuity, u.h.c. and l.h.c., which are quite different for general correspondences, coincide and are equivalent to continuity in the case of functions. It is therefore *multivaluedness* which plays the crucial role in making these concepts distinct from each other.

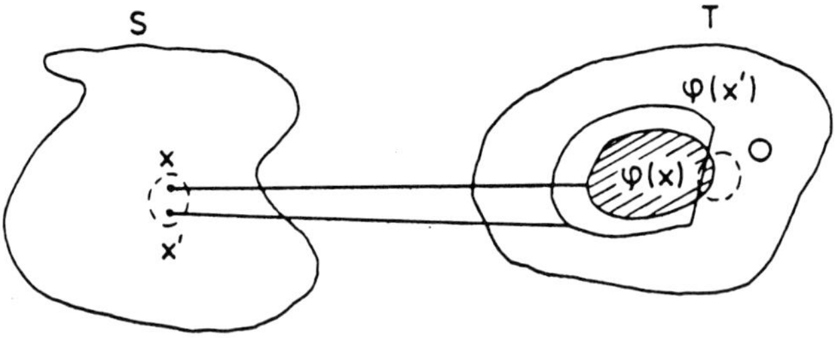

Figure AIII.7

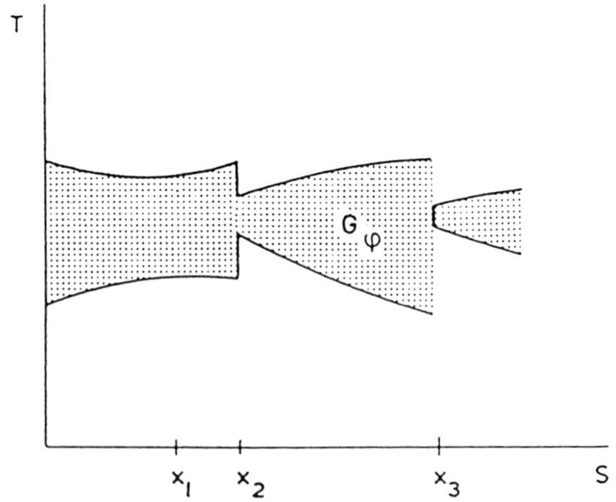

Figure AIII.8

As in the case of u.h.c. the operations of closure, union and composition of correspondences preserve l.h.c. This follows immediately from the definition. Hence, we have:

(i) The correspondence φ of S into T is l.h.c. at x if and only if the *closure* correspondence $x \mapsto \overline{\varphi(x)}$ is l.h.c. at x.

(ii) If the correspondences φ_i of S into T $(i = 1, \ldots, n)$ are l.h.c. at x then their *union*

$$x \mapsto \bigcup_{i=1}^{n} \varphi_i(x)$$

is also l.h.c.

(iii) Let the correspondences φ of S into T and ψ of T into U be l.h.c. Then the *composition* $\psi \circ \varphi$ is l.h.c.

The following result characterizes l.h.c. in terms of sequences. No compactness assumption is needed here.

Theorem AIII.2 (characterization of l.h.c. by sequences). The correspondence φ of S into T is l.h.c. at x if and only if for every sequence (x_n) converging to x and every $y \in \varphi(x)$ there exists a sequence (y_n) converging to y with $y_n \in \varphi(x_n)$.

In other words, every point y corresponding to x can be obtained as a limit of points y_n corresponding to points x_n near to x.

Proof. (a) Let φ be l.h.c. at x and let (x_n) be convergent to x and $y \in \varphi(x)$. For every integer r, let $B_r(y)$ denote the ball with radius $\frac{1}{r}$ and centre y. Since φ is l.h.c. at x, there exists for every r a neighbourhood V_r of x such that $z \in V_r$ implies $\varphi(z) \cap B_r(y) \neq \emptyset$. Since (x_n) converges to x there is for every r an integer n_r such that $n \geq n_r$ implies $x_n \in V_r$. Clearly, we can assume that $n_r < n_{r+1}$ $(r = 1, 2, \ldots)$. We now define the desired sequence (y_n). For n with $n_r \leq n < n_{r+1}$ choose y_n in the set $\varphi(x_n) \cap B_r(y)$. This is possible since $n \geq n_r$ implies $x_n \in V_r$, which in turn implies that $\varphi(x_n) \cap B_r(y) \neq \emptyset$. The sequence (y_n), constructed in this way, clearly converges to y since with increasing n the index r also increases and the ball $B_r(y)$ becomes smaller and smaller.

(b) Conversely, assume that φ is not l.h.c. at x, i.e., there exists an open set $\mathcal{O}$ with $\mathcal{O} \cap \varphi(x) \neq \emptyset$ such that every neighbourhood V of x contains a point z_V with $\varphi(z_V) \cap \mathcal{O} = \emptyset$. Therefore, there exists a sequence (x_n) converging to x with $\varphi(x_n) \cap \mathcal{O} = \emptyset$. Now let $y \in \mathcal{O} \cap \varphi(x)$. By assumption, there exists a sequence $(y_{n_q})_{q=1,\ldots}$ converging to y with $y_{n_q} \in \varphi(x_{n_q})$. However, since $\mathcal{O}$ is open and $y \in \mathcal{O}$ we have for large enough q that $y_{n_q} \in \mathcal{O}$. Thus, $\varphi(x_{n_q}) \cap \mathcal{O} \neq \emptyset$, a contradiction.

Q.E.D.

As in the case of u.h.c. correspondences the operations of *product, sum* and *convex hull* preserve l.h.c. There is, however, obviously no counterpart to Proposition AIII.1.

Proposition AIII.6 (l.h.c. of the product correspondence). Let the correspondences φ_i of S into T $(i = 1, 2, \ldots, k)$ be l.h.c. at x. Then the product correspondence

$$x \mapsto \varphi_1(x) \times \varphi_2(x) \times \ldots \times \varphi_k(x)$$

of S into the product space $T \times \ldots \times T$ is l.h.c. at x.

Proof. Let the sequence (x_n) converge to x and let $y = (y^1, y^2, \ldots, y^k) \in \varphi_1(x) \times \ldots \times \varphi_k(x)$. By Theorem AIII.2., y^i can be obtained as a limit of a sequence $(y^i_n)_{n=1,\ldots}$ with $y^i_n \in \varphi_i(x_n)$ $(i = 1, \ldots, k)$. Thus, $y_n = (y^1_n, y^2_n, \ldots, y^k_n)$ is the desired sequence.

Q.E.D.

Proposition AIII.7 (l.h.c. of the convex hull correspondence). Let the correspondence φ of S into $\mathbb{R}^m$ be l.h.c. at x. Then the convex hull correspondence

$$x \mapsto co\ \varphi(x)$$

is l.h.c.

Proof. Let the sequence (x_n) converge to x. Let $y \in co\ \varphi(x)$, i.e., $y = \lambda^0 y^0 + \ldots + \lambda^m y^m$, where $y^i \in \varphi(x)$, $\lambda^i \geq 0$, $(i = 0, \ldots, m)$ and $\sum_{i=0}^m \lambda^i = 1$. Since φ is l.h.c. at x there exists a sequence (y_n^i) converging to y^i with $y_n^i \in \varphi(x_n)$. Hence, $y_n = \lambda^0 y_n^0 + \lambda^1 y_n^1 + \lambda^2 y_n^2 + \ldots + \lambda^m y_n^m$ belongs to $co\ \varphi(x_n)$ and converges to y.

Q.E.D.

We remark that, in contrast to u.h.c. correspondences, the *intersection* of l.h.c. correspondences is, in general, not l.h.c.

4. Continuous Correspondences

Definition AIII.5. A correspondence φ of S into T is said to be *continuous* (at x) if φ is lower and upper hemi–continuous (at x).

We can best see the significance of this idea of continuity in the context of the general problem of choice in economics. Suppose that the elements of the set S each describe fully a possible "state of the world" for a given individual. In our exchange problem, for example, an element of S would be a price system, the individual's income and so forth. Now let the set T be all those actions which may at the outset be conceivable as choices for the individual. Thus, T in our case would be the consumption set. It is important to realize that T consists of all possible actions which could reasonably be contemplated by the agent and not those in actual fact available to him. Once the values of the environmental variables are fixed say at $s \in S$ then the choices that the individual can make are restricted to a subset $\beta(s)$ of T. Thus, in the exchange economy, once the prices and initial resources are stabilized the individual is restricted to choosing from his budget set. Now the agent has a criterion for making his choices, he can order the options available in T. This order is described by the preference relation $\succ$. This relation could depend in turn on the environment s, in which case we write $\succ_s$. Now consider the best elements (with respect to $\succ_s$) in $\beta(s)$. This defines a "choice correspondence" φ of S into T, i.e., $s \mapsto \varphi(s)$. A material question that arises is, what can be said about the continuity of $\varphi(\cdot)$? An answer is given by the following fundamental results.

Theorem AIII.3. Let β be a correspondence of S into T and for every $s \in S$ let $\succ_s$ denote an irreflexive and transitive binary relation on the set $\beta(s)$ with the following continuity property. The set

$$\{(s,x,y) \in S \times T \times T|\ x \succ_s y \quad x,y \in \beta(s)\} \text{ is open in } S \times T \times T \ .$$

If the set $\beta(s)$ is compact then the set $\varphi(s)$ of maximal elements for $\succ_s$ is non–empty and compact.

Further, if β is compact–valued, the correspondence φ is u.h.c. at every point s where β is continuous.

The continuity property says that if in a particular environment s, action x is preferred to action y then after a sufficiently small change of the environment from s to s' and a sufficiently small change of the actions x to x' and y to y', respectively, the agent will still prefer x' to y', i.e., $x' \succ_{s'} y'$.

For example, if the choice criterion $\succ_s$ is embodied in a utility function $u_s(\cdot)$ of $\beta(s)$ into $\mathbb{R}$, then the above continuity assumption is satisfied if $u_s(x)$ is a continuous function in *both variables* s and x. However, in general, there may be no such utility function since the relation $\succ_s$ of Theorem AIII.3. is not assumed to be derived from a complete and transitive preference–indifference relation $\succsim$.

Proof. Assume that $\varphi(s) = \emptyset$, i.e., for every $y \in \beta(s)$ there exists $y' \in \beta(s)$ such that $y \prec_s y'$. Let

$$\gamma(z) = \{y \in \beta(s) |\ y \prec_s z\} .$$

By the continuity property the set $\gamma(z)$ is open relative to $\beta(s)$. Further, since we assumed $\varphi(s) = \emptyset$, every element of $\beta(s)$ belongs to at least one set $\gamma(z)$. Thus the collection $\{\gamma(z)\}_{z\in\beta(s)}$ forms an open covering of the set $\beta(s)$. Since the set $\beta(s)$ is assumed to be compact there exists a finite sub-covering, i.e., there are $z_1, z_2, \ldots, z_n$ in $\beta(s)$ such that the union $\gamma(z_1) \cup \ldots \cup \gamma(z_n)$ contains the set $\beta(s)$. Now, the finite set $\{z_1, z_2, \ldots, z_n\}$ has a maximal element, say z_n, since the relation $\succ_s$ is transitive. Therefore, we have $z_n \notin \gamma(z_i)$ for $i = 1, \ldots, n-1$ and also $z_n \notin \gamma(z_n)$ since the relation $\succ_s$ is irreflexive. But since the sets $\gamma(z_i)$ cover the set $\beta(s)$ we obtain $z_n \notin \beta(s)$, a contradiction.

To show that $\varphi(s)$ is compact it suffices to show that it is closed since it is contained in the compact set $\beta(s)$. Thus, let $y_n \to y$ with $y_n \in \varphi(s)$. Assume $y \notin \varphi(s)$, i.e., there exists an element $z \in \beta(s)$ with $z \succ_s y$. The continuity assumption now implies that $z \succ_s y_n$ for n large enough. But this contradicts $y_n \in \varphi(s)$.

It remains to show that the choice correspondence φ is u.h.c.. Since $\varphi(s) = \beta(s) \cap \varphi(s)$ and the correspondence β is by assumption u.h.c. and compact–valued, it suffices by Proposition AIII.5. to show that φ is closed at s, that is to say, if $(s_n, y_n) \to (s, y)$ and if $y_n \in \varphi(s_n)$ $(n = 1, 2, \ldots)$ then it must follow that $y \in \varphi(s)$. Assume that $y \notin \varphi(s)$, i.e., there exists an element $z \in \beta(s)$ with $z \succ_s y$. Now we use the l.h.c. at s of the correspondence β. Indeed, there exists by Theorem AIII.2. a sequence (z_n) converging to z with $z_n \in \beta(s_n)$. By the continuity assumption the properties $z \succ_s y$, $z_n \to z$, $s_n \to s$ and $y_n \to y$ imply that $z_n \succ_{s_n} y_n$ for n large enough. But this means that $y_n \notin \varphi(s_n)$, a contradiction.

Q.E.D.

Mathematical Appendix IV

Fixed Point Theorems

The basic result which we will use in this section is

> **Brouwer's fixed point theorem.** Let C be a non–empty compact and convex subset of $\mathbb{R}^m$ and f a continuous mapping of C into C. Then there exists a fixed point $\hat{x}$ for f, i.e., $\hat{x} = f(\hat{x})$.

The proof of this result is not given since it may easily be found in the literature, e.g., Burger's (1963) or Scarf's (1973) book to which we referred earlier. However, as we have already remarked we are frequently faced with correspondences rather than functions in economics and we need a version of Brouwer's theorem for this. Such a result is the following theorem.

> **Kakutani's fixed point theorem.** Let C be a non–empty compact and convex subset of $\mathbb{R}^m$ and φ be a convex–valued correspondence of C into C which has a closed graph. Then there exists a fixed point $\hat{x}$ for φ, i.e., $\hat{x} \in \varphi(\hat{x})$.

The following fundamental lemma (Debreu, Gale, Nikaido) is a useful alternative version of Kakutani's fixed point theorem.

Lemma AIV.1. Let S be a closed and convex subset of the unit simplex Δ in $\mathbb{R}^{\ell}$. Assume that the correspondence Ψ of S into $\mathbb{R}^{\ell}$ has the following properties:

(i) Ψ is bounded, i.e., there exists a bounded set B in $\mathbb{R}^{\ell}$ such that $\Psi(p) \subset B$ for every $p \in S$,

(ii) the graph of Ψ is closed,

(iii) $\Psi(p)$ is convex for every $p \in S$,

(iv) for every $p \in S$ we have $p \cdot z \leq 0$ for every $z \in \Psi(p)$.

Then there exist $p^* \in S$ and $z^* \in \Psi(p^*)$ such that $p \cdot z^* \leq 0$ for every $p \in S$.

We remark that the following two cases are of special interest; they both imply $z^* \leq 0$. The first is $S = \Delta$, the second one is $p^* \in int\ S$ and $p^* z^* = 0$.

Proof. We can assume that the bounded set B in property (i) is convex. We shall define a correspondence of $S \times B$ into $S \times B$ to which we shall apply Kakutani's fixed point theorem. For every vector $z \in B$ we consider the set $\mu(z)$ of maximizers of $p \cdot z$ in S, i.e.,

$$\mu(z) = \{p \in S |\ p \cdot z = \max_{q \in S} q \cdot z\} .$$

Clearly, the set $\mu(z)$ is convex and it follows from Theorem AIII.3. of Mathematical Appendix III (or one can easily show directly!) that the graph of the correspondence μ is closed.

Consider now the correspondence of $S \times B$ into itself given by $(p, z) \mapsto \mu(z) \times \Psi(p)$. This correspondence satisfies all the conditions of Kakutani's fixed point theorem. Indeed, it is a convex–valued correspondence of a compact and convex subset of $\mathbb{R}^{2\ell}$ into itself, which has a closed graph. Therefore, there exists a fixed point $(p^*, z^*) \in S \times B$.

$$p^* \in \mu(z^*) \text{ and } z^* \in \Psi(p^*) .$$

The first inclusion implies by the definition of μ that $p \cdot z^* \leq p^* \cdot z^*$ for every $p \in S$. But the second inclusion implies by assumption (iv) that $p^* \cdot z^* \leq 0$, hence, $p \cdot z^* \leq 0$ for every $p \in S$.

Q.E.D.

Our aim in this Appendix is to show a simple way to generalize Brouwer's result to that of Kakutani. Clearly, Kakutani's theorem follows from Brouwer's theorem if we can show that for every $\epsilon > 0$ there exists a continuous function $f : C \to C$ such that the graph G_f of the function f is contained in the ϵ–ball around the graph G_φ of the correspondence φ (see Figure AIV.1), i.e., for every $x \in C$,

$$dist\ ((x, f(x)), G_\varphi) = inf_{z \in G_\varphi}\ d((x, f(x)), z) < \epsilon .$$

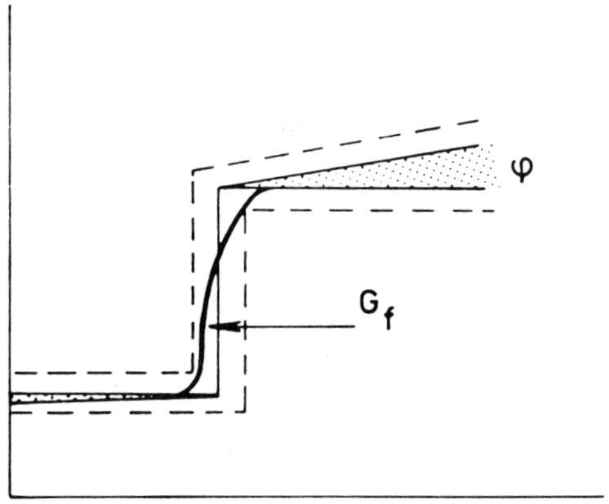

Figure AIV.1

Indeed, then we can find a sequence (f_n) of continuous functions $f_n : C \to C$ with the property: If $x_n \to x$ and $f_n(x_n) \to y$, then $(x,y) \in G_\varphi$, i.e., $y \in \varphi(x)$. Thus, if x_n is a fixed point of f_n, then every limit of a converging subsequence (x_{n_q}) is a fixed point of φ.

The existence of a continuous function whose graph is near (in the above sense) to the graph of a convex–valued correspondence follows from the following two elements, which are also useful in other applications[1)].

Lemma AIV.2. Let φ be a convex–valued correspondence of S into T where S and T are compact subsets of $\mathbb{R}^m$. Then for every $\epsilon > 0$ there exists a l.h.c. and convex–valued correspondence ψ of S into T such that $G_\psi \subset B_\epsilon(G_\varphi)$.

Proof. For every $\delta > 0$ define the correspondence φ^δ by

$$x \mapsto \varphi^\delta(x) = co \bigcup_{\substack{z \in S \\ d(z,x) < \delta}} \varphi(z) \,.$$

Clearly, the correspondence

$$x \mapsto \bigcup_{\substack{z \in S \\ d(z,x) < \delta}} \varphi(z)$$

is l.h.c., and therefore the correspondence φ^δ is also l.h.c. It remains to show that for δ small enough we have

$$G_{\varphi^\delta} \subset B_\epsilon(G_\varphi) \,.$$

---

1) This way of deriving Kakutani's theorem from Brouwer's is due to Cellina (1969).

Assume to the contrary that there is an $\bar{\epsilon} > 0$ such that for every $\delta > 0$ we have $G_{\varphi\delta} \not\subset B_{\bar{\epsilon}}(G_\varphi)$. Then there exists a sequence (x_n, y_n) in $S \times T$ with $y_n = \sum_{i=0}^m \lambda_n^i y_n^i$, where

$$y_n^i \in \varphi(z_n^i), \quad \lambda_n^i \geq 0\ , \quad \sum_{i=0}^m \lambda_n^i = 1 \ \text{ and } \ d(z_n^i, x) \leq 1/n$$

such that *dist* $((x_n, y_n), G_\varphi) \geq \bar{\epsilon}$ for every n. Since S and T are assumed to be compact, we can assume that $x_n \to x$, $y_n^i \to y^i$, $\lambda_n^i \to \lambda^i$, $z_n^i \to z^i = x$. Consequently, $y = \sum_{i=0}^m \lambda^i y^i$, where $\lambda^i \geq 0$, $\sum_{i=0}^m \lambda^i = 1$ and $(x, y^i) \in \bar{G}_\varphi$. Since $\varphi(x)$ is convex, we obtain $(x, y) \in \bar{G}_\varphi$, which contradicts that

$$\textit{dist}\ ((x_n, y_n), G_\varphi) \geq \bar{\epsilon} \qquad \text{for all } n\ .$$

Q.E.D.

Lemma AIV.3 (existence of a continuous selection). Let φ be a closed and convex–valued l.h.c. correspondence of S into $\mathbb{R}^m$. Then there exists a continuous function f such that $f(x) \in \varphi(x)$ for every $x \in S$.

Proof. We first show that for every $\epsilon > 0$ there exists a continuous function f such that

$$\textit{dist}\ (f(x), \varphi(x)) < \epsilon$$

for every $x \in S$. Note that this result is general enough for the proof of Kakutani's theorem. For every $y \in \mathbb{R}^m$ consider the set

$$U_y = \{x \in S |\ \textit{dist}\ (y, \varphi(x)) < \epsilon\}\ .$$

The sets U_y are open, since the correspondence φ is l.h.c. To see this, note that the set U_y is equal to

$$\left\{x \in S \mid \varphi(x) \cap \{z \in \mathbb{R}^m \mid d(z,y) < \epsilon\} \neq \emptyset\right\} .$$

The family $\{U_y\}_{y \in \mathbb{R}^m}$ covers the compact set S, and therefore there is a finite sub–covering, say $U_1 = U_{y_1}, \ \ldots \ , U_r = U_{y_r}$.

Define the function $\alpha_i(x) = dist\ (x, S \setminus U_i) \quad (i = 1, \ldots, r)$,

$$\beta_i(x) = \alpha_i(x) / \sum_{k=1}^{r} \alpha_k(x), \quad x \in S .$$

Thus $0 \le \beta_i(x) \le 1$, $\sum_{i=1}^{r} \beta_i(x) = 1$. Furthermore, $\beta_i(x) = 0$ if and only if $x \notin U_i$. Define now

$$f(x) = \sum_{i=1}^{r} \beta_i(x) y_i , \qquad x \in S .$$

Clearly, the function f is continuous since the functions $\beta_i \ (i = 1, \ldots, r)$ are continuous. Further, by definition, $f(x)$ is a convex combination of those points $y_i \ (i = 1, \ldots, r)$ for which the corresponding set U_i contains the point x. Hence, by definition of the sets U_i we have $y_i \in B_\epsilon\{\varphi(x)\}$, and consequently $f(x) \in B_\epsilon\{\varphi(x)\}$.

One can now easily show that this result implies that there is a sequence (f_n) of continuous functions which converges uniformly to a selection f of φ. Indeed, let f_1 be a continuous function such that $dist\ (f_1(x), \varphi(x)) < 1/2$. Consider the correspondence φ_2 defined by

$$x \mapsto \varphi(x) \cap \{y \mid d\ (y, f_1(x)) < 1/2\} .$$

The correspondence φ_2 is convex–valued, and one can easily verify that it is also l.h.c. Thus, by the first part of the proof there exists a continuous function f_2 such that $dist\ (f_2(x), \varphi_2(x)) < 1/2^2\}$.

In this way we define inductively the sequence (f_n), that is to say, given $f_1, \ldots, f_{n-1}$, we define f_n as a continuous function with the property that $dist\ (f_n(x), \varphi_n(x)) < 1/2^n\}$, where the correspondence φ_n is defined by

$$\varphi_n(x) = \varphi(x) \cap \{y|\ d(y, f_{n-1}(x)) < 1/2^{n-1}\}\ .$$

The sequence defined in this way has the property that

$$dist\ (f_n(x), \varphi(x)) < 1/2^n \text{ and } d(f_n(x), f_{n-1}(x)) < 3/2^n \text{ for all } x \in S.$$

Thus, the sequence (f_n) is uniformly in $x \in S$, a Cauchy sequence, and hence converges to a continuous function.

Q.E.D.

LIST OF MATHEMATICAL SYMBOLS

$x \in S$	means x is an *element* of the set S; x *belongs* to S.
$x \notin S$	means x is not an element of the set S.
$T \subset S$	means every element of the set T is also an element of the set S; T is a *subset* of S; T is contained in S.
$T = S$	denotes $T \subset S$ and $S \subset T$; we say that the two sets S and T are *equal.*
$\emptyset$	denotes the set without any element; the *empty set.*
$\{x, y, z, \ldots\}$	denotes the set whose elements are listed inside the braces, that is $x, y, z, \ldots$. Note that the order in which the elements are listed is immaterial as are repetitions. Thus, $\{x, y, z\} = \{x, x, y, z, x, y\}$.
$\#S$	denotes the *number* of elements in the finite set S, e.g., $\#\{a, b, c\} = 3$, $\#\emptyset = 0$.
$\{x \in S \mid \mathcal{P}(x)\}$	denotes the set of all objects x belonging to the set S for which the proposition $\mathcal{P}(x)$ is true.
$S \cup T$	denotes the *union* of the sets S and T, i.e., $S \cup T$ is the set of objects x which belong to S or T (here the word "or" means "and/or").
$\bigcup_{i \in I} S_i$	denotes the union of the collection $\{S_i\}_{i \in I}$.
$S \cap T$	denotes the *intersection* of the sets S and T, i.e., $S \cap T$ is the set of objects x which belong to S and T.
$\bigcap_{i \in I} S_i$	denotes the intersection of the collection $\{S_i\}_{i \in I}$.

$S \setminus T$	denotes the *complement of* T *with respect to* S, i.e., $S \setminus T = \{x \in S \mid x \notin T\}$.
$S \times T$	denotes the *Cartesian product* of the sets S and T, i.e., the set of *ordered pairs* (x, y) with $x \in S$ and $y \in T$. Note the distinction between the ordered pair (x, y) and the set $\{x, y\}$. Two ordered pairs (x, y) and (x', y') are equal if and only if $x = x'$ and $y = y'$.
$f : S \to T$	denotes a *mapping* (function) of the set S into the set T, i.e., the letter f stands for a well-defined rule which associates to *every* element $x \in S$ an element $f(x)$ of the set T.
$x \mapsto f(x)$	expresses that, with the element x is *associated* an object $f(x)$.
$sup(S)$	denotes the *least upper bound* for the set S of real numbers.
$max(S)$	denotes the *greatest number* in the set $S \subset \mathbb{R}$, thus if $sup\ (S) \in S$ then $sup(S) = max(S)$.
$inf(S)$	denotes the *greatest lower bound* for the set S of real numbers.
$min(S)$	denotes the *smallest number* in the set $S \subset \mathbb{R}$, thus if $inf(S) \in S$ then $inf(S) = min(S)$.
$(x_n)_{n=1,\ldots}$	denotes a sequence whose numbers are $x_1, x_2, \ldots$.
(x_n)	is the same as $(x_n)_{n=1,\ldots}$.
$(x_{n_q})_{q=1,\ldots}$	denotes the *subsequence* $x_{n_1}, x_{n_2}, x_{n_3}, \ldots$ of the sequence $x_1, x_2, \ldots$.
$x_n \to x$	means that the sequence $(x_n)_{n=1,\ldots}$ is *convergent* to x.

$lim\, x_n$	means that the sequence $(x_n)_{n=1,\ldots}$ is *convergent* and the *limit* is denoted by $lim\, x_n$.
$\lvert\lambda\rvert$	$\lambda \in \mathbb{R}$, denotes the absolute value of the real number λ, i.e., $$\lvert\lambda\rvert = \begin{cases} \lambda & \text{if } \lambda \geq 0 \\ -\lambda & \text{if } \lambda < 0. \end{cases}$$
$\mathbb{R}^\ell$	is the set of ordered ℓ–tuples (vectors) $(x^1, x^2, \ldots, x^\ell)$, $x^h \in \mathbb{R}$; the number x^h is called the h–th *coordinate (component)* of the vector x.
$\lvert x\rvert$	denotes the "sum norm" of the vector $x \in \mathbb{R}^\ell$, i.e., $\lvert x\rvert = \lvert x^1\rvert + \lvert x^2\rvert + \ldots + \lvert x^\ell\rvert$.
$\lVert x\rVert$	denotes the Euclidean norm of the vector $x \in \mathbb{R}^\ell$, i.e., $\lVert x\rVert = \sqrt[+]{x^1 \cdot x^1 + x^2 \cdot x^2 + \ldots + x^\ell \cdot x^\ell} = \sqrt[+]{x \cdot x}$.
$dist\ (x, X)$	denotes the distance between the vector $x \in \mathbb{R}^\ell$ and the subset $X \subset \mathbb{R}^\ell$, i.e., $dist\ (x, X) = inf\ \{\lVert x - y\rVert \mid y \in X\}$.
$\mathbf{1}_i$	i–th unitvector, i.e., the vector whose i–th component equals 1 while all other components are 0.
$\mathbf{1}$	vector with all components equal 1.
$\sum_{i=1}^m \lambda_i x_i$	$\lambda_i \in \mathbb{R}$, $x_i \in \mathbb{R}^\ell$, denotes the element $x \in \mathbb{R}^\ell$ defined by $x = \lambda_1 x_1 + \lambda_2 x_2 + \ldots + \lambda_m x_m$, where $x^h = \lambda_1 x_1^h + \lambda_2 x_2^h + \ldots + \lambda_m x_m^h \ (h = 1, \ldots, \ell)$.
$x \leq y$	$x, y \in \mathbb{R}^\ell$, means $x^h \leq y^h$ for every $h = 1, \ldots, \ell$.
$x < y$	$x \leq y$ and $x \neq y$.
$x \ll y$	$x^h < y^h$ for every $h = 1, \ldots, \ell$.

$\mathbb{R}^\ell_+$	denotes the positive orthant of $\mathbb{R}^\ell$, i.e., $\mathbb{R}^\ell_+ = \{x \in \mathbb{R}^\ell \mid 0 \leq x\}$.
P	denotes the strictly positive orthant of $\mathbb{R}^\ell$, i.e., $P = \mathbb{R}^\ell_{++} = \{x \in \mathbb{R}^\ell \mid x \gg 0\}$.
Δ	unit simplex in $\mathbb{R}^\ell$, i.e., $\Delta = \{x \in \mathbb{R}^\ell \mid x^h \geq 0 \ (h = 1, \ldots, l) \text{ and } \sum_{h=1}^{\ell} x^h = 1\}$.
$X \leq Y$	$X, Y \subset \mathbb{R}^\ell$, means $x \leq y$ for *every* $x \in X$ and *every* $y \in Y$.
$X + Y$	denotes the *sum* of the two sets X and Y, i.e., $X + Y = \{z \in \mathbb{R}^\ell \mid z = x + y \text{ with } x \in X \text{ and } y \in Y\}$.
$\overline{S}$	closure of the set S.
int S	interior of the set S.
co X	denotes the *convex hull* of X, and is defined as the intersection of all convex sets containing X.
$x \cdot y$	$x, y \in \mathbb{R}^\ell$, denotes the *scalar product* of the vectors x and y, i.e., $x \cdot y = x^1 \cdot y^1 + x^2 \cdot y^2 + \ldots + x^\ell \cdot y^\ell$.
$p \cdot X$	$p \in \mathbb{R}^\ell$, $X \subset \mathbb{R}^\ell$, denotes the set $\{\lambda \in \mathbb{R} \mid \lambda = p \cdot x \text{ with } x \in X\}$.
$H(p)$	denotes the hyperplane in $\mathbb{R}^\ell$ with normal $p \neq 0$, i.e., $H(p) = \{x \in \mathbb{R}^n \mid p \cdot x = 0\}$.

REFERENCES

Anderson, R.M. (1978) : An Elementary Core Equivalence Theorem; *Econometrica 46, 1483–1487.*

Aumann, R.J. (1964) : Markets with a Continuum of Traders; *Econometrica 32, 39–50.*

Aumann, R.J. (1966) : Existence of Competitive Equilibria in Markets with a Continuum of Traders; *Econometrica 34, 1–17.*

Burger, E. (1963) : *Introduction to the Theory of Games*; Englewood Cliffs NJ: Prentice–Hall.

Cellina, A. (1969) : Approximation of Set–Valued Functions and Fixed–Point Theorems; *Annali di Matematica Pura et Applicata 82, 17–24.*

Debreu, G. (1964) : Continuity Properties of Paretian Utility; *International Economic Review 5, 285–293.*

Debreu, G. (1970) : Economies with a Finite Set of Equilibria; *Econometrica 38, 387–392.*

Debreu, G. (1972) : Smooth Preferences; *Econometrica 40, 603–615.*

Debreu, G. (1974) : Excess Demand Functions; *Journal of Mathematical Economics 1, 15–23.*

Debreu, G. (1975a) : The Rate of Convergence of an Economy; *Journal of Mathematical Economics 2, 1–8.*

Debreu, G. (1975b) : Four Aspects of the Mathematical Theory of Economic Equilibrium; *Proceedings of the International Congress of Mathematicians, Vancouver 1974 , 65–77; reprinted in: Mathematical Economics, Twenty Papers of Gérard Debreu (1983),* Cambridge: Cambridge University Press, *217–231.*

Debreu, G., and H. Scarf (1963) : A Limit Theorem on the Core of an Economy; *International Economic Review 4, 235–246.*

Dierker, E. (1982) : Regular Economies; *in: Handbook of Mathematical Economics II, K.J. Arrow and M.D. Intriligator (eds.),* Amsterdam: North Holland, *795–830.*

Edgeworth, F.Y. (1881) : *Mathematical Psychics*; London: Paul Kegan.

Fenchel, W. (1953) : *Convex Cones, Sets, and Functions*; Lecture notes (mimeographed); Princeton NJ: Princeton University.

Fenchel, W. (1956) : Über konvexe Funktionen mit vorgeschriebenen Niveaumannigfaltigkeiten; *Mathematische Zeitschrift 63, 496–506.*

Finetti, B. de (1949) : Sulle stratificazioni convesse; *Annali di Matematica Pura et Applicata 30, 173–183.*

Gabszewicz, J. (1970) : Théories des noyaux et de la concurrence imparfaite; *Recherches Économiques de Louvain 36, 21–37.*

Hildenbrand, W. (1974) : *Core and Equilibria of a Large Economy*; Princeton NJ: Princeton University Press.

Hildenbrand, W. (1982) : Core of an Economy; *in: Handbook of Mathematical Economics II, K.J. Arrow and M.D. Intriligator (eds.),* Amsterdam: North Holland, *831–877.*

Hildenbrand, W. (1983) : On the Law of Demand; *Econometrica 51, 997–1020.*

Hildenbrand, W. (1987) : Cores; *in: The New Palgrave,* London: Macmillan, *666–669.*

Hildenbrand, W., D. Schmeidler, and S. Zamir (1973) : Existence of Approximate Equilibria and Cores; *Econometrica 41, 1159–1166.*

Kannai, Y. (1974) : Approximation of Convex Preferences; *Journal of Mathematical Economics 1, 101–106.*

Kannai, Y. (1977) : Concavifiability and Constructions of Concave Utility Functions; *Journal of Mathematical Economics 4, 1–56.*

Kirman, A.P. (1982) : Measure Theory with Applications to Economics; *in: Handbook of Mathematical Economics I, K.J. Arrow and M.D. Intriligator (eds.)*, Amsterdam: North Holland, *159–209.*

Kirman, A.P., and K.-J. Koch (1986) : Market Excess Demand in Exchange Economies with Identical Preferences and Collinear Endowments; *Review of Economic Studies 174, LIII , 457–463.*

Knaster, B., C. Kuratowski, and S. Mazurkiewicz (1926) : Ein Beweis des Fixpunktsatzes für n–dimensionale Simplexe; *Fundamenta Mathematicae 14, 132–137.*

Koopmans, T.C. (1972) : Representation of Preference Orderings with Independent Components of Consumption; *in: Decision and Organization; C. McGuire and R. Radner (eds.)*, Amsterdam: North Holland.

Leontief, W. (1947) : A Note on the Interrelation of Subsets of Independent Variables of a Continuous Function with Continuous First Derivatives; *Bulletin of the American Mathematical Society 53, 343–350.*

Mantel, R.R. (1976) : Homothetic Preferences and Community Excess Demand Function; *Journal of Economic Theory 12, 197–201.*

Mas–Colell, A. (1985) : *The Theory of General Economic Equilibrium: A Differential Approach*; Cambridge: Cambridge University Press.

Samuelson, P. (1947) : Some Special Aspects of the Theory of Consumer Behaviour; *in: Foundations of Economic Analysis, Ch. 7, Cambridge: Harvard University Press, 172–202.*

Scarf, H.E. (1960) : Some Examples of Global Instability of the Competitive Equilibrium; *International Economic Review 1, 157–172.*

Scarf, H.E. (1967) : The Core of an N–Person Game; *Econometrica 35, 50–69.*

Scarf, H.E. (1973) : *The Computation of Economic Equilibria*; New Haven Conn.: Yale University Press.

Scarf. H.E. (1982) : The Computation of Equilibrium Prices: An Exposition; *in: Handbook of Mathematical Economics II, K.J. Arrow and M.D. Intriligator (eds.)*, Amsterdam: North Holland, *1007–1061.*

Shapley, L.S. (1972) : On Balanced Games without Side Payments; *in: Mathematical Programming, T.C. Hu and S.H. Robinson (eds.)*, New York: Academic Press, *261–290.*

Shapley, L.S., and H.E. Scarf (1974) : On Cores and Indivisibility; *Journal of Mathematical Economics 1, 23–38.*

Shapley, L.S., and M. Shubik (1969) : On Market Games; *Journal of Economic Theory 1, 9–25.*

Shubik, M. (1959) : Edgeworth Market Games; *in: Contributions to the Theory of Games IV, R.D. Luce and A.W. Tucker (eds.), Annals of Mathematical Studies 40*, Princeton: Princeton University Press, *267–278.*

Sonnenschein, H. (1972) : Market Excess Demand Functions; *Econometrica 40, 549–563.*

Sonnenschein, H. (1973a) : Do Walras' Identity and Continuity Characterize the Class of Community Excess Demand Functions?; *Journal of Economic Theory 6, 345–354.*

Sonnenschein, H. (1973b) : The Utility Hypothesis and Market Demand Theory; *Western Economic Journal 2, 404–410.*

Walras, L. (1926) : *Eléments d'économie politique pure, édition définitive, revue et augmentée*; Paris: Pichon et Durand–Anzias.

Author Index

Anderson, R.J., 186
Aumann, R., 182
Bowley, A., 2
Brouwer, L., 90, 107, 277
Burger, E., 277
Caratheodory, C., 256, 266
Cellina, A., 280
Debreu, G., 85, 108, 111, 169, 173, 203, 207, 224, 278
Dierker, E., 224
Edgeworth, F.Y., 1, 2, 13, 16, 33, 34, 75, 127
Fenchel, W., 85
Finetti, B. de, 85
Gabszewicz, J., 191
Gale, D., 147, 278
Gillies, 75
Hildenbrand, W., 88, 120, 153, 184, 189, 194, 196, 198, 216, 259
Kakutani, S., 90, 108, 277
Kannai, Y., 86, 88
Kirman, A., 179, 211
Knaster, B., 133
Koch, K.J., 211
Koopmans, T., 85
Kuratowski, C., 133
Leontief, W., 85
Mantel, R.R., 207
Marschak, J., 58
Mas-Colell, A., 85, 88, 224
Mazurkiewicz, S., 133
Nikaido, H., 278
Samuelson, P. A., 85
Scarf, H.E., 75, 105, 111, 131, 141, 147, 149, 169, 232, 277
Schmeidler, D., 120
Shapley, L., 75, 134, 135, 141, 147, 149
Shubik, M. 75, 149
Smith, A., 102
Sonnenschein, H., 202
Walras, L., 7, 27, 29, 34, 42, 48, 82, 89, 102, 176, 181
Zamir, S., 120

Subject Index

Allocation, 71
  feasible, 71
  for continuum economy, 180
  improve upon 16, 74, 127, 181
  utility, 124
  Walras, 92

Balanced, 128
  family, 129
  game, 129
  strongly, 156
  weights, 129
Binary relation, 60
Boundary point, 245
Bounded (set), 246
Budget set, 8, 78

Closed correspondence, 265
Closed set, 241
  relative, 245
Coalition, 73
Commodity bundle, 54
Commodity space, 53, 54
Compact subset, 247
Competitive equilibrium, 7
Competitive sequence, 195
Completeness, 56, 60
Comprehensive sets, 125
Consumption plan, 55
Consumption set, 54,55
Continuous correspondence, 271
Continuous function, 247
Continuous relation, 58, 60
Continuous selection, 279
Continuum economy, 178
  of agents, 214
Convergence economy, 153
  of preferences, 87
  sequence in, 240, 241
Convex relation, 64
Convex set, 249
Core of a continuum economy, 181

Core of a game, 127
Core of an economy, 16, 74
Correspondence, 80, 255
  closed, 265
  compact valued, 260
  continuous, 271
  lower hemi–continuous, 267
  total demand, 96
  upper hemi–continuous, 258

Demand, 9
  law of, 215, 227
  set, 81
  excess, 9
  mean, 180
Distance, concept of, between two points, 240
Dominant diagonal, 225

Economy, continuum, 178
  exchange, 70
  regular, 220, 223
  replica, 166
  type, 191
Edgeworth box, 2
Endowments, collinear, 212
  initial, 70
Equilibrium, competitive, 7
  Walras, 82, 181
  price system, 82
Excess demand, 9
Excess supply, 10

Feasible allocation, 71

Game, general definition of, 126
  with transferable utility and characteristic function, 158
Graph, 60
Gross substitutability, 225

Homogeneous commodity, 53
Hyperplane, 251

Income distribution, 212
  density of, 213
  relative, price independent, 208
Income effect, 217
Income, individual, 78
Indifference curves, 4
Indifferent, definition of, 56
Initial resources, 54

Limit of sequence, 240
Lower hemi–continuous correspondence, 267

Monotonicity, 215
  restricted, 219
Monotonic preference relation, 64

Negative definitness, 216, 219, 226
Neighbourhood of a subject, 244
Numéraire, 227, 236

Open set, 243

Pareto optimum, 14, 72
Preferences, 56
Preference relation, 4, 60
  convex, 64
  homothetic, 207, 229
  monotonic, 64
  strongly convex, 65
Prices, transitive, 58

Redistribution, 71, 180
  efficient, 72
Reflexivity, 60
Regular economies, 220, 223
Relation, binary, 60
  preference, 4, 60
Replica economy, 166
Resources, initial, of economic growth, 54

Set, 283
  closed, 241
  convex, 249
  demand, 81
  open, 243
  relative closed, 245
Slutzky substitution, 217
Stability, 232
  global, 236, 237
Structure, 202

Tâtonnement adjustment process, 233, 236
Total demand correspondence, 96
Total excess demand function, 107
Transitive preference relation, 58
Transitivity, 60
Type economy, 191

Unequal treatment in an economy, 174
Uniqueness, 222
Upper hemi–continuous correspondences, 258
Utility allocation, 124
Utility function, 66

Walras allocation, 82
  equilibrium, 181